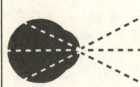

This Large Print Book carries the
Seal of Approval of N.A.V.H.

RITZ & ESCOFFIER

Ritz & Escoffier

THE HOTELIER, THE CHEF, AND THE RISE OF THE LEISURE CLASS

Luke Barr

THORNDIKE PRESS
A part of Gale, a Cengage Company

GALE
A Cengage Company

Farmington Hills, Mich • San Francisco • New York • Waterville, Maine
Meriden, Conn • Mason, Ohio • Chicago

Thorndike Press® Large Print Popular and Narrative Nonfiction.
The text of this Large Print edition is unabridged.
Other aspects of the book may vary from the original edition.
Set in 16 pt. Plantin.

LIBRARY OF CONGRESS CIP DATA ON FILE.
CATALOGUING IN PUBLICATION FOR THIS BOOK
IS AVAILABLE FROM THE LIBRARY OF CONGRESS.

ISBN-13: 978-1-4328-4976-4 (hardcover)

Published in 2018 by arrangement with Clarkson Potter/Publishers, an imprint of Crown Publishing Group, a division of Penguin Random Publishing Group, LLC

Printed in Mexico
1 2 3 4 5 6 7 22 21 20 19 18

For Yumi

CONTENTS

PART 1. THE GRAND OPENING, 1889

1. The Hotelier and the Impresario . . 11
2. A London Debut. 36
3. An Offer Too Good to Refuse . . . 62

PART 2. BOOMTOWN, 1890

4. Taking Charge 81
5. A Celebrity Guest and an
   Infamous Dinner 104

PART 3. DECADENCE AND SUSPICION, 1890–1893

6. The Shareholder Meeting 143
7. Flying High 155
8. Expansion Plans and
   New Pressures 178

PART 4. SCANDAL, 1894–1898

9. The Prince of Wales vs.
   The Duc D'Orléans 199

10. Ritz Makes a Move 232
11. A Secret Investigation 247
12. Calamity. 264

PART 5. PARIS, 1898–1899
13. A New Beginning 287
14. The Cookbook 306
15. The Perfect Hotel 321

PART 6. RETURN TO LONDON, 1899–1902
16. Revenge is Sweet 355
17. The Toast of the Town 373
18. A New King and a Nervous
    Breakdown 389
Afterword: Paris, 1925 415

ACKNOWLEDGMENTS 427
NOTES AND SOURCES 429
BIBLIOGRAPHY 449

■ ■ ■ ■

PART 1
THE GRAND
OPENING, 1889

■ ■ ■ ■

1

THE HOTELIER AND
THE IMPRESARIO

In early August 1889, César Ritz left Cannes on an overnight train, the 8:43 p.m. bound for Calais. He was en route to London, ensconced in a private cabin, traveling alone.

He wore a suit with a high-collared shirt, a tie and waistcoat, and a bowler hat. As usual, he was dressed impeccably, a white carnation in his lapel, his moustache carefully waxed. Ritz was a young man, but his hairline had begun to recede above his high brow and intelligent, watchful eyes. He looked around the compact cabin: it was wood-paneled, with brass coat hooks, a mirror, and a number of storage compartments for his personal items. (His trunk had been taken by a porter when he boarded the train.) Now Ritz hung his jacket in the small closet and placed his hat on the rack. The weather was hot, and he was glad to be traveling at night.

Ritz loved to travel, the thrill and speed of it, the trains rushing toward the future. The Calais-Mediterranean Express train he was on now, for example, had launched a few years earlier, in 1886, and was state of the art, with a restaurant car and onboard lavatories, precluding the need for rest stops at stations along the way. The train ran slowly along the French Riviera, stopping at resort towns like Menton and Monte Carlo before speeding north through Lyon and Paris and on to the English Channel. From there, Ritz would board a ferry and then another train, to London. The trip would take a full night and day.

It was remarkably fast, Ritz thought. The express trains were transforming European travel and, especially, the towns along the Mediterranean. The English had been coming to the Côte d'Azur for a century already, traveling by carriage and on boats. Rail lines had made the trip far easier. There were numerous competing train companies using the tracks — the long-established Marseilles-to-Nice service along the coast dated back to the 1860s, which was when the Cannes station had been built, a small white building with a roof covering both tracks. But the express trains heralded a new era, bringing throngs of visitors from all over Europe. This was good for Ritz: he was in the hotel business.

Why was he going to London, anyway? He hated London. Well, he'd never been to London, actually, but he hated the idea of it: the gloom, the fog, the dour English propriety and cool reserve. The mediocre food. He was Continental, in every sense of the word. His business was pleasure. Ritz was a hotel man, welcoming guests with well-practiced charm at his two small properties, one in Cannes, the Hôtel de Provence, the other in Baden-Baden, Germany, the Hotel Minerva, where he also ran the Restaurant de la Conversation.

He was thirty-nine years old and had been working in the business his whole life — in Lucerne, Paris, and Vienna; in San Remo, Monte Carlo, and Trouville; all over Europe, following the glamorous trail of vacationing aristocrats and wealthy tourists as they took their cures and baths and sought mountain air in the summer and Mediterranean sun in winter. They were an international tribe, increasingly mobile — the Orient Express, with its luxurious sleeping cars, had just launched the first nonstop train between Paris and Constantinople — and Ritz had cultivated a following among them. The dapper young Swiss hotelier was effortlessly

13

multilingual (if heavily accented), and never forgot a name or a face. Not only that, he also took careful note of his clients' whims and desires: who preferred what for breakfast, who required a carafe of water on his bedside table at night.

Ritz was also a showman, an orchestrator of evening entertainments and gala dinners. Indeed, it was because of one such grand dinner that he now found himself, however reluctantly, on the train to London.

It had been almost a year ago, that dinner, at Ritz's recently opened restaurant in Baden-Baden. The Restaurant de la Conversation was already the talk of the town. He had advertised both the hotel and restaurant extensively, printing lavish brochures, and installed electric lights above the terrace, twinkling in the branches of the plants and trees. He was soon attracting a glamorous crowd. (Kaiser Wilhelm I, the German emperor, had eaten dinner there, and Ritz had made sure everyone knew it.) Baden-Baden was a summer resort, a place people came to for the casinos and the racetrack, and of course for the hotspring baths — *baden* is German for "bath" — and it was a town where, in the evening, elaborate dinner parties were held. So when Prince Radziwill, a leading member of the Kaiser's circle and Berlin society, told Ritz that he wanted to host a dinner that would be remembered — "something original," he said — and that cost was not a concern, Ritz seized the opportunity.

This was the sort of challenge Ritz loved: to create a spectacle. And all the better to do so with an unlimited budget. This would be more than a dinner; it would be an event. He landed upon a simple, summery idea: to bring the outside in. He covered the entire floor of the restaurant with grass, and the walls with roses, hundreds and hundreds of them. He placed potted trees among the tables and brought a stone fountain and pool into the restaurant and filled it with exotic goldfish. At the center of this theatrical indoor woodland scene was an enormous fern. Ritz had seen it at one of the local horticultural gardens and managed to rent it for the night. (That alone had cost a small fortune.) Then he built a table around the towering plant and covered that with yet more flowers. (Ritz was a great believer in flowers — vast, extravagant quantities of them. He sometimes thought he was single-handedly keeping the local florists in business.)

He hired an orchestra, designed the menu, and then basked in the delight of the prince and his guests. The scene was magical, transporting the diners into a kind of *Midsummer Night's Dream* stage-set fantasy, and the evening, despite all the logistical hurdles, was a stunning success.

It was just after dinner when Ritz was approached by an Englishman named Richard D'Oyly Carte. "This is the sort of thing," D'Oyly Carte said, his arm sweeping across the room, "I'd like to do at my new hotel in London."

D'Oyly Carte was a few years older than Ritz, in his mid-forties, a short, wiry, frenetic man with a full beard and piercing brown eyes that seemed to have an orange tint. He owned the Savoy Theatre on the Strand in London — this was "Theatreland," they called it, a raucous stretch of the Thames Embankment that was the center of bohemian London's nightlife. D'Oyly Carte was now building a large luxury hotel next door to his theater, also called the Savoy, one that he said would be the best in the world.

D'Oyly Carte had made his fortune producing Gilbert and Sullivan's comic operas, hugely popular entertainments that included *The Pirates of Penzance* and *The Mikado,* in the 1870s and '80s. The hotel was a long-held dream of his: a place for theatergoers

16

to eat dinner and, if they were from out of town, stay the night. D'Oyly Carte had traveled widely and was convinced that London was ready for a truly modern hotel.

The two men had met before, two years earlier, in Monte Carlo. D'Oyly Carte had stayed at the Grand, which Ritz was then managing, and had been effusive in his praise: "There is not a hotel in London," he proclaimed, "where you can get a decent meal . . . much less one where you can dine like a god, as one does here."

He went on to tell Ritz when they spoke in Monte Carlo that London desperately needed a good hotel with a good restaurant. Or, better yet, a great hotel with a great restaurant. Yes, what London needed was a man like Ritz. "You'd make money hand over fist," D'Oyly Carte said. "Hand over fist!" There were plenty of large hotels in London (the Langham, the Westminster Palace), but their food and service were mediocre. Unsophisticated. And as for the leading restaurants, they were banal. Stolid chophouses mostly, along with a few decent French restaurants, such as the Café Royal and Kettner's, both favored by the literary set. Still, there was nothing that could compare to the glamorous atmospherics and sophisticated cooking on the Continent.

Now, amid the trees and ferns and roses at the Restaurant de la Conversation, surrounded by German, French, and English high society, the orchestra playing, everyone drinking, Prince Radziwill holding court at the center of the room, D'Oyly Carte was no longer making idle small talk about the hotel business. He was offering Ritz a job: come to London, he said. See it for yourself. The Savoy was going to change everything. And he needed a man like Ritz to manage the hotel and restaurant.

Ritz had only smiled. London? No one even ate in restaurants there, at least not the aristocratic types he served in Provence and Baden-Baden. The English elites were tradition-bound, in Ritz's experience. They all ate at their private clubs, or entertained at home, either in town or at their country estates. Why would they come to a hotel for dinner?

And furthermore: Ritz had only just gone into business for himself, independently, taking charge of the restaurant in Baden-Baden and the nearby Hotel Minerva, and opening his hotel in Cannes. Not to mention he was newly married, just last year: his young wife, Marie, awaited his return from Baden-Baden even as they spoke. His plate was full. He had to say no.

D'Oyly Carte understood completely. But . . . and now a new idea formed. Why not come to London for the grand opening, just for a short visit — a week or two? Ritz could survey the operation and offer advice. His knowledge and expertise would be invaluable, said D'Oyly Carte. He would be a consultant, his very presence at the Savoy conferring legitimacy and guaranteeing its success. In fact, if Ritz agreed, D'Oyly Carte would announce to the press that the renowned César Ritz was overseeing the debut of the restaurant. And for this, D'Oyly Carte would be willing to pay a significant sum: £350.

He looked at Ritz in his keen, assessing way. It was a baldly mercenary offer, a form of prostitution, really: Ritz's reputation in exchange for cash. Still, £350 was a lot of money, the equivalent of a decent annual salary.

"He wants the clientele I can give him," Ritz told Marie when he arrived at home in Cannes — the guests he had courted and served over the years both there and in Baden-Baden, and before that in Monte Carlo and Lucerne, relationships he'd nurtured for years. First and foremost, "the Marlborough House set — Lord Rosebery, Lord and Lady Elcho, Lord and Lady Gosford, Lord and Lady de Grey, the Sassoons." They were members of London's social, political, and business elite: the Prince of Wales's inner circle, named for his residence on Pall Mall. Not far from Buckingham Palace, Marlborough House was a grand London mansion and had been home to Queen Victoria's eldest son and heir to the throne since the 1860s. The prince was a man of great appetites and good taste, and he traveled often. He was Ritz's most important client.

But it wasn't only English aristocrats who favored Ritz's hotels and who D'Oyly Carte hoped would come to the Savoy: there were "the Roman Princes, Rudini, the Crispis, the Rospigliosis, the Radziwills, and so forth," Ritz continued — all the great royal families of the Continent. "And the best of the theater and opera crowd — Patti, the de Reszkes, Coquelin, Bernhardt; the Grand Dukes, and the smart Parisian crowd — the Castellanes, the Breteuils, the Sagans." And, of course, the European and American financiers: "He wants the Vanderbilts and Morgans, he wants the Rothschilds."

There was nothing that gave Ritz more pleasure than contemplating this list of his most illustrious, glamorous guests — the prestige, money, and honor their names represented, prestige that had now attached itself in some way to his *own* name. And for a man who'd grown up herding cows and goats in the Swiss Alps, that was saying something.

Ritz was known in this rarified world. Respected. He had made something of himself. Ritz had been serving the Prince and Princess of Wales since the early 1880s; the royal couple had come to the Hôtel de Provence with their five children the previous year over Easter, and had addressed him as a friend. They had stayed for two weeks, their royal patronage a most valuable endorsement of Ritz's new venture: where the prince went, others invariably followed. And the prince was loyal.

Now D'Oyly Carte was hoping for a similar result in London, and hoping Ritz could help. If the prince and his friends were to embrace the Savoy, that alone would justify the cost of paying Ritz an exorbitant fee to attend the opening.

"He wants to make his hotel the *hotel de luxe* of London and of the world," Ritz told Marie.

"And he thinks your name alone can do it?" Marie asked.

"He says I am one of the titans of the hotel and restaurant world," Ritz said, laughing. "And he's right in thinking that my name now has a certain value. It will attract the crowd he wants — but it won't keep them. He hasn't the least idea how much work and care, how much imagination and effort, go into the proper running of a hotel."

Still, he was flattered — and curious. And so here he was on the train to London. The Savoy Hotel was opening the following Tuesday, August 6, 1889. Ritz would be there in his dark suit, a flower in his lapel, a temporary figurehead, a symbol of the Continental style and luxury the Savoy promised. Would it deliver? He felt a twinge of unease at the risk he'd taken on — the risk to his own reputation. Would it be tarnished if the Savoy failed to live up to expectations? Ritz didn't think so. He was his own man, with his own hotel. And this visit to London would also be an excellent opportunity to remind some of his many longtime English customers about his new, independent ventures in Cannes and Baden-Baden.

In London, meanwhile, Richard D'Oyly Carte was frantic. He was a theater man; he was used to opening nights. But there had never been one like this — three of them, actually, over the course of an eleven-day span:

First there was to be a "housewarming supper" hosted by Hwfa Williams, one of the seven directors of the Savoy Hotel Company, and his wife, Florence. Williams was a confidant of the Prince of Wales, a sportsman and man-about-town, founder of Sandown Park, the horseracing track in Surrey. His wife was a prominent member of London society, famously well dressed, one of the premier hostesses in a city full of them. A glittering assortment of well-titled aristocrats and other prominent couples was expected to attend.

Next was a larger event, this one for investors who'd bought shares in the company, for the many theater people associated with the Savoy, and for the press. D'Oyly Carte was billing this as a "private viewing," and he had invited hundreds.

Finally, the following week, came the actual, official opening of the hotel and restaurant.

D'Oyly Carte found himself consumed with anxiety, the deep and existential kind that accompanies great risk undertaken in public. He had put it all on the line for this hotel: his money, his friends' money, his reputation. Of course, he was accustomed to pressure. He was a producer, a man who wrangled and cajoled, persuaded and inspired. The egos and hysterics and the never-ending scramble for money were all in a day's work in the theater business. Still, this was different.

He had enlisted a group of high-profile investors: in addition to Williams, the company directors included the Earl of Lathom, who was the Lord Chamberlain (a political position within the royal household); A. G. Weguelin and R. B. Fenwick, both wealthy financiers; Michael Gunn, a theater impresario from Dublin; and Sir Arthur Sullivan, the composer — and of course D'Oyly Carte himself. This small group had put up the money to buy the land, construct the building, and launch the company, which had then raised £200,000 by selling shares. The share subscriptions, at £10 each, had been offered to the general public after the hotel was built but before it opened.

D'Oyly Carte had spent five years building the Savoy Hotel, and now was the moment of truth.

The structure itself was a technological marvel: seven stories high and built entirely of fireproof materials. The lighting was all electric, in every room, available twenty-four hours a day. Indeed, one could turn the bedroom light on or off, using a conveniently placed switch, *without getting out of bed.* D'Oyly Carte loved telling people this.

There were six American-made elevators, four for service and two for guests, all running twenty-four hours a day. The guest elevators were the largest ever seen in Europe, and were luxuriously appointed. D'Oyly Carte referred to them as "ascending rooms." The use of elevators erased any distinction in status or convenience between floors: the seventh-floor rooms were equal in height and in every other way to the rooms on any other floor — and cost the same, too. (This was unusual: most hotels charged far less for rooms on higher floors, which had traditionally been servants' quarters.) Also, there were speaking tubes, pipes that could carry voices over long distances, connecting every floor of the hotel to the kitchen, so guests could order breakfast, lunch, dinner, or supper and, within a few minutes, be served, D'Oyly Carte proudly exclaimed, "in the most perfect manner in their own rooms."

There was a total of four hundred guest rooms in the hotel, two hundred fifty of which were in suites, with sitting rooms and varying numbers of bedrooms. Many of the suites had their own private bathrooms and toilets, with hot and cold running water. In fact, there were sixty-seven bathrooms in all — an astounding number. When D'Oyly Carte showed the plans for the hotel to his builder, Mr. G. H. Holloway, he'd been met with incredulity. Was he planning to host amphibious guests at his hotel? the builder asked sarcastically. Sixty-seven bathrooms was unheard of — the Hotel Victoria, for example, recently opened on Northumberland Avenue, had a total of only four bathrooms for five hundred guests. Each room had a flat bath stored under the bed, and guests would ask servants to bring large canisters of hot and cold water to the room. The Savoy did away with such inconveniences; it was entirely modern.

This, however, is what worried D'Oyly Carte: there was a certain English disdain, at least in some quarters, for anything faddish, newfangled, or American. Indeed, it had been on his many trips to America, booking performances of Gilbert and Sullivan operas for his traveling theater company, that he had first stayed in hotels with elevators and private bathrooms. The enormous Palace Hotel in San Francisco had impressed him the most: it had five elevators and more than four hundred bathtubs

— and it had been built fourteen years ago, in 1875. The idea that elevators or modern plumbing might be viewed with suspicion was preposterous, but D'Oyly Carte understood that he needed to educate his clientele.

He had faced a similar challenge when opening the Savoy Theatre in 1881. It was one of the first buildings anywhere, and certainly the first theater in London, to be lit entirely by electricity, a fact that aroused much curiosity, but also fear. Was it safe? Just how flammable, exactly, was a lightbulb? D'Oyly Carte had printed reassuring information in the Savoy playbills about the building's fire-safety equipment:

The theatre is protected against fire by an elaborate system of water "sprinklers" placed over the stage, and also by the HARDEN STAR GRENADES (as adopted by Her Majesty).

The "grenades" were blue six-inch-tall spherical glass bottles filled with a liquid-chemical fire extinguisher. They were meant to be thrown at a fire, at which point they would explode and douse the flames. Harden Star Grenades were considered the best.

On the theater's opening night, D'Oyly Carte himself had taken the stage. He walked out with a standing lamp and switched it on. The audience fell silent. The lights were absolutely, perfectly safe, he said, as he covered the lightbulb with a thin muslin cloth, in the manner of a magician performing a trick. "You see there is no deception," he proclaimed — and then took out a hammer and smashed the glass bulb. The crowd gasped, tittered, and applauded. The point was made. The bulb had *not* exploded in a fireball, much to everyone's relief. The muslin cloth, furthermore, amazingly, was unsinged: D'Oyly Carte held it up for inspection, to loud cheers. The cheers continued even after he'd left the stage, and so he returned for another bow. Enjoy the show, he said.

Beyond electricity, the Savoy Theatre had been groundbreaking in other ways, pioneering standards that D'Oyly Carte knew would make the show better but that took some getting used to. For example: reserved seating and an organized queue. No longer would there be a rush to the best seats, leaving the less agile at the back of the house. There would be order. He also forbade tips of any kind, offered programs and coat check service free of charge, and served decent-quality, nonwatered-down whisky and real coffee (not chicory) at the theater bars.

He had, in other words, modernized not only the theater but the theatergoing experience itself. Powered by the hit musicals of Gilbert and Sullivan, and the dazzling performances of the "Savoyards," as the actors in the company came to be called, the Savoy was a runaway success, piling up huge profits year after year. Now the question was: could he do the same for the restaurant dining and hotel experiences?

Just as he had at the theater, D'Oyly Carte planned to eliminate all extraneous charges at the hotel, aiming for smoother and less irritating service. "No charge for Baths, Lights, or Attendance," announced the full-page advertisements for the hotel that D'Oyly Carte took out in the London papers. Such charges for basic services were common at most hotels, and infuriated him endlessly. Indeed, the multitude of fees and tips levied at hotels and inns was a remnant of the early Victorian era, and bitterly bemoaned as far back as the 1850s, when Albert Smith published his darkly comic treatise, *The English Hotel Nuisance,* a book that outlined every shabby indignity, over-priced candle, unusable bar of soap, inedible steak, uncomfortable room, and gouging fee charged for indifferent service at English hotels:

Let us first take, as an example of the spirit of Extortion brooding over most hotels, the elaborate and expensive process of washing one's hands, which is as follows:

The first stage: You go into the coffee-room, and, previous to dining, wish to wash your hands.

The second stage: You ring the bell, and the waiter appears, to whom you communicate your wish. He says "Hands, sir, yes — sir," and goes away.

The third stage: After waiting a considerable time, you ring again.

The fourth stage: He then conducts you to the foot of the staircase, and calls up it to the chambermaid.

The fifth stage: You stand in expectancy with the waiter for a little while upon the rug, and then the chambermaid appears.

The sixth stage: She precedes you up some stairs, and down others, and along passages on different levels, and round corners, and at last introduces you to a bedroom.

The seventh stage: She next draws the bed-curtains, and pulls down the blind —

not because such is wanted, but from mere mechanical habit, and then leaves you to your own devices.

The eighth stage: You find some hard water that would curdle the soap, if it would dissolve; but you might as well wash with a bit of chalk, as with the singularly hard white cake in the soap dish. There is one towel, damp and hard, and very like embossed paste-board.

The ninth stage: With these aids you make what toilet you may, and then come out to find the attendant waiting for her fee at the door.

This is no exaggeration: I am certain there are few of my readers who will not bear me out in the truth of the picture.

D'Oyly Carte had great ambitions for the hotel restaurant, which would be open to the public, and not only to guests. He had announced the formation of a "restaurant committee," an offshoot of the board of directors, a group of influential Londoners who would consult and advise on matters related to food and wine. D'Oyly Carte hoped they would also be frequent guests, and bring their friends. The committee included Earl de Grey, Reuben Sassoon, Arthur Sullivan, and Hwfa Williams — all men of renowned good taste.

As D'Oyly Carte said to César Ritz when they first met, there was no world-class restaurant in London, and he meant to change that. "The restaurant is intended to be cosmopolitan," he said — it would "equal such famous establishments as Bignon's, the Café Anglais, and others in Paris; Delmonico's or the Brunswick, in New York; the Belle-Vue, in Philadelphia; and Pfordte's, in Hamburg." These were the great restaurants of the nineteenth century: the Café Anglais dated back to 1802, Delmonico's to 1827, chef Louis Bignon's Café Foy to the 1840s, Franz Pfordte's namesake establishment to 1859. They served mostly French or French-influenced dishes in warrens of wood-paneled private dining rooms, attracting fashionable crowds — generally men, as was typical of the period. Each was well known in its city and beyond, at least among sophisticated travelers, just the sort of renown D'Oyly Carte planned to achieve at the Savoy.

As for the food: it would be mainly French, of course, but not exclusively. D'Oyly Carte wanted the menu to include English, Russian, German, and Indian dishes, too. "A marked importance will be given to the special products of the United

States — canvas-back ducks, terrapin, clams, American oysters, green corn and other luxuries being imported as in season, so that the traveling Americans will be well catered for."

Americans were coming to London in ever-greater numbers, crossing the Atlantic in ever-larger and more luxurious ocean liners, and they had money. D'Oyly Carte knew that they would be one of the keys to his success. At the same time, he needed to convince the old guard of London society to leave their private clubs and entertain in a more public venue — and to do so alongside these wealthy Americans.

He had hired François Rinjoux, the maître d' at the Grand Hotel in Monte Carlo, to oversee the restaurant's operation. Rinjoux was the epitome of the French maître d'hôtel, known to one and all by his first name. "François!" customers called out when they saw him. Monsieur Charpentier, meanwhile, who had been the chef at White's, the venerable gentlemen's club on St. James's Street, would run the kitchen. He was a classic and proper French chef, of the old school. And as for general manager, after Ritz had declined the job, D'Oyly Carte hired W. Hardwicke, who had long experience running the staff of a large private home. Hardwicke's senior staff were likewise mostly former high-level private service personnel — butlers and footmen.

It was all coming together. The truth was, D'Oyly Carte enjoyed the pressure, the rush of putting on a show. It was exhilarating, if a little panic-inducing, particularly the financial end of things. The Savoy Hotel Company stock subscription had gone well enough, but his future was riding on the success of the venture. He had sunk a good portion of his own wealth into the business. He was invested in every way.

As usual, he put thoughts of money and balance sheets out of his mind. He was not prone to dwell on such details. D'Oyly Carte was a man of instinct and forward-charging energy and passion. Always one eye on the next big thing, the next opening. He was famous at the theater for doing everything at the same time. He might be found dictating telegrams from his box at the Savoy, watching a dress rehearsal, consulting with the director about last-minute production changes, all while also giving an interview to a newspaper columnist about his new hotel, and eating lunch.

Now he was drowning in last-minute logistics — scheduling, deliveries, staffing, supplies; everything late, expensive, and not quite right. It was just like a play: yes, it would all come together in the end. Opening night, they would be ready. Not every show succeeded; he knew that. You launched them as well as you could and hoped for the best.

2

A LONDON DEBUT

The Hwfa Williams housewarming supper at the Savoy didn't start until midnight on Saturday, July 27, 1889, after the performance at the Covent Garden opera ended and guests had made their way to the hotel. The late hour served only to accentuate the slightly giddy, celebratory ambience.

Horse-drawn carriages pulled up into the Savoy courtyard from the Thames Embankment, one after the other, as guests climbed the steps to the entrance, admiring the nighttime view: the row of gaslights along the waterfront, the looming outline of Cleopatra's Needle, cloaked in misty darkness. Inside, the hotel dazzled with over-bright electric lights. The décor was formal, even grand: carved wooden wall panels beneath a golden frieze, and ceilings in gold and red. There were flowers on all the tables, and at the far end of the room, the London Military Band had begun to play.

Helen D'Oyly Carte surveyed the scene as she and her husband welcomed guests and thanked them for their good wishes. The Savoy was splendid, they all said. What a delightful room!

Helen was Richard's second wife, and it was complicated. They had married the previous year, but she'd been working for him since the 1870s (more than ten years), and they'd been in love for most of that time. His first wife, Blanche, had died of pneumonia in 1885 after a long illness, at the age of thirty-two. Helen and Richard had waited an appropriate amount of time, puzzling through the oddness of their circumstance, going from employer and employee to married couple and full partners. Of course, Richard took the lead. It was his business. But the truth was, Helen was indispensable. She ran whole swaths of her husband's theater operations, and was intimately involved in the launch of the hotel, too. She was canny and intelligent. What she was particularly good at was the actual business part of business: the details, the money, the contracts, the negotiations, the schedules, all of it.

Helen had made more than a dozen trips to America over the past decade, many more than Richard, overseeing the Savoy's touring company and establishing copyright protections for Gilbert and Sullivan's works. (This was not always successful — the staging of unauthorized versions of the hit musicals was rampant — but she did her best.) There were frequent visits to San Francisco, Philadelphia, and New Orleans with the touring company, but mostly Helen had worked out of a small office in New York, on the corner of Broadway and Thirty-Second Street. It was from there, for example, that she helped arrange American lecture tours for D'Oyly Carte clients, including essayist Matthew Arnold and playwright Oscar Wilde.

The Wilde tour had been a sensation, timed to coincide with the 1882 New York opening of Gilbert and Sullivan's *Patience.* The play was a satire of the aesthetic movement — the effete, decadent, sensuous art and poetry of the 1870s — and of the self-serious aesthetes themselves. The main character, Bunthorne, wore a velvet jacket, knee breeches, and a monocle; carried a sunflower wherever he went; and offered pronouncements on art and beauty. Bunthorne was loosely modeled on the painter James McNeill Whistler and the poet Algernon Swinburne, but it was Wilde, who had just published his first collection of

38

poetry, whom D'Oyly Carte had hired to tour the United States. There was a great deal of interest in the aesthetic movement, and in the endlessly witty and peculiarly dressed Wilde. In city after city, he gave lectures on the decorative arts and poetry, traveling from New York to St. Louis to San Francisco. The tour was an enormous success, and was extended to last almost a year. Helen made all the arrangements.

Helen was unusually well educated for a woman of the time. Born and raised in Scotland, where her father was a bank manager, she had attended London University as one of the first four women honors candidates granted admission there. She had received certificates, as reported in the London *Times,* for passing exams in mathematics and mechanical philosophy (the term for technology) and in logic and moral philosophy. She was on the path to a career in education but soon found herself drawn in another direction. Teaching, as it turned out, bored her. She worked for a while as a tutor to daughters of wealthy families in London, but spent all her free time going to the theater. Soon she was taking classes in singing, dancing, and elocution, and dreaming of a career as an actress.

"Helen Lenoir" became her suitably glamorous stage name, and she moved to Dublin to take a small role in a comedy called *Aladdin and His Wonderful Lamp,* at the Theatre Royal. This was a fortunate engagement, for it was in Dublin that she met Michael Gunn, the manager of the theater, and it was he, in turn, who gave her a letter of introduction to his old friend Richard D'Oyly Carte in London.

She appeared in D'Oyly Carte's office on the Strand — R. D'OYLY CARTE, MUSICAL AND THEATRICAL AGENT, read the sign on the door — at noon one February day in 1877 and presented the letter. Her name was Helen Lenoir, she said, and she was looking for work as an actress.

"Oh no," said D'Oyly Carte. "All my actors are coming back from pantomimes and I cannot find places for any of them. And I am sorry, but now I have to go out to lunch. But at present I do not need anyone at all."

"Oh yes you do, Mr. Carte," said Helen. "You need someone to tidy this office."

That was always how she told the story anyway, casting herself as the plainspoken and well-organized aide to the brash and permanently harried D'Oyly Carte.

And thus had begun her career in the theater, though not quite as she'd planned. She soon found herself working as a secretary for D'Oyly Carte and his three other employees. She pursued a few acting jobs that year (a small role in a legal comedy called *The Great Divorce Case*), but discovered that her real talent was managing and organizing: D'Oyly Carte was a dynamo, fiery and impulsive, and Helen's calm and meticulous rigor were just what the business needed as it grew. Richard and Helen proved to be an excellent team.

Gilbert and Sullivan, on the other hand, the creative source of much of D'Oyly Carte's success, were a temperamental pair, and it fell as often as not to Helen to smooth things over. W. S. Gilbert, in particular, the librettist, could be difficult, his sense of grievance always close to the surface. Arthur Sullivan, who wrote the music, was more congenial. His signing on as a director of the Savoy Hotel Company, for example, was a show of support for D'Oyly Carte, and he had of course agreed to come to the hotel opening that evening.

He was one of a number of theater people in attendance, including Michael Gunn, from Dublin, who had introduced Helen to Richard those many years before. Like Sullivan, Gunn had invested in the hotel out of loyalty to D'Oyly Carte, and joined the board of directors. The theater people were scattered around the dining room, offering a dash of bohemian raffishness to the otherwise genteel proceedings.

Although D'Oyly Carte had overseen the organization of the party, and made sure to invite his friends and confidants, Hwfa Williams was the event's official host. A large and glamorous assortment of high-society regulars had come. There was the beautiful Consuelo Montagu, the Duchess of Manchester, an American socialite in her late thirties who had married into the British aristocracy. Lord and Lady Dudley, Lord and Lady de Grey, Lord Hartington, and Lord Hardwicke were all in attendance — leading lights of London society. Lady de Grey in particular was a prolific hostess and patron of the arts. She made a point of inviting artists, writers, musicians, and various foreign intellectuals to her luncheon parties — the French author Jules Claretie, for example, and Oscar Wilde. Lady Randolph Churchill, another American — she was born Jennie Jerome in Brooklyn — had also come. Though her husband was a politician, and they had two young sons, John and Winston, her dark eyes, seductive manner, and friendliness with the Prince of Wales were a topic of much gossip and speculation.

Sullivan sat at a further table of aristocrats, including Lady Claud Hamilton, Lord and Lady Gosford, and Lord Dunraven, and charmed them all. There was also a contingent from the English branch of the Rothschild family, the wealthy banking clan, and from the American Forbes family. His Imperial Highness Prince Ernst Hohenlohe of Württemberg, a kingdom in southern Germany, was also in attendance.

There were no members of the British royal family at the party. Richard and Helen had grumbled to each other privately about this, but what could they do? As circumstance would have it, the wedding of the Prince of Wales's eldest daughter, Princess Louise, had taken place that very day at Buckingham Palace, and this evening the prince was hosting a reception in celebration at Marlborough House. Numerous European royals were in London for the wedding, including the King of Greece and the Crown Prince of Denmark; D'Oyly Carte hoped that some of them would find their way to the Savoy that week. Indeed, given the royal wedding, it was remarkable that Hwfa Williams and the Savoy had drawn such a glamorous crowd, including a good showing from the Marlborough House set. (Not every member of this diffuse social circle had been invited to the royal wedding, apparently.)

In the constellation of London society, no one was more important than the Prince of Wales. He had ushered in a new era of license and pleasure in the 1880s. Unlike his famously remote mother, Queen Victoria, ensconced in a world of court tradition and formality, the prince was a man-about-town. He liked to eat and drink, surrounded himself with bons vivants, and carried on affairs with numerous women — some of them married to his friends. He presided over a generation of London society that was more open, more wealthy, more dashing, and more fun. This was precisely the new London for which D'Oyly Carte had designed the Savoy, so of course the prince's absence was keenly felt.

Still, it didn't really matter: the prince's friends were there, and that would have to be good enough.

At the large oval head table, in the center of the room, Mrs. Hwfa Williams, in a pink-and-gray gown, laughed with Lady Churchill. All around the room were women in dresses in a great variety of designs and colors — Lady Dudley in all white, Lady Clarendon in black with pink roses. Some of the gowns were slim and high-waisted;

others made use of a rigid bustle, although this figure-enhancing fashion was by now on the way out. "Charles Frederick Worth now eschews even the semblance of a bustle," reported the *Rational Dress Society Gazette* in the fall of 1888, referring to the prominent Parisian dressmaker. "The news seems almost too good to be true. We will actually be able to lean back in a carriage or on a chair once more." So-called rational dress had become a political cause: suffering for fashion in a girdle or a bustle was not only unhealthy — it was wrong.

The 1880s had seen huge changes in women's fashion, a liberation of sorts. Liberation from the constrictions of the girdle, yes, but also from the previously strict rules about morning dresses, walking dresses, visiting dresses, dinner dresses, and ball gowns, and when exactly to wear each of them. "Now, women dress for dinner in as many different ways as the meal is served," the magazine *The Woman's World* had just announced. "Low gowns, half high gowns, or tea gowns which are akin to dressing gowns, or tea gowns that closely resemble the revised court bodice, inspired by the modes of mediaeval times — all these are popular!"

Just a few years old, the magazine was one

of a slew being published in London for modern, forward-thinking women. Oscar Wilde was the editor.

A similar liberation was under way when it came to the staging of an event such as the opening of the Savoy. Married couples, for example, were not seated together or even necessarily at the same table. Prior to the opening, there had of course been much agonizing about who would sit where, all of which had been handled by Mrs. Hwfa Williams. The evening's hostess had a perfect understanding of the politics of rank and prestige that was so thoroughly codified among the titled aristocrats, but also a good sense of drama, the pleasure of mixing things up.

Waiters circulated with glasses of champagne, and everyone was talking and drinking and watching everyone else talk and drink. It had been a wonderful season in London, they all agreed: so many lovely dinners and soirees. The late-night debut of the Savoy was a fitting conclusion to the summer festivities. The room was beautiful, the crowd was noisy, and the champagne was excellent.

The menu had been designed by Charpentier, and it was simple: a midnight sup-

per and not a full dinner. There was to be
no dessert.

CROUSTADES DE CREVETTES DIEPPOIS
Shrimp croustades with Dieppois sauce

❈

CAILLES DE VIGNE
Quail wrapped in grape leaves

❈

DEUTZ & GELDERMANN GOLD LACK, 1880

The croustades (thin rounds of pastry)
were served with shrimp in a light white
wine-and-cream sauce made with mussels
and mushrooms (the Dieppois); the quail
was roasted with grape leaves and slices of
bacon. The waiters continued to pour the
Deutz and Geldermann vintage champagne,
bottle after bottle.

D'Oyly Carte was enjoying himself immensely. He listened as Algernon "Algy"
Bourke, who owned White's gentlemen's
club and whose chef D'Oyly Carte had
poached, remonstrated with him half-
jokingly about his loss. Charpentier was the
best in London, Algy declared, destined for
great things.

There was a long history of French chefs
working in England, in private homes and

clubs; employing a French chef was a sign of status and refinement going back decades. Louis-Eustache Ude, for example, had been the well-known chef at Crockfords, the exclusive London gambling club on St. James's Street, in the 1820s and '30s; Alexis Soyer was the famous chef at the Reform Club on Pall Mall in the 1830s and '40s. Both had written cookbooks aimed at an English audience — Ude's was called *The French Chef* — offering up simplified and sometimes bastardized versions of French dishes. Indeed, the predicament of the French chef in England had long been that the English sometimes liked the idea of French food more than the food itself. They wanted a joint of mutton, but they wanted to call it a *gigot d'agneau.* Pheasants tasted better when they appeared on the menu as *faisans.* And so on.

But that was starting to change. Charpentier's quail were excellent. London was ready for real French cooking; D'Oyly Carte was sure of it.

Hwfa Williams agreed wholeheartedly — he only wished he could transport the entire Savoy restaurant out to his racetrack, Sandown Park. That would be something! D'Oyly Carte laughed and laughed.

After dinner, there were no formal toasts

or speeches. This was not that sort of party, thank God, thought Helen D'Oyly Carte. (Pompous speeches were a common hazard at many such events, populated as they were by politicians and other men who loved to talk.) Instead, there was dancing. The band began to play again, and couples took their turns around the small dance floor, the younger among them spilling out into the carpeted anterooms and lobby, where they soon discovered the thrill of the elevators. Elevators! These were a novelty, and now couples crowded into them for a ride up to the seventh floor and back again. This went on all night.

Helen observed the scene from her seat in the dining room. She could see her husband savoring the glory of the evening's success. What had been an abstraction, a dream, was now real, and he was surrounded by his investors, acolytes, and friends — and a few society columnists, too, who would be sure to report on the party.

For her part, Helen was watchful, fully alert to the foibles and failings of the newly hired restaurant staff. The service was fine, but there were rough edges, and she took note of every delay, every empty champagne glass awaiting a refill, every fumbled pronunciation of *croustades de crevettes Diep-*

pois. This was her role: to attend to the details. She was a nervous, meticulous person, and fiercely protective of her husband. She would talk to Hardwicke and Rinjoux in the morning about getting the staff in shape.

Ritz had never seen anything like it. London was a metropolis of five and a half million people — more than twice the population of Paris, the next-biggest city in Europe, and far bigger than New York City, Canton, Berlin, Tokyo, Vienna, or any other city in the world, for that matter. It was the booming center of a global empire. There were vast amounts of money here, and an unrivaled concentration of business, politics, and trade. There were new buildings going up, new streets being built, old streets being widened, and an underground electric railway, the first in the world, under construction. Shops and department stores were opening and expanding: jewelers, dressmakers, shoemakers, milliners, cabinet-makers, grocers, sporting goods suppliers, emporia of all kinds catering to the shopping needs of the leisure class. The larger establishments employed huge staffs who lived in nearby residence halls. The city was teeming with commerce.

Ritz arrived at Charing Cross Station at ten o'clock at night, a week after the Hwfa Williams supper at the Savoy on July 27. He'd been traveling for more than twenty-four hours, and he marveled at the speed of the journey. London was another world, and it amazed him that in a single day, more or less, he had come so unfathomably far.

Outside the station, the roads were crowded with horses and carriages, the cobblestone streets clattering with traffic, dust and dung everywhere, shouting cab-men looking for fares, unwieldy horse-drawn trams and omnibuses lumbering by, plastered with advertisements for Pears Soap, Oakey's Knife Polish, Horlick's Malted Milk, Colman's Mustard, and many other things. There were billboards on top of buildings and posters on the sides of taxi stands. Street lamps lit up the Strand and other thoroughfares, while smaller streets and alleys disappeared in total darkness. Ritz hailed a cab and directed it to the Savoy.

There was no denying it: the hotel was magnificent. Ritz was given a large suite of rooms, exquisitely decorated. There was too much drapery and wallpaper for his taste, but he said nothing as the attendant took care of his suitcase and D'Oyly Carte showed off the view from the balcony. The river flowed silently below, and all of London was laid out before them, glowing here and there in the dark. To the west were Westminster Bridge and the Houses of Parliament, D'Oyly Carte explained, pointing; and to the east, one could see St. Paul's Cathedral and the Tower of London. Due south, far in the distance, was the Crystal Palace.

D'Oyly Carte had taken the trouble to greet Ritz in the lobby, to accompany him to his room. He was understandably proud of the hotel. "I do not know that there is any view so beautiful from any hotel in Europe as is the view by night from the balconies of the Savoy Hotel," he said, and he was right. The hotel's location could not have been better.

Now he showed Ritz a sheaf of recent newspaper clippings. The Savoy had not yet opened but was already the subject of intense interest: there were fawning descriptions of the Hwfa Williams supper, which included long lists of every grand person in attendance; there were similar accounts of the open house for investors the previous week, also listing all the "theatrical celebrities" who'd made an appearance; there were articles written in the arch, knowing style of high-society gossip: "Clara Jecks, just back from Switzerland, led the way in climbing the Alpine heights of the top story, inwardly wondering why they don't have a lift up Mont Blanc as well as at this hotel," read the *Oracle,* noting the actress's presence. And there were countless news reports about the hotel's preopening preparations, describing the facilities and staff — many of them taking note of Ritz's expected presence at the hotel.

This was what D'Oyly Carte wanted him to see.

Look here, he said, in *Era:* "M. Ritz, proprietor of the Hotel Minerva, Baden-Baden, is at present in London directing the opening of the restaurant."

Ritz saw announcements of his arrival in London in a number of papers, and he was flattered — and impressed with D'Oyly Carte's uncanny ability to win the attention of the press. It made sense, given his background in theater. The sheer quantity of articles was also an indication of London's ferocious and fantastic popular press: there were articles about the Savoy in the *Times,* the *Sunday Times,* the *Observer,* the *World,* the *Globe,* the *Economist, Society, Lighthouse, Sporting Life,* the *Morning Advertiser,* the *Financial Times,* the *Daily News,* the *Pall*

Mall Gazette, the *Pall Mall Budget,* the *News of the World,* the *Daily Telegraph,* the *City Press, People, Oracle, Vanity Fair,* the *Daily Chronicle,* and the *Society Herald* — all before the hotel had opened its doors.

D'Oyly Carte had arranged for Ritz to examine every aspect of the hotel and restaurant operations over the coming days. He would tour the building from top to bottom; he would meet the staff; he would dive into the minutiae of how dinner orders were to be handled in the kitchen and how the front desk would respond to special requests from guests. D'Oyly Carte wanted Ritz's advice and guidance, he said — Ritz knew better than anyone what the Savoy's clientele expected and, more than that, what might delight them.

And so Ritz threw himself into the job, if only for two weeks, and was immediately pulled into the grand extravaganza of the Savoy's opening week, and of London high society in general. The hotel was set to open on Tuesday, August 6, a few days after he arrived. It was the end of the so-called season, the spring and summer months in London that brought society families from their country estates and into the city for balls, dinners, and debutante coming-out parties, for the horse races at Ascot and for meetings of Parliament. Some families kept a house in the city for this purpose; others rented one for the summer, bringing a number of their household staff with them. But if now, in August, the season was mostly over, everyone was still in town, it seemed, and they were all making appearances at the Savoy.

Ritz was perfectly attuned to the rhythms of the social calendar — he'd spent his entire working life in thrall to it: in Cannes, Lucerne, Monte Carlo, and Baden-Baden. Yet everywhere he'd welcomed aristocratic guests over the years, it was always precisely *not* during the London season that he'd welcomed them: they came to the Alps in late summer and the Cote d'Azur in the winter. Indeed, Ritz's guests came to his hotels as often as not, it seemed, to recuperate from the rigors of all those London masquerade balls and late-night suppers.

Now here he was, in the thick of it.

A cascade of royalty, glamour, and money poured through the doors of the Savoy for lunches and dinners; there were parties and receptions at the hotel, and processions and gala opera nights all over the city that brought visitors to the restaurant afterward. The recent royal wedding of Princess Louise had drawn numerous aristocrats from the Continent, and they were still in London. The Shah of Persia was in town. Ritz saw the Duc d'Aumale, the Duc d'Orléans, and even the exiled French ultranationalist general Georges Boulanger, who had fled to England after being accused of treason a few months earlier. Theater and opera stars thronged the Savoy, not surprising given D'Oyly Carte's background, as did prominent businessmen, who attended dinner parties in the smaller private dining rooms.

It was as if, all these years, Ritz had been on the outside looking in and now he was inside and the music was louder and the lights were brighter and it was much more crowded and wonderful than he'd ever imagined. This was the very heart of a world that had shaped him, a world of privilege and luxury in which he had forged a place for himself, against all odds. Ritz had not been born to this life. Raised in Niederwald, a tiny village (population 123) in the foothills of the Swiss Alps in Valais, he was the last of eleven children, and had left home at the age of twelve. He was a self-made man. And beneath his placid, imperturbable Swiss poise lay enormous ambition.

He knew immediately that the Savoy had every reason to succeed. It was the right time and the right place for a modern luxury hotel: London was booming. On a visit to the opera one night to see the American soprano Emma Eames perform in Charles Gounod's *Roméo et Juliette* — longtime clients often invited him to the theater — Ritz looked at the audience and swore he'd never seen so much flamboyant money, so many beautiful women wearing so many diamonds, not even in Second Empire Paris in the 1860s. Yes, the Savoy should succeed — except . . .

Except that as the days went by, his doubts crept in.

The restaurant, for example: His old friend from the Grand Hotel in Monte Carlo, François Rinjoux, was running the show as the maître d'hôtel, and that was good. Still, there was no way, Ritz could see already, that the kitchen would live up to D'Oyly Carte's grand ambitions for the place. It was not organized properly for à la carte dining. True, it was on the same floor as the dining room (rather than below-ground, as was common), which ought to have increased efficiency. But service was slow. Achieving the speed and precision that would allow for large numbers of many different dishes to be served at the same time (as opposed to a banquet with a limited menu) would require further division of labor in the kitchen. Nor was Charpentier's menu ambitious enough. The food was fine, consisting of competent executions of mostly French classics, but it was not great; it was not awe-inspiring.

It was not Escoffier.

Ritz knew better than anyone the importance of the kitchen in creating a truly luxurious hotel experience. He had built his success in the hotel business in tandem with the brilliant chef Auguste Escoffier. At the Grand Hotel in Monte Carlo and the Grand Hotel National in Lucerne, where they had both worked for years, Escoffier had dazzled guests with his cooking, inventing new dishes and finding new ways of presenting classics. Ritz often thought that Escoffier, in fact, was the key to his own success. The Savoy's Charpentier was not on the same level.

And then there was Hardwicke, the manager of the Savoy. He was a charming man but had none of the verve or watchfulness the job required. Running a hotel was not the same as running a household. It required equal parts self-effacement and bold, quick-witted imagination. As with the restaurant, the hotel staff seemed unprepared to deliver personalized service. In general, the service was too formal, not light on its feet. The ambience of the Savoy was too somber.

Ritz was well aware that his real purpose was to offer a sheen of Continental sophistication to the proceedings — his mere presence was mostly what D'Oyly Carte wanted. He was not there to direct and organize the staff, but to offer advice, which he did politely, and to welcome some of the restaurant guests familiar to him from his years working in resort hotels. To those guests who recognized him, he represented elegance, reassuring them that the Savoy, for all its technological marvels, would also be truly luxurious.

Still, he could see every flaw, and how to fix them.

The décor of the hotel, the restaurant in particular, was overly dark and masculine — clublike, with all that mahogany wainscoting and wallpaper. The furnishings were in good taste, but heavy: imposing armoires and in-set mirrors. And all the drapery and wallpaper everywhere (Japanese designs, tapestries) — it was overwhelming. The lighting, meanwhile, was too bright, unflattering to the ladies in their evening gowns.

D'Oyly Carte had told Ritz proudly that it was his wife, Helen, who had taken charge of the décor, so Ritz held his tongue. Unlike her husband, who was voluble and enthusiastic, Helen was harder to fathom. She was obviously capable, if a bit nervous. She was a slim, tiny woman, vivacious and not quite beautiful. She was also not particularly friendly.

Helen herself showed Ritz the lobby's sitting and reading rooms, for which she had purchased a large number of desks and cabinets, filled with glass and china knickknacks. They were nice enough, but there was too much of everything, Ritz thought.

There was no point in antagonizing Helen with his views on hotel design, so he didn't. And anyway, the real problems were deeper. Alone in his room at the end of his two-week stay, Ritz contemplated the Savoy's future.

"It will not succeed," he thought. "Not under its present management. The equipment is excellent. The staff is fairly good, and could easily be whipped into shape. Needs a little weeding out, that's all. The *cuisine* . . . is uninteresting. It should be much better. The directors are eager to make a success of it and seem very generous in their ideas. But, in my opinion, the management and organization will have to be improved, or the thing will not be successful."

He had no regrets about turning down the

job D'Oyly Carte had offered. Ritz had
spent years working for others and was now,
finally, a hotel owner himself. Of course he
had investors and, yes, his hotels were small,
but they were *his*. And seeing the wealth in
London, and the many travelers passing
through, only reinforced his desire for
independence — and his confidence in his
own success.

3
AN OFFER TOO GOOD
TO REFUSE

Ritz had been so preoccupied in London
that he failed to send his wife a single letter.
He'd never been much of a writer, but usually sent Marie regular notes while traveling. This time all she got were two brief
telegrams, one announcing that he'd arrived
in London and, two weeks later, another
saying that he was leaving and would be
back in Cannes the next day.

Marie Ritz was twenty-one years old. She
had grown up in the hotel business, working at her mother's modest, old-fashioned
Hotel de Monte Carlo, and at her aunt and
uncle's luxurious Grand Hotel, also in
Monte Carlo. Another aunt and uncle
owned the Hôtel des Iles Britanniques, in
nearby Menton, and it was here that she'd
first encountered her future husband, who
was managing the hotel for the winter
season in 1877. She'd been a child, eleven
years old, and noticed only that Ritz was

old and well dressed, and that he chided her and her cousin once for giggling. They'd fallen in love in the mid-1880s, after she was finished with school and César had moved on to managing the Grand, her family's best hotel. (He continued to work in Switzerland during the summer.)

She was young, beautiful, and well-off; César had grown up in relative poverty, and had proposed marriage only after he'd left the employ of her family and gone into business for himself. Ritz was proud, but also full of what Marie thought were silly insecurities: about his Swiss peasant family background, his lack of education.

She loved to tease him. Ritz was overly self-conscious about his appearance, and something of a dandy, doing everything in his power to eliminate any trace of his meager origins. He had spent his youth as a waiter serving the high and mighty, observing just exactly how his customers comported themselves, how they spoke, how they wore their jackets . . .

When he arrived in Paris from Switzerland, at the age of seventeen, the first thing he did was change his name. Well, the spelling of his name anyway. Growing up, he'd been Cäsar, spelled with an umlaut and pronounced the German way, with an initial

"Tse" sound. Once in Paris, though, he quickly replaced the *ä* with an elegant French *é,* and adopted the French pronunciation, with a soft *C.* He was César now, César Ritz. He liked the sound of it.

Within a few years, Ritz had worked his way up as a waiter at some of the best Parisian restaurants. In the early 1870s he was working at the Hôtel Splendide; he still remembered serving the American railroad tycoon Jay Gould. At the end of the meal, Gould had offered Ritz some advice: "It's a mathematical certainty the new age is going to be an age of electricity and steel," he said. "Bank on it. But don't let machinery govern you. Take off your coat now and again and work in a garden. That's what the new generation must learn to do if it wants to keep sane."

Gould went on to describe his love of manual labor, of working outside, of digging his hands into the soil and how invigorating it all was. "When you're working, all sorts of ideas come to you," he said.

Ritz had grown up on a farm, herding livestock on an alp in Switzerland from a very young age. He knew all about hard outdoor work, and the irony of the robberbaron millionaire telling him, oh so wisely, about the benefits of working the land were not lost on him. Everything Ritz had done in his life he had done in order to *escape* that fate. He had seen too much of the hardscrabble, desperate life of peasants to romanticize it.

Of course, he could say none of this to Gould, and only smiled as he cleared the dishes from the table.

Later, he told Marie the stories of his early life, his struggles, his ambition, his fears. And she alone understood. His silence at that moment, listening to Jay Gould, listening politely to all the rich men who gave him their dinner orders, and to all the employers who'd chastised and corrected him over the years — it was that silence that propelled him now. He had persevered. "You'll never make anything of yourself in the hotel business," his boss at one of his very first jobs, in Brieg, Switzerland, had told him. "It takes a special knack, a special *flair,* and it's only right that I should tell you the truth: you haven't got it." Well, he'd got it now.

Marie was blonde, with dark eyes and a self-confident manner. She was her husband's closest confidante, and also his muse. He adored her. She inspired him, and calmed him. Ritz's high-strung perfectionism would sometimes turn, in private, to introspection and doubt, and Marie was the one who soothed his nerves. After a long day at work, sitting with his black-and-tan terrier at his feet, Ritz would ask Marie to play the piano. When they were alone, he called her by her nickname, Mimi.

"Oh, but I'm tired!" he would sigh. "Tired, tired, tired." He'd take her hand and kiss it. "Now, let's have some music. Play something soothing . . . sing some quiet music."

Marie would sit at the piano and play "Ave Maria" for César and listen to him talk about the hotel business.

But when he got back from his trip to London, he was far from tired. No: he returned in a "fever of excitement," as Marie described it. He told her about the Savoy in every detail, about London's immense wealth and energy, all the celebrities and royalty he'd seen there, the parade of women's fashion, and, finally, about his considered, expert opinion that the hotel would not succeed.

It would not succeed without *him* was what he meant.

Marie could sense her husband's anguish. He had seen the future in London, and he wanted so much to be a part of it. César was happiest when he was busy, going

66

nonstop, and the challenge the Savoy represented was tantalizing to him. At the same time, he was proud and immensely protective of his recent independence. He would not go back to being an employee.

But he couldn't stop talking about it. The Savoy had made an impression.

Marie was particularly taken with César's descriptions of the fashionable women crowding into the hotel, swanning through the lobby and into the restaurant in dresses without elaborate trains or bustles. At twenty-one, she herself was a member of a new generation, an exemplar of what the newspapers and magazines would soon be calling the "New Woman," one who had every intention of maintaining her independence, and never wearing a bustle.

It was a moment in time when the future seemed to be arriving faster than ever — socially, culturally, technologically. A sense of change was in the air. Earlier that year, Marie and César had gone to Paris together and visited the Paris Exposition. The Eiffel Tower, César declared, was the crowning achievement of the nineteenth century. The tallest structure in the world and made entirely of steel, it was the new symbol of France. They watched Buffalo Bill perform feats of horsemanship with his troop of

American cowboys; the star of the show was the sharpshooter Annie Oakley, who was especially popular among women. They also saw all kinds of inventions that César said would reduce kitchen labor and improve hotel keeping. There were, for example, Thomas Edison's "speaking machine," or phonograph, and other electronic gadgets. A bank of telephones had also been set up at the exposition, connected to telephones at the Paris Opéra and the Opéra Comique. Listeners could hear live performances from across the city, amazingly, as crowds gathered around, watching them listen, waiting for a turn. Soon enough, César was sure, guests would be calling hotels on the telephone to make reservations, rather than sending letters.

Marie had gone clothes shopping — that was why she'd come to Paris. Both Worth and Jacques Doucet, the leading dressmakers, were showing shockingly masculine-looking tailored dresses, and she wanted one. "So mannish!" she thought. César was dubious. "Would it suit your type?" he asked. The jacket had pockets, just like a man's suit. And the skirt was short, almost revealing her ankles. She ordered the outfit in dark green and wore it with a green *toque,* a newly popular style of narrow-brimmed hat. Even César, always rather conservative when it came to clothes, thought she looked dashing.

It was only a few months later, in the late fall of 1889, that D'Oyly Carte contacted Ritz again. The board of directors at the Savoy had come to the conclusion that Hardwicke, the manager of the hotel, was not up to the job. They wanted Ritz to take over. He could name his own price.

Once again Ritz was flattered, and once again he explained to D'Oyly Carte why he could not take the job: he had just opened two hotels; he had just gone into business for himself. It wasn't simply a matter of money, of "naming his own price," as the board of directors had proposed.

What Ritz didn't know was just how desperate D'Oyly Carte had become. The opening weeks at the Savoy had been brilliant, but the novelty of the new hotel had worn off. Business had dropped precariously.

This was not an unfamiliar situation for D'Oyly Carte. After all, how many times had he seen plays open to acclaim, selling out, only to fade into oblivion and half-empty houses weeks or months later? It happened all the time. With a play, you might make adjustments, revisions, add or subtract a song, change the cast or even the ending. It was no different with a hotel, was it?

D'Oyly Carte needed to get people talking about the Savoy again. He still remembered the dinner Ritz had put on for Prince Radziwill in Baden-Baden — the radical and magical transformation of the restaurant Ritz had orchestrated. That's the kind of excitement we need at the Savoy, D'Oyly Carte said. He had built the most technologically sophisticated hotel in Europe, and now he needed Ritz to make it great.

The two men began sending each other telegrams — many, many telegrams. This went on for weeks. What finally emerged was an agreement that was favorable to Ritz in every way. Or at least it seemed that way at the time. He would bring his own team to London and be given free rein to organize the staff at the Savoy as he saw fit. Most important of all, he would continue to run his hotels in Cannes and Baden-Baden, and he would stay in London for only half the year, leaving his deputies in charge at the Savoy during the winter. He would, in other words, maintain his independence.

What made it all work were the complementary high-travel seasons for the various groups of leisurely and aristocratic clientele

Ritz catered to: in London, the social season ran from spring to summer; in Baden-Baden, as in the Swiss Alps, the high season was summer; in Cannes, the high season was winter and early spring. Of course, Ritz would find himself pulled in multiple directions as he oversaw multiple hotels, but he was sure he could make it work.

The deal was struck. Ritz would be paid £1,200 per year, a large sum, more than he'd ever been paid before. The salaries for his staff would be similarly generous.

In the early months of 1890, he set about gathering his men. He would take his best staff members with him to London, all people he'd worked with for years, mostly at the Grand Hotel in Monte Carlo. They were his "little army of hotel men," as Marie called them. The Provence, in Cannes, and the Minerva and the Restaurant de la Conversation, in Baden-Baden, meanwhile, would need to operate more or less self-sufficiently.

Louis Echenard would be his deputy. Echenard was supremely competent, and would run the Savoy whenever Ritz was not there. He was also a true connoisseur of wine, and would oversee the wine list at the restaurant.

William Autour, currently managing the Provence and Minerva hotels, would come to London as third in command.

Henry Ellès, half French and half English, would manage the restaurant, along with François Rinjoux, an original D'Oyly Carte hire, who would stay on as maître d'hôtel.

In charge of accounting would be Mr. Agostini, Ritz's longtime head cashier. He was Italian, trustworthy, and absolutely loyal.

And most important of all, running the kitchen would be *chef de cuisine* Auguste Escoffier.

Auguste Escoffier was a few years older than Ritz, forty-three to Ritz's thirty-nine. A disciplined and scientific Frenchman — calm, quiet, and thoughtful — he was a brilliant and innovative cook, inventing new dishes and always keeping careful notes of what he served to important guests, so as never to make them the same thing twice. He and Ritz had worked as counterparts since the mid-1880s, at the Grand Hotel in Monte Carlo and at the Grand Hotel National in Lucerne, making their names together.

They were an odd couple, and ideal partners. Like Ritz, Escoffier had grown up poor, in a tiny village — he was the son of a blacksmith, and had been raised in

Villeneuve-Loubet, in the hills of Provence near Nice. They'd both left home at an early age to work as apprentices, Ritz as a waiter, Escoffier as a cook.

Temperamentally, however, they were opposites.

Ritz was outgoing, debonair, and excitable, while Escoffier was cerebral and methodical. Ritz was extravagant, ambitious, and prone to self-doubt, while Escoffier was self-assured and precise. He had organized the kitchens at the Grand and the National hotels according to an entirely modern brigade system, with specialist chefs working in parallel, allowing for far faster service. He was imperturbable, soft-spoken, and wore a carefully trimmed, professorial moustache. He was a small man, and quite handsome.

They had crossed paths by chance. But as it turned out, it was a fateful meeting.

This had been back in 1884. Ritz was managing the Grand in Monte Carlo (the hotel owned by Marie's aunt and uncle, the Jungbluths) and had great success attracting a fashionable clientele. But his talented chef, Jean Giroux, had just been hired away by the hotel's main competitor, the newly opened Hôtel de Paris at the Monte Carlo Casino. The casino owners had realized that to compete with Ritz, they needed an excellent restaurant, and had offered Giroux a fantastic amount of money to defect.

Giroux had been good, but Ritz remembered something: the chef had often sung the praises of his master in Paris, at the Petit Moulin Rouge restaurant, a man named Auguste Escoffier, who'd taught him everything he knew. And so Ritz tracked down this Escoffier and hired him.

Ritz had come to the realization that his success in the luxury hotel business depended in large part on having a superb restaurant at the hotel. His customers were rich. They sought comfort, of course, and beauty — the cool, clean linens on their beds, the flowers in the lobby — but they also wanted to be tempted and surprised, *seduced,* and there was no better way to do that than with dishes like *Les cailles Richelieu* or *Poularde aux raviolis à la Garibaldi,* dishes Escoffier would make famous at the Grand, dishes they would find nowhere else. Dishes so perfectly and carefully prepared they were fit for a king, or a prince, or a wealthy American industrialist. The food Escoffier prepared was generally lighter than was usual, the portions smaller, the sauces more delicate, the ingredients always of the highest quality.

Escoffier, meanwhile, had also come to a realization: he was a brilliant chef, and he needed an appreciative audience, one that was willing to pay for those filets and ravioli, and happy to try something new. Working with Ritz had solved that problem: Ritz was on his way to being the premier hotelier in Europe. His clientele included opera stars and princesses. And now Escoffier found himself acquiring a bit of fame, too: recognition for his culinary inventions at the Grand. His success meant that he had access to the best and rarest ingredients: caviar, foie gras, wild game, anything he wanted.

Quite apart from their own self-interested reasons, it turned out that Ritz and Escoffier worked exceedingly well together. Ritz loved to give encouragement and suggestions in the kitchen, tasting new sauces and preparations. He was as enthusiastic about new dishes as Escoffier was. And their collaboration extended to the dining room, where Ritz welcomed Escoffier's suggestions about décor and dishware, how the tables should be set, and how exactly food should be presented to customers.

Escoffier and Ritz were a team, each contributing crucially to the other's triumphs. They were also friends, and had stayed in touch even after Ritz left the Grand and the National the previous year to go out on his own. He could not yet afford a chef of Escoffier's caliber at the Hôtel de Provence or the Minerva.

But the Savoy would bring them together again.

"I am counting on your support in this affair, Auguste," Ritz said, when he came to Monte Carlo to make his case. "I want you to take on the organization and management of the kitchens." He then launched into a long discourse about the Savoy, how brilliant and modern it was, how glamorous and wealthy its clientele. This was their chance, he said, to open the best restaurant in the world.

Ritz could not do it without Escoffier — not only because Escoffier was a great chef, but also because he had perfected the modern organization of the restaurant kitchen. For all the problems Ritz had seen at the Savoy restaurant (the slow service, the merely decent food), Escoffier was the solution.

Still, Escoffier resisted the idea of going to London. He didn't speak a word of English. He had just bought an estate in Monte Carlo, the Villa Fernand, where he planned a more settled life for his wife, Delphine, and their two sons. He had no interest in leaving his family behind. But Ritz was persuasive, as only he could be. Just come for the summer season, he said, to set things up. This was their opportunity to do something on a larger stage — on the international stage.

Escoffier finally agreed. He told the Pfyffers, the owners of the National Hotel in Lucerne, that he wouldn't be coming that year, and they understood. (Ritz had worked at the National for years, and had brought Escoffier to the hotel to begin with. What could they say?)

So it was that in April 1890, Ritz and Escoffier were on their way. They would take London by storm. They were going to change the world.

■ ■ ■ ■

Part 2
Boomtown, 1890

■ ■ ■ ■

4
TAKING CHARGE

When Escoffier walked in to the kitchen at the Savoy on Sunday morning, April 6, 1890, the first thing he noticed was the smell. It was awful.

What the hell happened? he asked.

The kitchen had been trashed. One of the cooks was sweeping up broken dishes and glasses from the floor. He explained that the previous night — well, Monsieur Charpentier, the chef, had been angry. He'd lost his job after only eight months, as had a number of his deputies, and so they had sent a vicious message in response, in the form of sabotage: Meat and fish had been left out to spoil, milk and cream poured down the sinks. Fruits and vegetables had been bruised and crushed underfoot. There was no usable food in any of the storage rooms, no flour, rice, sugar, or much of anything at all.

It was an unpleasant welcome to London,

though Escoffier wasn't all that surprised: restaurant kitchens were intense, sometimes brutish places. The men who worked in them were frequently drunk. Everyone shouted all the time — orders coming in, dishes going out. The heat from the charcoal-fired ovens was inescapable. Everyone sweat and swore profusely. Kitchens were hot, dirty, and loud, and the mess at the Savoy that morning reminded Escoffier of the restaurant kitchens of his youth, and how much he'd hated them.

Escoffier had been working in kitchens since he was thirteen, and had always despised the uncivilized cacophony and abuse they seemed to foster. He could remember being swatted about and bullied as a young apprentice — including by his own uncle François, who owned the Restaurant Français in Nice, where Escoffier had first started out. Escoffier was not a tall man, and he'd been even less tall then, which made him an easy target. Even more problematic, with his small stature, he often found his face precariously close to the flames that roared out of the stove.

There was an easy, partial solution to the height problem, which he deployed to this day: he wore boots with heavy built-up heels. As to the other problem, the wretched conditions of kitchen work — that had taken years longer to solve. Indeed, he was still working on it.

Escoffier was not an educated man, but he had quickly discovered that he had a real talent for cooking, which he saw as both a science and an art. The *chef de cuisine,* long considered no more than an ordinary servant, deserved more respect, he thought. And the state of the kitchen ought to reflect that.

Over the course of the previous decade, working in Paris at the Petit Moulin Rouge, and then especially with Ritz in Monte Carlo and in Lucerne, Escoffier had organized restaurant kitchens to his own exacting specifications. He had instituted a rational, modern division of labor, and a level of specialization that went far beyond the distinction between the grill man and the pastry chef. He had begun to establish a new ethos for the professional kitchen, one that depended on respect: respect for the chefs, respect for the ingredients, respect for the artistry of cooking.

In the traditional kitchen organization, cooks were separated into sections, and each section was responsible for certain dishes, which they prepared entirely independently. This was how it had been in kitchens in

Europe for centuries, going back to the aristocratic households of seventeenth-century France, where the *office,* responsible for hors d'oeuvres and desserts, was a completely separate department from the *cuisine.* Modern kitchens maintained this separation, relying on self-contained teams turning out cold dishes and soups, grilled meats, fish, sautéed dishes, and desserts. This meant, inevitably, that there was a certain amount of duplicated labor, as multiple teams prepared the basic sauces and stocks they'd need, for example.

Escoffier would require his staff to work more closely together, collaborating across sections, with each section led by a *chef de partie.* This would allow the kitchen to prepare dishes with greater speed.

Now, as he gathered his staff around him in the large kitchen at the Savoy, he explained that this was a new day, a new beginning. The room was filled with sunlight, streaming through the windows and onto the white brick walls. This was, all by itself, a powerful sign that the Savoy would be different. Every kitchen Escoffier had ever worked in had been dark, smoky, and underground. It was a luxury for the cooks to be working on the first floor. There was electric lighting illuminating the stoves. All the equipment was brand new. It was a beautiful kitchen.

Escoffier continued: He wanted an atmosphere of calm and cooperation, he said. He wanted serenity. There would be no vulgar language, no swearing. There would be no shouting. In fact, he said, the *aboyeur,* the man who called out incoming orders from the waiters in the restaurant, would now be called the *annonceur,* and he would not shout. Never. He would speak. *Aboyeur,* the traditional term, means "barker." *Annonceur* was a more civilized title — and if the "announcer" did not shout, then everyone in the kitchen would need to stay quiet in order to hear him.

"The rush hour in the kitchen is not a time for a rush of words," Escoffier said.

The terms were French, of course, the language of Escoffier's kitchen. His staff was predominantly French, Swiss, and Italian, but they all spoke French, or at least kitchen French.

Escoffier pointed at the men's white aprons and uniforms. They were stained, splattered, some of them quite filthy. Escoffier spoke in his quiet, precise way: I want all your uniforms to be perfectly white at the beginning of each day here in this kitchen. And when you leave the restaurant you will change into a proper jacket, tie, and hat. This is a matter of self-respect. We are professionals. We will present ourselves professionally.

The cooks looked at one another. They were responsible for their own uniforms and equipment; indeed, each carried his own knives to and from work each day, held in a scabbard on his belt. These were the tools of the trade. Escoffier was now telling them that their appearance, their *cleanliness,* was just as important as the sharpness of their blades.

And not only that: There will be no beer in this kitchen, Escoffier said. There will be no drinking of any alcohol. There will be no smoking of cigarettes.

The men groaned. The kitchen got hot, they protested, and they got thirsty.

This was another tradition dating back decades, if not centuries: cooks in the kitchen getting drunker by the hour. Escoffier could well remember his early days in Paris: the hot basement kitchens and the drunken, shouting chaos of the dinner rush. He'd hated it.

We are not drunks, he said. We're cooks.

He looked around the room. For all his stern lecturing and unsmiling absolutism, he felt protective of these men. These were his people: itinerant Frenchmen, mostly, and others from the Continent. The young assistants, the *commis,* reminded him of himself all those years ago, so far from home. The kitchen was a kind of family, and Escoffier was now at the head of it, at least for the time being. He had agreed to come to London with Ritz, to set up and organize the Savoy kitchens and devise the menu, but he had no intention of staying long. He would be here through the summer and then head back to Monte Carlo for the winter season.

François Rinjoux, the maître d'hôtel, caught his eye. He had the reservation book in his hands, and now he held it up to remind Escoffier of its existence.

Enough talk, Escoffier said. There would soon be customers in the restaurant, ordering lunch, and there was no food in the kitchen. And it was Sunday. And all the shops and supply houses were closed.

He asked the *chefs de partie* to oversee the cleaning of their stations and to salvage what they could from the supply rooms. He himself would go in search of provisions.

He went to see Ritz.

Ritz was in his office in the warren of rooms off the hotel lobby. He, too, had introduced himself and his team to the staff, and was now writing personal notes to his many longtime clients, families who had stayed at the Grand in Monte Carlo and the National in Lucerne for years. They knew the quality that he and Escoffier represented, he wrote, and "they would find no flaws in food or service at the Savoy, but instead perfection."

He was eager to establish a new ambience at the Savoy, one that was less like a gentlemen's club and more Continental; less stuffy, more sophisticated. Partly this would be a matter of décor, and he planned extensive changes on that front. Partly it was a matter of style. What kind of service did modern travelers want?

"Never bother a guest with too much attention — people like to be served, but invisibly! They like when in hotels to have some peace!" he declared.

Service ought to be unobtrusive for the most part, anticipating what people wanted before they asked for it, yet also responsive to any request they made. "The customer is always right" was one of his oft-repeated maxims. Service should be unquestioning and solicitous and swift. This was in many ways the secret to Ritz's success: speed. His nickname as a waiter back in the 1870s had been "César le Rapide."

He'd made a little speech about all this to the staff, yet he knew that the key would be to lead by example. Yes, there were protocols to be followed, but it was his manner and comportment, the way he addressed himself to others with calm and reserve but also genuine warmth, that he wanted to impart to his staff. That, and the importance of quickness. Too many of the doormen, waiters, and bellhops had a lugubrious manner about them. They were polite, dutiful, and slightly unfriendly, in the manner of English servants. This would have to change.

He spoke to the staff in his Swiss-accented English, exuding a debonair confidence he didn't quite feel. Would he be able to train his mostly English employees to follow his lead? He hoped so.

The men he had brought with him to London were already steeped in his hotel philosophy; they modeled themselves on Ritz, and would help set a new tone. He could remember when Agostini, the cashier, had first come to work for him years ago, how he had soon begun dressing just like Ritz, even asking for the name of his tailor. When Ritz adopted side whiskers (large, extravagant sideburns), so did Agostini, along with many of the others on staff. When he ordered a new frock coat in the latest style, they all followed suit. They jokingly referred to Ritz as "the Beau Brummel of the hotel trade," Brummel being the quintessential symbol of the too-fashionable man even sixty years after his death. In the 1790s, Brummel had been a friend of the prince regent, the future King George IV. He had proudly, and possibly apocryphally, claimed that it took him five hours to get dressed every morning. Ritz laughed off the comparisons to Brummel but was secretly glad to be seen as a dandy.

There was a knock on the door, and Escoffier walked in. He was furious. That bastard Charpentier had ruined the kitchen, he said. It was dishonorable, deplorable. What kind of self-respecting chef would do such a thing?

Welcome to London, said Ritz. They both allowed themselves a wry laugh. Obviously D'Oyly Carte had not handled the situation well, or put much care into smoothing ruffled feathers. He had recruited Ritz and Escoffier in secret, and dismissed the previous regime without any notice at all. In fact, Ritz told Escoffier, he had heard that Hardwicke, the previous hotel manager, was planning to sue the hotel for breach of contract.

We need supplies, Escoffier said. He told

Ritz about the state of affairs in the kitchen.

What about Louis? Ritz asked.

I was thinking the same thing, Escoffier said.

Louis Peyre was an old friend of Escoffier's who ran the kitchens at the Charing Cross Hotel, a few blocks away on the Strand. Surely he would loan them what they needed to make it through the day. There was a fraternity of sorts among the many expat French chefs and cooks in London; they may have been competitors, but they were Frenchmen first. (Charpentier, needless to say, felt differently.) Escoffier and Peyre went way back — they'd known each other as young men in Paris.

You should go yourself and make the request in person, Ritz said.

They walked out of Ritz's office together, Escoffier off to plead his case with Peyre (successfully, as it turned out) and Ritz to walk through the lobby and restaurant, greeting guests and talking to staff, thinking and planning.

Helen D'Oyly Carte wouldn't like it, but he would be removing some of the drapery and heavy décor. He didn't like the bright lights in the restaurant; they ought to be shaded, and more subtle. And flowers: there weren't nearly enough flowers in the hotel;

he wanted them everywhere.

Ritz walked out into the interior courtyard, where there was an imposing Della Robbia–style fountain, ornate in the Italian manner, covered with carvings. It was illuminated by electric lights at night, a novel effect first seen at the Paris Exposition. There were plants and flowers set around the square, but again, not enough, thought Ritz. This was where guests arrived, their coaches entering through the narrow archways of a double porte cochere, a covered entryway, and they needed to feel they had arrived in an oasis of calm and beauty.

He made lists in his mind: changes to be made, initiatives to be launched. Yes, the Savoy was state of the art, but the electric lights and elevators and bathrooms meant little if the overall effect was not one of impeccable luxury. The magic of the place D'Oyly Carte was advertising as "the hotel de luxe of the world" would be conjured from a thousand decisions and details, and would transcend them all.

Over the coming weeks, Escoffier and Ritz imposed themselves on the Savoy.

Every morning, Ritz gathered his staff for a meeting, looking at the day ahead. Who was checking in? Who was coming to dinner? Were there any special events, private parties to be planned? Ritz had established this formal, all-hands morning meeting at both the Grand and the National, and made it the foundation of his management. It was a novel concept: to include the entire staff, and to welcome anyone to raise any pertinent topic or question. It was a democratic meeting in which all were heard. With one exception: Ritz did not invite the accounting or finance staff. The morning meeting was not the venue for talk about budgets and money.

As he had promised, Escoffier instituted and refined his signature level of specialization in the kitchen. The staff of eighty was already specialized to a degree — the *chef pâtissier* and the *chef poissonnier* and the *chef rôtisseur* all did very different things, taking charge of pastry, fish, and roasts, respectively. But they needed to learn to be less independent, more collaborative.

All the cooks in the kitchen had learned their trade in the traditional way, coming up as apprentices working for one of the *chefs de partie,* the senior cooks in charge of each of the stations. The *commis,* the junior cooks, worked for their chefs and paid little attention to the rest of the kitchen, as each unit worked independently. Each *chef de partie* listened to the orders coming in, dividing the labor for his station's dishes among his group of cooks and then delivering the finished dish to the *chef de cuisine* for inspection before it went out into the dining room.

Or, more likely, waited for its counterparts to arrive — the rest of the order. The timing was never right.

Of course, the *chef de cuisine* knew that a filet of sole would be ready faster than a stuffed, roasted breast of chicken, and he might indicate to the *chef poissonnier* to hold off on the fish when he knew it needed to be served alongside the chicken. In practice, though, the rush of orders meant that every station turned out its dishes as fast as it could, which was not very. A single station producing all the components of a single dish was inevitably slower than multiple *chefs de partie* taking on the job, subdividing the cooking of that same dish.

In order for Escoffier's system to work efficiently, it required the *chefs de partie* to manage the orders coming into their stations, while also coordinating seamlessly with their counterparts at the other stations who were working on the same dish. It also required the *commis* at each station to specialize in different tasks. (They would rotate as part of their training.) Timing was everything. As Escoffier explained, they had to work together like a perfectly balanced machine — to work in synchronicity, to work with precision. This was why they needed the kitchen to be as quiet as possible: so that they could all communicate.

Apart from Escoffier himself, there was his sous-chef, who helped manage the *chefs de partie.* There were six of them:

The chef saucier *prepared all sauces.*
The chef rôtisseur *roasted and braised meat. His station also took charge of grilling and frying.*
The chef poissonnier *cooked fish and shellfish, including doing all necessary cleaning and boning.*
The chef entremétier *prepared vegetables, eggs, and soups.*
The chef garde-manger *was in charge of cold dishes and hors d'oeuvres, including salads, pâtés, and charcuterie, and also oversaw the pantry.*
The chef pâtissier *made desserts and sweets, including ice cream.*

There would now be far more collaboration among the chefs. When an order came in from the *annonceur,* it would not simply go to whatever station seemed appropriate. Instead, Escoffier or the deputy chef would divide the job right from the start, so that an order of *Deux oeufs sur le plat Meyer-beer,* for example, would go simultaneously to the *chef entremétier,* the *chef rôtisseur,* and the *chef saucier.* Each of these stations would assign an assistant *commis* to the task: the eggs were cooked in butter, the lamb's kidney was sliced and grilled, and *sauce Périgueux* was made with meat glaze, Madeira, and truffles. The *chef entremétier* would then put the cooked eggs on a plate and pass it to the *chef rôtisseur,* who would place the grilled kidney between the eggs and then pass it to the *chef saucier,* who would pour the truffle sauce over it. The dish would then be inspected by Escoffier before being sent out to the dining room.

This assembly-line process achieved two things, both enormously important: speed and quality. The time it took to get a dish out, from order to delivery, dropped from fifteen minutes to five. Meanwhile, the checks and balances of the interlocking responsibilities demanded a high level of cooking precision. Dishes were more uniform, and subject to more oversight by the *chefs de partie.* The difference was nothing short of revolutionary: better food, served faster, and at the right temperature.

The food itself was less complicated than it had been, shorn of unnecessary ornamentation, inedible decoration, and too many sauces. Food should be food, said Escoffier. *Surtout, faites simple* was his motto — "above all, make it simple." The era of Marie-Antoine Carême, who had epitomized the royal French style of cooking in the early part of the century, was long gone. Carême had served huge numbers of dishes — more than one hundred fifty at a dinner for forty people was not unheard of — and presented them all at once in a grand architectural display. There were tiered trays and numerous *pièces montées,* fantastical structures and centerpieces upon which food was displayed, including miniature Roman ruins made of lard and Greek temples made of marzipan and spun sugar. (Carême had trained as a confectioner and had an abiding interest in classical architecture, both of which informed his cooking.) Guests gathered around the table to admire the food and its presentation, and then sat down and helped themselves to what was in reach. This was called *service à la française.*

There were a number of drawbacks to this approach. For one thing, by the time it was eaten, the food was generally lukewarm at best, rather than hot. For another, guests at dinner could eat only those dishes positioned close by. (It was considered bad manners to reach too far across the table trying to serve oneself a roasted squab.) *Service à la française* had been replaced in recent years with what was called *service à la russe,* named for a Russian ambassador to Paris in the early nineteenth century, Alexander Kurakin, who had introduced the idea. With *service à la russe,* by the 1880s the predominant custom both on the Continent and in London, dishes were served one after the other.

Escoffier's streamlined, assembly-line kitchen organization was built to handle the rigors of the modern, à la carte dining, with dishes cooked to order.

Carême's influence could still be felt in the overly elaborate displays of food at banquets, for example: piles of desserts rising on structures made of marzipan were still a common enough sight. Escoffier, too, had a great talent for the dramatic presentation of his dishes — he was prodigiously creative in the kitchen, researching international preparations and new cooking tools — but ultimately, he wanted the ingredients to shine through.

In the dining room, Ritz and Escoffier

watched their guests and soon identified another problem: they could not read the menu. It was in French, for one thing, and for another, the names of the dishes (like those *Deux oeufs sur le plat Meyerbeer*) were not always entirely descriptive. A further complication was that English diners were unsure about the proper balance of the meal — how to arrange a pleasing series of courses for themselves — so even translating the menu into English would not have helped.

The solution was simple, and proved to be hugely popular: the prix fixe meal. For any party of at least four people, Escoffier would create a personalized seven-course menu for a set price. (Smaller parties ordered à la carte, with the help of the waiter.) When such a reservation was made, a note would be brought to Escoffier with the name of the party, the time of the dinner, their preferences, and any special requests.

He had always paid attention to the choices of his important guests over the years, at the Grand and National hotels, making sure that the Prince of Wales, say, was not served the same dessert he'd received the last time he visited — unless, of course, he requested it. Escoffier had made notes in his diary. It started simply as a way of keeping track of the menus he created for important guests, but he soon began including further details — who particularly liked *brochettes de rognons,* or who was less enthusiastic about lentil soup. It was a haphazard record, based on what he gleaned from conversations as he passed through the dining room, or learned from guests when they made their reservations.

But now Escoffier instituted a more systematic record keeping: in his files, organized by customer name, he kept the original chit from the maître d'hôtel who'd taken the reservation, and a copy of the resulting personalized menu. Over time, it was this record of predilections, favorite dishes, and likes and dislikes that made possible Escoffier's seemingly magical, uncanny ability to design the perfect meal for his regular guests, every time.

The ambience in the hotel and restaurant was stylishly formal, suiting their status as gathering places for the London and international elite. Ritz had followed through on his plan to remove much of the bric-a-brac and decorative glass from the hotel lobby and drawing rooms to create a more streamlined, modern style. Ritz was all for grandeur, but he was also devoted to hygiene:

anything that would gather unnecessary dust or that could not easily be cleaned displeased him.

In the restaurant, he dressed the waiters in ties and aprons, the headwaiters in black ties, while he and his deputy, Echenard, and others among the senior staff wore morning coats with tails. Escoffier would sometimes wear the traditional chef's whites and *toque blanche,* usually on Sunday, but generally he wore a long frock coat, cut just above the knee, and a tie, exuding professionalism.

Richard D'Oyly Carte welcomed the changes and adjustments, agreeing to expand the kitchen according to Escoffier's specifications, adding more equipment, and to create a new, more informal *salle à manger,* with its own entrance off the hotel lobby. This dining room was needed, Ritz explained, to serve guests who did not require a formal dinner, or who just wanted a snack or a quick lunch, and would increase the Savoy's capacity. Here, the meals would be offered at a set price — breakfast for two shillings per person, for example, and dinner for seven shillings, sixpence. As was typical of the time, the cost of dinner rivaled the cost of a room at the hotel; a single room at the Savoy cost seven shillings, sixpence; a double room (with bath) went for twelve shillings. (By way of comparison, a half pound of good tea cost a shilling, and a silk hat might go for about seven shillings.)

The main restaurant catered to hotel guests and the general public alike, and prices were higher, starting at ten shillings, sixpence per person for a prix fixe menu. Guests entered from the lobby into a white-and-gold-papered anteroom in which there were two fireplaces, comfortable terra cotta–colored armchairs, and numerous palm trees in large pots — a place where a gentleman might wait for his dinner guests. The restaurant radiated a sense of sophistication.

The alterations were expensive, and required knocking down walls, moving the restaurant lavatories to a different position, and redecorating the new *salle à manger* (previously a private banqueting room), which Ritz took in hand personally. D'Oyly Carte made no complaint about the costs. Business was picking up again, and he was only too happy to see the Savoy in capable hands. His wife, Helen, on the other hand, had her doubts. Ritz struck her as imperious. He was a perfectionist, and she respected that, but he was also a spendthrift

— and he was spending other people's money.

5
A Celebrity Guest and an Infamous Dinner

In late June 1890, Sarah Bernhardt arrived at the Savoy accompanied by a retinue of French opera producers, her dog, and a Japanese boy who spoke neither English nor French. No one seemed to know who he was, but such was the glamour and mystery of Bernhardt that no one asked.

The most famous actress in the world, "the Divine Sarah" had made her name in Paris in the 1860s and '70s. She was eccentric, liberated, and beautiful, setting fashion trends in dress and hairstyles. At forty-five years old, she appeared to be much younger, and had numerous lovers, including the Prince of Wales. She was in London to perform the lead role in *Joan of Arc* at Her Majesty's Theatre.

There was palpable excitement at having someone so famous in the hotel. It permeated the building. And no one was more thrilled than Escoffier.

104

Escoffier and Bernhardt had met years earlier, in Paris, in 1874, when he was the chef at the Petit Moulin Rouge. They had a mutual friend, it turned out: the sculptor and printmaker Gustave Doré, whose studio was around the corner from the restaurant, not far from the Grand Palais. He was a regular customer.

Escoffier was an artist at heart — an artist manqué. As a young boy of thirteen, finished with primary school, he'd dreamed of being a sculptor, imagining a career in fine arts. "Unfortunately," he would later write, "I was forced to give up this dream." His father, insisting on a more reliable profession, had sent him to apprentice at his brother's restaurant in Nice. "I was informed that I was to be a cook, and I was given no option but to obey." At least he'd been spared blacksmithing, his father and grandfather's profession — Escoffier was too small for work at the forge.

And so he'd brought his artistic temperament to bear in the kitchen. And in his free time, what little there was, alone in his Paris apartment, he carved wax flowers. It was sculpture on a miniature scale, nothing more than a hobby, but the meditative focus on craft gave him great pleasure. He mentioned the flowers to Doré one day, shyly, and soon found himself in the artist's studio receiving informal lessons on the finer points of carving. It was here that he first met Bernhardt.

Bernhardt was in rehearsals for a role as an artist's model for an upcoming play, and her lover at the time, the painter Georges Clairin, had introduced her to Doré, who agreed to give her lessons in his studio. They ordered dinner from the nearby Petit Moulin Rouge, which Escoffier took great care in preparing and brought to the studio himself. He made Bernhardt *Timbale de ris-de-veau aux nouilles fraîches,* veal sweetbreads with fresh noodles, served with foie gras and thinly sliced truffles. She loved the dish, and a friendship was born.

Over the years, Escoffier had seen her in most of her famous roles — as Feuillet's Sphinx, as Racine's Phèdre. He would sit in the theater, alone, watching the drama unfold onstage. As with the wax carving, his love of theater connected him to a world of pure sensation, emotion, and beauty, all transcending the everyday practicalities of the restaurant kitchen.

Bernhardt seemed to subsist mainly on champagne, and was no gourmet, yet she recognized Escoffier's soulful ambition to create something sublime. She said he made

106

the best scrambled eggs in the world. (His secret, which he never told her, was stirring them quickly over low heat with a garlic clove speared on the end of his fork.)

Escoffier visited Bernhardt in her room the day she checked in, to welcome her to the hotel. He brought her a bottle of Moët et Chandon champagne in an ice bucket. She was staying in a suite on the fourth floor, with a tremendous view of the Thames. There were baskets of flowers and other gifts from well-wishers all over the room.

She was delighted to see him, as always, and was as glamorous as ever, wearing a white corded silk peignoir with puffed-up shoulders and tight sleeves, red velvet slippers peeking out from beneath the folds of the robe. They talked about the role she was playing, Joan of Arc, debuting the following night — she was already feeling the opening night jitters. He would be there, he said, of course. He wouldn't miss it for the world.

Ritz, meanwhile, was contending with an avalanche of requests and reservations. It was June, and the London season was well under way: the restaurant was full, the private dining rooms booked every night.

Each morning, Ritz scanned the newspapers to see who was in town that day. The papers all ran columns announcing the arrivals and departures of prominent people, and listing their hotels. The Savoy was consistently the lead item on these lists, he was happy to see. American travelers were flocking there, as were European aristocrats. The German Prince and Princess of Fürstenberg had just checked in.

Still, Ritz agonized about the crowds in the restaurant. His goal, and D'Oyly Carte's, too, was for the Savoy to occupy the very heart of cosmopolitan London, to bring together in spectacular fashion socialites and celebrities, royalty and bohemian artists, and newly minted millionaires, night after night — all the energy and drama of the city in one place. Instead of hosting elaborate dinner parties at home, leaders of society began having their dinners at the Savoy. Ritz hoped to make this an everyday occurrence.

The social life of the city was changing; everyone could feel it. This was the fin de siècle, and the old order was shifting — with a little encouragement.

For example, it was D'Oyly Carte who proposed the after-opera supper. This was a common enough phenomenon during the season — private banquets at which guests arrived after 11:00 p.m. for post-theater dinner and dancing. Indeed, the Hwfa Williams housewarming party at the Savoy the previous August had been just such an affair. Starting this month, though, the Savoy announced it would be serving an "opera supper" after every performance, every night of the week but Sunday.

The late-night suppers were an instant success, drawing not only theatergoers but also the stars of the operas themselves (Adelina Patti, Emma Eames, the de Reszke brothers), along with leading patrons of the arts such as the Earl and Countess de Grey, Lord and Lady Hindlip, and the brothers Reuben and Arthur Sassoon, prominent tradesmen. All the papers took note, some of them wondering how such a supper was even possible: "Although we have all heard and read a great deal about the Opera Supper at the Savoy," wrote one columnist, "few goers have been told how it is to be done. Clearly the Licensing Act — the most abominable example of grandmotherly legislation extant — will not permit the ordinary opera-goer to sit over his light refreshment after licensed hours, unless he has a bedroom at the hotel."

In fact, an exception had been allowed by the legislature in this case — a number of the Savoy's board members were well connected in Parliament — although the law still forbade serving dinner on Sundays. This was another thing Ritz was hoping to change, but one that would take time.

Old habits died hard: a great number of the events and dinners at the Savoy seemed to involve large groups of men, rather than mixed company. The venerable Cecil Club, for example, a political group allied with the Conservative Party and presided over by Lord Balfour of Burleigh, held its annual dinner at the Savoy in June 1890, which was attended by a few dozen members of Parliament, many of them standing, one after the other, to give long toasts. They discussed constitutional principles, and the rise in importance of the opinion of "the man in the street" and what that meant for politics and democracy.

That same week, there'd been the annual dinner of the Council of the Association of Municipal Corporations; a dinner to celebrate the establishment of the Italo-Britannica Royal Mail Steam Navigation Company; and the dinner of the Edelweiss Club, a group of about thirty American businessmen who were also amateur Alpine climbers and who traveled every year to Switzerland to hike. They met in the Sorcerer Room — all the private dining rooms at the Savoy were named after Gilbert and Sullivan operas. Tradition held that the menus printed for their annual dinner be decorated with real edelweiss flowers, which grow on high Alpine meadows in summer, above the snow line. These proved hard to procure — there were none to be had in London or Paris — but a supply was finally found in Geneva and imported at great expense.

It was a sign of the Savoy's vitality and modernity that it had immediately become the preferred location for exhibits and demonstrations of new inventions and technologies. Inventor Henry Schallehn hosted a *matinée musicale* during which various musicians performed with his "perfect transposing pianoforte," a piano with a sliding mechanism that allowed it to play in any key and was declared "the instrument of the future" in newspapers. A representative of Thomas Edison, meanwhile, hosted a party for the press to demonstrate his amazing talking dolls, built with mechanical phonographs hidden inside. Wound up, one doll sang the first four lines of "Twinkle, Twinkle, Little Star," while another recited "The Spider and the Fly." He had shown the dolls the previous week to the nine-year-old Princess Wilhelmina, heiress to the throne in Holland, the salesman explained. The one she chose said, "Good morning, mama. Do you love baby? Baby loves you."

Ritz made his rounds throughout the day, welcoming guests, talking with his staff, checking on any special arrangements for private events and dinners, and generally monitoring every detail of the hotel's operation, down to the last flower arrangement. He learned the rhythms of the building itself, the daily comings and goings of messengers and deliverymen, and he listened carefully (like a spy, gathering intelligence) to every conversation he heard. What were guests talking about? What were staff members complaining about?

What people were talking about at the Savoy in June 1890 — apart, of course, from the never-ending wonders of modern technology, including talking dolls — was the food they were eating. This was a striking development, and a welcome one. As the "Diana's Diary" column in the *Illustrated Sporting and Dramatic News* reported:

Conversation during the repast never flagged, for it was all about food. (Am beginning to think that the most brilliant of dinner talk is about food. So appropriate, and a dissertation on each dish increases the enjoyment of it.) One dish, which was much discussed, struck me as more odd than nice; it was called *Omelette en surprise.* An omelette with an ice inside it. If the ice doesn't melt before one eats it, it would indeed be a surprise. Of course, this dish must almost be prepared at the table to produce the proper effect.

The meringue-and-ice-cream dessert was a relatively recent invention, popularized at Delmonico's in New York, where it was called the "Alaska, Florida." Various versions had appeared on menus in France in recent years as well. Escoffier liked the dish for its inherent drama: the hot, toasted-brown meringue exterior giving way to cold, sweet ice cream. And the columnist was wrong: the ice cream did not melt — at least not immediately.

Yes, Escoffier's cooking was attracting attention, and that was of utmost importance to the Savoy's success. It was the cooking that would entice new visitors, and bring them back.

Just that morning, Ritz had received a request from two businessmen who wanted to host an extravagant gourmet dinner. And when they said "extravagant," they meant *extravagant.* L. H. Phillips was the proprietor of the City Fur Warehouse, on Newgate Street, an enormous discount fur emporium. He was also a member of the Court of Common Council, part of the London city government. E. Ulph was also a tradesman. The two wanted to host a dinner for ten.

"It must be superb, unbeatable," Phillips said to Ritz. "The menu must be memorable. Spare no pains."

Needless to say, this was the sort of assignment that Ritz relished: the over-the-top dinner, with no limit on the budget, the best Escoffier could muster, as many courses as could be humanly consumed, the best wine to be had. A grand feast.

He told Escoffier about the dinner, and the requirement that it be spectacular. Phillips and Ulph were rich, and wanted to show off both their wealth and their taste. They wanted a dinner so fantastic it would make the morning papers. (Ritz himself, with his clients' permission, would call the papers with the item, in the hope of garnering publicity.)

Escoffier had an idea: he would create a menu drawing from the traditions of various cuisines, including — he had just come across this — a Chinese bird's nest soup.

Qu'est-ce que c'est? Ritz asked.

As the name says, it's a soup made from a swallow's nest, Escoffier explained, one of which is served in each guest's bowl. The nests are delicate, and they dissolve quickly, thickening the soup. It's a rare and stupendously expensive Chinese delicacy. One of Escoffier's suppliers of exotic and imported ingredients had told him about the nests.

Perfect, said Ritz. That was just what these men were looking for: something to talk about for years to come. Bragging rights.

And there might be a stew of American turtle, Escoffier continued, and a Ukrainian borscht. Of course, there would also be French delicacies: *poularde royale* with truffles and foie gras; roasted ortolans, tiny songbirds eaten whole; and many other things.

Ritz also consulted with Echenard, his wine expert, who oversaw the Savoy cellars. Echenard selected particularly rare wines for the dinner.

Ritz was sure Phillips and Ulph would be pleased, and indeed, they didn't blink when he outlined the menu Escoffier proposed, nor when he told them the price would be fifteen pounds per person. That would include the cost of wine, but was nonetheless an astronomical sum. Fifteen pounds was a respectable monthly wage for a bank clerk, for example; it was some thirty times the Savoy's standard rate for a prix fixe menu. Of course, this dinner would be anything but standard.

Phillips and Ulph were members of the nouveau riche, as the press referred to them, meaning they had earned their money — doing unseemly things like selling fur coats, in this case — rather than inherited it, and were in possession of no titles or social prestige whatsoever. Still, it was the new money of men like Phillips and Ulph, and the far wealthier stars of global finance like Alfred Beit, Ludwig Neumann, Cecil Rhodes, and Barney Barnato, that was transforming the social life of the city. Some of them were Jewish, a further challenge to the establishment order. Ritz paid close attention when he saw the so-called gold and diamond millionaires Beit, Neumann, Rhodes, and Barnato conducting business meetings over lunches and dinners at the Savoy. Beit was said to be the richest man in the world; he and the others had all made their fortunes in South Africa, financing gold and diamond mines. Their rough-and-tumble backgrounds, their dangerous adventures on the "Dark Continent," and their unfathomable wealth all served to make them objects of fascination and gossip.

And scorn: *Punch* magazine, the satirical weekly, had been poking fun at the nouveau riche since the 1870s. George du Maurier was well known for his comic illustrations in the publication, which included a number of recurring fictional characters — the social climber, "Mrs. Ponsonby de Tomkyns," for example, always angling for an invitation to the best dinner parties, forever hoping to befriend an elusive duchess. And then there was the businessman "Sir Gorgius Midas," who was rich, fat, and ridiculous, pretending to sophistication with ostentatious vulgarity — showing off his house and clothes and his too many servants, while the true aristocrats looked on in dismay, modest yet superior. In one cartoon, Sir Midas complains bitterly that he has not been made a peer (given the title of "Lord") and his language and accent, dropping some *h*'s and adding others, betray his lower-class roots:

Why it's enough to make a man turn radical, 'anged if it ain't, to think of sich services as mine bein' rewarded with no 'igher title than what's bestowed on a heminent sawbones, or a hingerneer, or a literary man, or even a successful hartist.

Du Maurier's depiction of the type was unforgiving, his disdain palpable, and quite typical. The past ten years had seen the rise of new money — from business and industry, from imports and trade, from stock market speculation — and high society had been forced to adjust. The Upper Ten Thousand, as they were called, those titled members of society with a capital S, may have looked down on the striving businessmen and industrialists who were reshaping the economy, but they could no longer ignore the Midases of the world. Indeed, more and more, some in the aristocratic class had begun to enter into business themselves. They needed the money. It was now quite common to find lords, barons, and earls taking positions as company directors. The Savoy board of directors, for example, included the Earl of Lathom, a prominent Conservative politician.

The nouveau riche were welcomed at the Savoy, their dinners and parties often even more glamorous and expensive than those of royalty. Indeed, they were among the earliest to gravitate to the new hotel.

"Trust them to find out new luxury hotels at once," thought Ritz. "American millionaires will do the same."

But it wasn't their money Ritz was after,

though he welcomed it of course. No, it was something else: there was a sense of theater that accompanied these men. They spent their money in exceedingly public ways. They took pleasure in their wealth. They may have been considered tasteless by some members of English society, but they carried themselves with panache. Ritz could still remember the day A. G. Weguelin, a London financier and member of the Savoy board of directors, walked into the restaurant wearing a chinchilla coat. Chinchilla! Ritz had never seen a man wear such a coat, and neither had anyone else in the restaurant. It was a moment that signaled a new and brazen kind of money, a new and brazen sense of style. His entrance that day caused a sensation.

And Barnato, who'd grown up in the Jewish slums of London's East End, now famously carried a handful of diamonds in his pocket, which he would take out and play with, as if to remind himself of the precariousness of his great fortune — he might just drop one — but also of the shameless audacity it took to acquire it. He was young, around forty, and had made his money both in South African diamonds and on the London Stock Exchange, where he bought and sold the shares of South African gold mining companies. He took out his diamonds, and he didn't care what others thought. (They whispered behind his back.)

This overt, public pleasure taken in luxury, including in gourmet cooking, was new. The English upper classes had been raised to eschew such public displays. Talking about food at the dining table was considered bad manners; expressing delight at an *Omelette en surprise* was beyond the pale. It was downright *American*.

Yet attitudes were changing. The Prince of Wales was a man of great appetites, and he set the standard for the younger generation of royals and their friends. He loved to eat, and to eat well. He was a gourmet. He was also open-minded about the nouveau riche, whose invitations he sometimes accepted, over the objections of some court advisers. He was also notably less anti-Semitic than others of his class, having had a long association and friendship with Baron Nathaniel Rothschild, and with other wealthy Jewish families. It was more than a simple friendship: the prince also borrowed large sums of money from Rothschild, including £100,000 in 1889, when he found himself running a deficit. He also borrowed money from another friend, Baron Maurice de Hirsch, an Austrian-Jewish banker. When

Hirsch invited the prince to St. Johann, his estate in Hungary, to shoot partridges, there were sneers and expressions of shock in some anti-Semitic quarters at the prince being the guest of a Jew. He went anyway.

This was all important in unspoken ways, as others of the Marlborough House set followed his lead, and nonaristocratic families gained some acceptance in society. As Daisy Brooke, Lady Greville, one of the prince's mistresses, later described it:

> We resented the introduction of Jews into the social set of the Prince of Wales, not because we disliked them . . . but because they had brains and understood finance. As a class we did not like brains. As for money, our only understanding of it lay in the spending, not the making of it.

And so when Alfred Beit threw a party at the Savoy, which he was already planning to do, it would be the most extravagant party ever thrown, and people might roll their eyes condescendingly, but they would accept the invitation.

In the dining room at the Savoy, people were paying attention to one another as never before, transfixed by the intermingling of wealth, status, and notoriety. Here were actors, members of Parliament, American millionaires, and Continental aristocrats; here were Sarah Bernhardt and Hwfa Williams, and Barney Barnato rolling his diamonds around in his hand as waiters served food of a quality never seen before in London, and much remarked upon. Here was the Prince of Wales himself being shown to one of the private dining rooms. (The prince always entertained in private.) This was the beginning of a new theater of the restaurant, invented at the Savoy.

Ritz was awakened by the sound of knocking at his door. It was the middle of the night — 4:00 a.m. There was an emergency, he was told. Sarah Bernhardt was gravely ill.

He dressed quickly and rushed to her room, where he encountered an ashen-faced maid. Madame had taken chloral, she explained. Bernhardt's play, *Joan of Arc,* had opened that night, and she had been so keyed up afterward that she'd apparently consumed an entire bottle of the sleeping aid, a tranquilizer. Instead of putting her to sleep, though, it had sent her into an incoherent panic, the maid said — the actress had called for help and then passed out completely.

Ritz took one look at the lifeless figure on the bed and sent for a doctor. The situation was delicate, needless to say, so he directed the request to the French embassy, which referred them to Dr. Vintras, head of the French Hospital in London. Bernhardt had been treated by Vintras years earlier, also after an opening-night performance. It had been *Phèdre,* in June 1879, and after the show, she'd vomited blood and collapsed of exhaustion. Vintras had stayed for hours, putting crushed ice between her lips every five minutes and administering a "potion" that contained opium.

Now the doctor arrived at the Savoy, and once again he found Bernhardt close to death. If he hadn't arrived just in time, he claimed self-importantly, the world would never again have seen another performance by the great tragedienne.

Escoffier, meanwhile, paced the hall outside Bernhardt's room, distraught. Ritz had sent word to the chef, knowing of his close friendship with her. Escoffier had been at the theater the previous evening. Sarah had been magnificent, he said, though it was true that she'd seemed nervous the previous day, when he'd visited her in her room. What had she done?

His voice cracked, and Ritz shook his head

reassuringly. I'm sure she'll pull through, he told Escoffier.

The doctor emerged from the room at 8:00 a.m. It had been a close call, he said. One hundred twenty grains of chloral, the contents of the bottle Bernhardt had consumed, was an exceedingly dangerous amount. But she was sleeping now. All was well.

For the moment, this was true. Later that morning, though, the doctor spoke to a reporter for the *Pall Mall Gazette* — off the record of course, not for attribution — about the brilliant rescue of his celebrity patient. The item ran in the afternoon paper, and by the next day it was all over the press, from London and Paris to New York. "Narrow Escape of Madame Bernhardt" and "Madame Bernhardt in Danger," the headlines announced. Dr. Vintras was described in all the stories as having arrived just in time to save the actress's life.

It was a stunning betrayal of confidence, but Bernhardt didn't much care: she liked the attention. Still, she didn't want people thinking she was at death's door. "I have not been very well, as you know," she told a reporter for the *New York Herald* two days later, "but I am not ill. I am tired and somewhat nervous. I wish you would deny the story published yesterday of my having taken an overdose of chloral. It was absurd. I was so nervous after the opening performance that I took some chloral in order to sleep. That was all. I do not see anything remarkable about that."

Once again, the headlines proliferated: "A Sensational Story Contradicted," announced all the papers. But the truth was that Bernhardt was unwell. She made it less than halfway through Friday night's performance before collapsing onstage in a faint. The curtain was abruptly lowered, and the audience erupted with excitement. After a few minutes, a doctor came out and explained that Madame Bernhardt had lost her voice and could not continue with the performance. Now the audience erupted once again, quieted only by the theater manager, who invited them to return the next day for a special matinee show. Bernhardt would be fully recovered, he assured the crowd.

Yet, of all the talk about Bernhardt that week, one rumor struck closer to home: Escoffier had been seen by others on staff at the Savoy as he wept outside Bernhard's room the night of her overdose, and now they speculated that he and the actress were lovers. This would be a topic of conversation for a long time to come.

The following week, Escoffier found himself in the kitchen, overseeing the Phillips and Ulph dinner. The restaurant was serving an astonishing twenty-two dishes for the meal. As promised, the menu incorporated preparations from around the world, expanding the definition of gourmet cooking to include Chinese, American, and Eastern European flavors. Still, the menu was printed in French:

HORS D'OEUVRES À LA RUSSE
Russian hors d'oeuvres

MELON CANTALOUP
Cantaloupe

❀

POTAGE AUX NIDS D'HIRONDELLES
Bird's nest soup

POTAGE BORTSCH
Borscht

❀

LAITANCES DE CARPES À LA LUCULLUS
Soft carp roe

TIMBALE D'ÉCREVISSES NANTUA
Timbales of crayfish mousse

POULARDE ROYALE
Roast chicken with foie gras and truffles

NOISETTES D'AGNEAU MAINTENON
Medallions of lamb with mushroom sauce

COLUMBINES GLACÉES
Iced columbines

ORTOLANS CENDRILLON
Roasted ortolans

MARQUISES AU PORTO
Sorbet in port

CAILLES DE VIGNE
Quail wrapped in grape leaves

SALADE IMPÉRIALE
Green salad

ASPERGES D'ARGENTEUIL
Purple asparagus

AUBERGINES À LA PROVENÇALE
Eggplant Provençal

NAGEOIRES DE TORTUE
À LA AMÉRICAINE
Braised turtle fins

❀

MOUSSELINE D'ANANAS DANS
SON FRUIT
Pineapple mousse with fruit

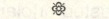

COMTESSE MARIE
Vanilla ice cream in strawberry ice

GÂTEAU REGENT
Chestnut cake

❀

SOUFFLÉS AU PAPRIKA
Paprika soufflés

❀

PÊCHERS, PRUNIERS, CERISIERS,
CEPS DE VIGNE, AVEC FRUITS MÛRS
Peach trees, plum trees, cherry trees, and
grapes vines, with ripe fruit

DESSERT
Various sweets

It was a long meal. Some of the dishes were presented in pairs — the caviar and smoked fish hors d'oeuvres and the melon, for example, were followed by the two soups.

The Chinese bird's nest soup was other-worldly, a thin chicken broth with the gelatinous strands of the nest dissolving in the center of the bowl, looking like very fine, transparent vermicelli. (The edible nests were those of a swallow-like bird called a swiftlet. They had been soaked in water for twenty-four hours, and any bits of feather carefully removed with a needle.) The borscht, on the other hand was robust — the beets, leeks, and cabbage braised with breast of beef and a roasted duck for four hours and then served with a sauceboat of sour cream.

Next was another pairing, the extremely delicate sacks of poached carp milt — the soft roe — sliced and served on grilled toast, and the timbale filled with a mousse of crayfish and mushrooms and topped with very thin slices of black truffle. The Nantua sauce was a classic preparation, a béchamel enriched with cream and flavored with crayfish. Indeed, Escoffier made liberal use of classic, familiar recipes even as he introduced new and rare ingredients on the same menu.

The chicken was served according to Escoffier's method, the breasts removed from the whole bird and deboned just before being brought to the dining room. It had always frustrated him to see the inexpert and clumsy carving of a bird at the restaurant table, resulting in a haphazard distribution of meat and stuffing, already getting cold. "For indeed," he said, "how often does not the diner find himself presented with a plate of fowl which is neither appetizingly dainty nor yet sufficiently hot!" Deboning the breasts and then reassembling the whole chicken with mousseline forcemeat and rice solved the problem. The chicken was presented with its garnish (in this case, tartlets filled with slices of foie gras), and the breasts quickly sliced and served.

The parade of dishes continued for hours, as did the parade of wines, all chosen by Echenard:

Magog, 1815
Johannisberg Cabinet, 1862
Pommery and Greno, 1874
Magnums of Perrier-Jouët, R. Cuvee,
1874
Magnums of Château Mouton Rothschild,
1875
Mussigny, 1858
Château d'Yquem, 1868
Old Crusted Port, 1815
Grandes Liqueurs

The room was decorated with large, potted palm trees and many flowers, creating an exotic backdrop; the conversation revolved around the food: the tiny, perfectly roasted ortolans, eaten whole, bones included, each served on an artichoke bottom; the purple-green asparagus, rarely seen outside France; the garlicky eggplant and tomato gratin. Along with the borscht, asparagus would become one of Escoffier's trademark dishes — before he introduced the green varieties, only white asparagus had ever been served in London. The garlic in the eggplant à la Provençal was also noteworthy — it was a controversial ingredient, long considered unrefined and repulsive. Escoffier had spent years upholding what he called "the cause of garlic" against ignorance and "inexplicable contempt." He loved garlic.

The lamb noisettes were seared and then topped with a rich dome of oniony soubise sauce thickened to a paste with finely chopped mushrooms and quickly broiled. It was a decadent dish. The quail, meanwhile, were stuffed with peeled grapes and spit-roasted after being wrapped in vine leaves and bacon. The stewed turtle fins were an American delicacy, made from a large, 120-pound turtle, cooked for many hours, and finished with Madeira port.

The pièce de résistance in a dinner filled with them was the penultimate dessert, the fresh fruit. The ten men at the table were presented with miniature grape vines, and tiny peach, plum, and cherry trees, all laden with perfectly ripe fruit. Each diner was then presented with a small pair of golden scissors with which to harvest the fruit — and to keep as a souvenir of the grand meal.

The image of these ten wealthy and possibly vulgar men harvesting their fruit from living trees with golden scissors in a private dining room at the Savoy was so perfectly decadent, it was no wonder newspapers jumped on the story. What got everyone's attention, of course, was the price: "A Dinner at £15 per Head" was a typical headline.

Snobbery and anti-Semitism seeped into the articles: "Even in these days of luxurious living, £15 a head for dinner is a rather high figure," reported the *Figaro*. "The sybarites at the Savoy who, the other evening, plucked fruit from real trees, and reveled under the shade of palm trees specially provided, were not members of the Royal family, or peers. There was not a baronet at the party." *Society* described Mr. Phillips, the host of the dinner, as "a very large specimen of the Hebrew fraternity, and if his manners are not quite as polished as the Earl of Beaconsfield, it is not to be wondered at." The article went on to speculate snidely that Phillips might one day, eventually, "cultivate the arts and graces of polite society."

Pelican, meanwhile, sounded a more populist note: "In times like these, when the struggle for bare existence to thousands of people in this city is almost too terrible and too awful to think of — in times when there are strikes and rumors of strikes on all sides — it is strange to find men eating dinners at £15 a head, oddly enough, close to the Embankment, within a stone's throw of lots of poor devils of men and women, who in their blind despair hardly dare to wonder where their next meal in this world is going to come from."

The reactions to the dinner were a sign of the times. Progressive, reform-minded politics were ascendant — but so was fin de siècle decadence. Ever-greater wealth coexisted with vast urban poverty, particularly in London, the biggest city in the world. Various socialist groups, including the Fabian Society, sought to promote the rights of workers and children, even as the titans of industry and trade were noted in gossip columns alongside royalty.

Indeed, the sudden appearance of "epicures" and "gourmands" on the scene was a revelation. Anyone — anyone with money, that is — could eat like a king at the Savoy, and that had never been true before. The nouveau riche had arrived, but until now, there had never been anywhere for them to go to announce their arrival. They had rarely been invited to the exclusive dinner parties or private clubs of high society. But now there was the Savoy. The restaurant may have served the most refined, daring, and sometimes shockingly expensive food in the world, but it was not exclusive. All were welcome, including Jewish fur tradesmen. The Savoy offered a new and democratic kind of luxury, and cooking was very much at the center of it.

In August 1890, Marie Ritz and Delphine Escoffier came to London to visit their husbands. They were friendly but not close — Delphine was older than Marie by more than a decade, and was traveling with her two sons, Paul, age ten, and Daniel, five.

Right from the beginning, Delphine did not like London. Auguste was totally immersed in his work, and had almost no free time for his family. She did not speak any English, and found the city unfriendly and cold. Delphine was the daughter of a book publisher, and was herself a well-regarded poet. She was devoted to her husband but considered this London venture at the Savoy a temporary situation. He would soon be moving back to Monte Carlo to continue at the Grand for the winter season, and then head to the National in Lucerne for the summer, as he always had in the past. She was surprised, however, to find that Escoffier had taken a liking to London. He had found something here: a recognition of his genius, a real appreciation for his talent. He was written about in the newspapers. He was famous.

It made no sense to Delphine. To leave the Riviera to live in this overcrowded, dirty, teeming metropolis? But that's what Auguste wanted. D'Oyly Carte had made him a very generous offer to stay on at the Savoy on a permanent basis, and he planned to accept.

Marie, meanwhile, was transfixed. "It seemed to me a wonder city," she later said.

"Society in London was still ostentatious. It showed itself, dressed to the nines, at the theater, the opera, the park, and even, thanks to the drawing power of Ritz's name, the public restaurant at the Savoy." She had never seen a hotel as large or as grand as the Savoy — or with so many bathrooms!

Marie was young, impressionable, and in love. César showed her the best of London: she rode the new electric trams, went to see Lillie Langtry in *Esther Sandras,* and saw opera stars Adelina Patti, Nellie Melba, and other celebrities dining in restaurants. (Melba wore a black-and-dark-green lace dress with black roses sewn onto the skirt, and a necklace that showed off an enormous diamond. She was stunning.) Most of all, Marie was impressed with the formal English style — "their perfect arrogance."

"They say Mrs. R —: you see her, with that tiny waist: they say she has recently been operated on, my dear," said Mrs. Hwfa Williams, who had offered to take Marie on a shopping tour of London, and was full of gossip. This was the first time Marie had ever heard of the concept of plastic surgery. She was amazed. This was an era when even makeup was considered somehow shameful, and applied only very discreetly. "No whisper in a ballroom was ever more damning," Marie later wrote, than the words "She paints!"

César took her to the Savoy Theatre to see *The Yeomen of the Guard,* and introduced her to W. S. Gilbert and Arthur Sullivan. She told them she loved the show, although the truth was she'd been dumb-founded by it: "What very odd music that is!" she said to César. She didn't get it: the comic opera had none of the grandeur or passion she expected from a night at the theater, and the jokes were unfunny, she thought, even after they'd been explained to her. "My fault," she said, "and my loss, doubtless!"

Still, she understood the thrill of London. Even if she didn't take to the Gilbert and Sullivan production, she was fully enter-tained by the audience in the theater. The spectacular dresses, the jewels, the wealth on display, the beautiful women — it was just as César had described it when he came back from his first visit to London the previ-ous year: the most glamorous city in the world. The atmosphere was electric.

Marie took particular note of the women she met, how they were dressed, how they talked, how they navigated the city, how they made their entrances and exits at the Savoy Hotel. They were, compared to the women in Paris, far more likely to make a point of being seen in public — eating at the Savoy, for example.

Women did not traditionally eat in restau-rants. They entertained at home, and their husbands ate at their private clubs. This was

137

something Ritz was determined to address: of all the numerous changes he'd made at the Savoy, many of them, one or way or another, were meant to abolish the gentlemen's-club quality of the place and introduce a sense of lightness and femininity. Partly this was a matter of décor. But more important was to attract a new clientele. He wanted men to bring their wives to dinner at the Savoy, for he knew it was women who would make the restaurant fashionable. Wealthy men in private rooms ordering twenty-course dinners was fine and good, but the success of the restaurant depended on the element of theater and people-watching that only a mixed crowd could produce.

The turning point turned out to be a single dinner.

It was Ritz's idea: a ladies' banquet. He and D'Oyly Carte asked Lady de Grey to host a small dinner for her friends — all women. Lady de Grey was a patron of the arts and a leading member of high society (her husband, Earl de Grey, was on the Savoy restaurant committee). Of course she agreed, and invited a dozen prominent women to her dinner at the Savoy.

The dinner broke the rules of social protocol: these were unaccompanied women, at a public restaurant. They sat in the main dining room, not hidden away in private, though Ritz did position a few screens around the long table to shield the women from full view, and for the sake of decorum. Still, the purpose of the dinner was to challenge decorum and change the rules, and at this they succeeded. The screens only attracted more attention, as did the string ensemble Ritz had hired for the occasion. The women's laughter could be heard throughout the restaurant, and soon everyone was talking about Lady de Grey's ladies' banquet, how fashionably daring it had been, how of the moment.

As similar women's luncheons and dinners became more popular, Ritz soon dispensed with the screens. After all, the idea was to be *seen*.

The thrill of the Savoy was its embrace of the modern. London at this moment felt like the future, and nowhere more so than in the dining room at the Savoy. And of all the social, cultural, political, and technological changes under way, none was more important than the emergence of women on the public stage. At least, none was more important to Escoffier and Ritz, whose new brand of cosmopolitanism fueled and was fueled by this shift. By the end of the summer season of 1890, the Savoy was booming, its central role in changing fin de siècle London assured.

But booming or not, the Savoy's finances were in fact on shaky ground, as Ritz would soon discover.

■ ■ ■ ■

PART 3
DECADENCE AND
SUSPICION,
1890–1893

■ ■ ■ ■

6
THE SHAREHOLDER MEETING

Richard D'Oyly Carte cleared his throat.

"It is hardly necessary for me to refer to the fact, no doubt already known to most if not all of you," he said grandly, "that the Savoy Hotel has established a reputation for being unrivaled for luxury and perfect comfort, that the cuisine is acknowledged to be the finest in London, and second to none in the world."

He paused briefly, looking out at the audience. They were in the largest banqueting room at the Savoy, more than a hundred keenly interested investors gathered for the company's first ordinary general shareholders' meeting. It was Friday afternoon, September 26, 1890, just over a year after the hotel had opened. D'Oyly Carte was glad that Ritz had placed flowers all around the room, highlighting the beauty and sophistication of the hotel. He and Helen had been astounded at the amount of money Ritz spent on flowers, Helen in particular complaining bitterly in private about the manager's profligate habits. Ritz and his damn flowers! she would exclaim. But at this moment, D'Oyly Carte was counting on the enveloping ambience of opulence to soothe and reassure the crowd. He needed all the help he could get. He had unwelcome news to deliver.

The men in the room were professionals — lawyers, tradesmen, small-time investors. They weren't rich, but they dreamed of wealth, their shares in the Savoy representing the possibility of profit, yes, but also something more ephemeral: the promise of access and glamour. They owned a piece, however small, of London's new luxury, opened for the first time to those not born into aristocratic wealth.

"The hotel and the restaurant have been frequented during the past London season by the elite of society here and by the most distinguished foreigners and Americans," D'Oyly Carte continued, "and the class of business done in the restaurant has been really exceptional and extraordinary, showing that there is a large public which is ready to come forward and pay good prices when there is really something high class offered."

He went on to explain that the business

was showing great improvement since the hiring of César Ritz as hotel manager, less than six months earlier. "We are now in really good working order," he said. After a rocky start, "into the details of which it is perhaps not necessary or desirable to go," the hotel was profitable. All was well. Things couldn't be going better. Since April, when Ritz had started, the monthly earnings had been steadily increasing. Partly this was because of the London social season, partly because Ritz and Escoffier had brought a new standard of service and luxury to the city. In any case, they were back on their feet. However . . . unfortunately . . .

Unfortunately, they would not be able to pay a dividend to the ordinary shareholders — not yet.

The men in the audience looked at each other in surprise and began to murmur, but D'Oyly Carte continued speaking.

"We should, of course, have preferred to be able to declare a dividend to the ordinary shareholders," he said. "As explained in the report, and as will be readily understood, in the opening of a great place of this kind and of this class there were many expenses, and the trading operations for this period were largely in the nature of installation, establishment, and advertisement — items which could not properly be put to capital account, but could also not be considered a fair charge against the profit and loss of one year." He himself, along with two other directors of the hotel, had put up the £30,000 to cover the losses. This was a loan for which they generously agreed to accept only 6 percent interest.

Furthermore, D'Oyly Carte said, "the directors have not charged their fees, and their present intention is not to do so until a dividend is declared to the ordinary shareholders. We care much less about our fees than about getting a good dividend."

Some of the audience applauded. "Hear, hear," they shouted.

D'Oyly Carte continued with a detailed accounting of all the expensive improvements and alterations the Savoy had required, including expanding the kitchens to suit Escoffier's needs; adding luggage rooms, larders, and other staff rooms in the basement; converting one of the banqueting rooms into the casual *salle à manger* and connecting it to the restaurant and the hotel; furnishing the new reception room and reception halls; and purchasing vastly more china, glass, cutlery, and linens than had been originally budgeted, due to the restaurant's popularity.

There were a number of things D'Oyly Carte did not mention, of course, among them the large payout to Hardwicke, the first general manager of the hotel, who had sued after being fired; and the exceedingly generous salaries paid to Ritz and Escoffier. More fundamentally, he gave no hint of just how close to disaster the Savoy had really come the previous fall and winter — the scramble for cash amid Hardwicke's disastrous tenure. "You will have gathered," he told the shareholders, "that we do not think it is in the interests of the shareholders to publish our accounts, and thus to give others in the same business a number of details and information."

The shareholders present today, D'Oyly Carte explained, were welcome to inspect the books themselves. The accounts were on a table at the front of the room. They would see that the company's income was growing quickly: "The takings for January were £6,504; for February, £6,205; March, £6,999; April, £8,167; for May, they were £10,511; and for June, they reached the large sum of £15,848."

The audience applauded once again. The numbers were good, but cash was in short supply — hence the problem of the wine.

D'Oyly Carte explained the situation:

Owing to the special reputation of the restaurant, and to the extraordinarily large amount of business done in that department, the monthly consumption of wine is very great — far greater, we are given to understand, than that of other hotels — and the directors have had under their serious consideration the question of the means of obtaining a sufficiently large stock for future use, especially of 1880, 1884, and 1889 champagnes. These vintages are rapidly rising in price, and must continue to do so, for there has been no good champagne since 1884, except that of 1889, which is, of course, not yet fit to use.

The hotel needed to invest, therefore, in a large supply of champagne, which it could not afford. D'Oyly Carte had a solution: he proposed the formation of a new, separate company that would stockpile wine and sell it to the Savoy "at a reasonable profit"; the company would also sell wine to other hotels at market prices. Given the limited supply of the best brands of champagne of the desirable vintages, this business would certainly be very profitable, D'Oyly Carte predicted, and he and a few of the other directors were ready to make the initial investment, in the hope that others, the shareholders there in the room, would also purchase shares of the new wine company.

More applause, and now the meeting drew to a close.

The official accountant, Mr. Dever of Deloitte, Dever, Griffiths, and Company, stood to vouch that the books were in order, and D'Oyly Carte said he would be pleased to answer any questions.

One man stood to ask about the accounts: Was it proper to keep them secret? Should not the Savoy — which had, after all, nothing to hide — publish its accounts like every other publicly traded company? (It was indeed highly unusual, though not illegal, for a business to keep its accounting private.)

D'Oyly Carte answered: "The directors do not think it desirable to publish the accounts, but if the shareholders express a strong opinion that we do so, we will give this matter our careful consideration."

Several shareholders now stood to say they approved of the policy of not opening the books, and D'Oyly Carte moved that the annual report and accounts be adopted. The motion was carried unanimously, and the meeting adjourned.

■ ■ ■ ■

The meeting had gone well, all things considered. Or, at least, it could have gone much worse: D'Oyly Carte had faced the crowd and told them they would not be receiving a dividend, and he had survived. He was pleased.

But the newspapers were merciless. The event had been open to the press, as all such annual shareholder meetings of public companies were. The *Lighthouse* ran a long and sardonic report on the meeting; the headline went straight to the point:

His presentation, the newspaper claimed, had been "nothing more than a burlesque" — "It was so excessively funny and witty, the ideas were so preposterously absurd, the fancies so highly fanciful, and the disappointments so beautifully and tastefully explained away that the work of Mr. W. S. Gilbert showed itself in every sentence; in fact, in every term used." D'Oyly Carte was nothing more than a showman, a fraud, a fantasist.

He was attacked for failing to pay a dividend, and for failing to publish the company's accounts. "We maintain that the Savoy accounts should have been published, just the same as all other hotel accounts are, and the mere fact of their not being so, throws doubt and suspicion upon the undertaking. What are the Savoy Hotel directors ashamed of that they do not take the shareholders into their confidence? Is it the heavy and absurd salaries paid to some of the officials?"

Ritz, being one of the very officials receiving what the *Lighthouse* considered an "absurd" salary, was also raked over the coals:

> We have not a word to say against the distinguished foreigner who enjoys the position of manager, but if we are rightly informed, he has never before had the management of a large hotel, but it would be ridiculous to pay him £1,200 per annum, and a commission on profits, even had he been proprietor or manager of the largest and most successful hotel in the universe. . . . Then comes Mr. "Chef" with his £800 per annum, Mr. "Reception-Bureau Clerk" with his £250, and so on. We ask any experienced hotel manager in London if he ever heard of such salaries under such conditions?

How had the *Lighthouse* managed to get a

hold of the salary figures? D'Oyly Carte wondered. It was embarrassing. Presumably one of the shareholders had looked through the books, and then given the information to a reporter.

D'Oyly Carte's plan to spin off a separate company to import wine was also met with scorn and derision. The directors of the company were fleecing the shareholders, the paper argued, and now they proposed to extract a commission on all the wine consumed at the hotel. "There is something radically wrong with the management of the Savoy," the article concluded.

The press was bad, but the truth was, D'Oyly Carte knew, business was improving — and it was thanks to Ritz and Escoffier. Yes, their salaries were high, but then again, he had been desperate. And now they'd turned the corner, or at least so he hoped. The revenue numbers were better, but they needed to stay better.

Anyway, he had other things on his mind: D'Oyly Carte was suddenly contending with a rupture in the Gilbert and Sullivan partnership. It was about money, of course. And respect: Gilbert had long felt less than equal to Sullivan. He was the librettist, and they wrote comedies, but Sullivan wanted to compose more serious music — real operas. This had led to countless arguments about the direction of their most recent operetta, *The Gondoliers*.

The play was well received, but when D'Oyly Carte reported to Gilbert and Sullivan that the expenses of the production — to be borne by the three of them — were £4,500, Gilbert was dismayed. He demanded to see the accounts, which included expensive costumes (multiple dresses at £100 each) and £500 for new carpets for the front of the house at the Savoy Theatre.

It was the carpet that got him. Why should he, Gilbert, be liable for the general upkeep of D'Oyly Carte's theater? he complained bitterly, his anger compounded further when Sullivan seemed to take D'Oyly Carte's side in the dispute. (This was not a surprise, given how close Sullivan and D'Oyly Carte were, with Sullivan on the board of directors of the Savoy Hotel Company. It was an affront to Gilbert nevertheless.)

It fell to Helen D'Oyly Carte to try to smooth things over as best she could. Nevertheless, Gilbert went to court to sue D'Oyly Carte, who would not bend on the question of the expenses, or the carpet. The court found for Gilbert, and ordered D'Oyly Carte to produce the theater's accounts in full for examination.

It seemed astounding that these men, who had each made a fortune working together, were now squabbling in public over a few hundred pounds. It was bad for all their reputations. And it was, perhaps, a sign of things to come at the Savoy Hotel, where small grievances (and some creative accounting) could conceivably cause trouble, too.

7
FLYING HIGH

Ritz had never been happier. He had also never been more frantic. He was managing three hotels and two restaurants in three countries: a recipe for always needing to be somewhere else. His operations in Cannes and Baden-Baden were mostly self-running, but he was in perpetual demand nevertheless: important clients arriving, dinner parties to be arranged, staff members to hire for the coming season — and there was always another season gearing up somewhere else.

He kept in touch with all the hotels via a stream of letters back and forth. He also traveled constantly. He would stand in front of his wardrobe pulling out clothes and throwing them into piles destined for different suitcases and different destinations: "Paris! Switzerland! Germany!"

He had studied the train schedules between London, Cannes, and Baden-Baden, and found the fastest connections and the best routes. No one could travel faster than Ritz. He had devised, for example, an innovative route between Paris and London that got him there in just under eight hours — a remarkable speed. Marie wrote down his itinerary for him:

Leave Paris at 3:45 p.m.
Change at Amiens
Pick up the Bâle Express
Arrive at Calais at 8:20 p.m.
Take the steamer to Dover
Thence by train to London,
arriving 11:40 p.m.

There was a restaurant car on the Bâle Express, which served dinner between Amiens and Calais. Ritz was a regular.

Train travel was a topic of much conversation, as travelers compared routes and train companies and bragged wearily about the thousands of miles they'd logged. Max Beerbohm, the young writer and caricaturist, wrote an essay about the brightly colored destination labels stuck to his hatbox — a record of his travels. "For the most part, they are crudely colored, crudely printed, without sense of margin or spacing; in fact, quite worthless as designs. No one would be a connoisseur in them." Except that he was. Not only for the memories they evoked, but for the subtle status they imparted:

> Many of them signified beautiful or famous places. There was one point at which Oxford, Newmarket, and Assisi converged, and I was always careful to shift my hatbox round in such a way that this purple patch should be lost on none of my fellow passengers. The many other labels, English or alien, they, too, gave their hints of a life spent in fastidious freedom, hints that I had seen and was seeing all that is best to be seen of men and cities and country-houses. I was respected, accordingly, and envied. And I had keen delight in this ill-gotten homage. A despicable delight, you say? But is not yours, too, a fallen nature? The love of impressing strangers falsely, is it not implanted in all of us?

Beerbohm, a member of Oscar Wilde's literary set and a frequent guest at the Savoy, had wryly identified the sense of prestige that now accompanied travel: mobility was a new kind of status, something to brag about. When Ritz told people about his Paris-to-London itinerary, they eagerly compared notes. Everyone spent an inordinate amount of time studying train schedules — each company published its own — highlighting connections and planning future trips.

Lillie Langtry, the actress and onetime mistress of the Prince of Wales, to whom she remained close, had toured America, as had Sarah Bernhardt and Oscar Wilde. They all talked about trains and hotels with wit and authority. American hotels were far more modern than Continental ones (with elevators and electric lights, just as at the Savoy), but none could match the Savoy's elegance and service, or the quality of its restaurant, they all agreed.

Wilde loved the restaurant at the Savoy, and ate there frequently, but he complained bitterly (though only half seriously) about the hotel's modern amenities. "Who wants an immovable washing-basin in one's room?" he said. "I do not. Hide the thing! I prefer to ring for water when I need it."

As for electric light, it was "everywhere, except where you need it! A harsh and ugly light, enough to ruin the eyes. And not a candle or a lamp to read by." And the elevators: they moved much too fast.

Wilde was a dandy, an aesthete, a provocateur. He embodied the flamboyant, unapologetic celebration of pleasure that was very much at the heart of the Savoy's appeal. Though he traveled in different social circles, he would likely have approved of Phillips and Ulph's extravagant fifteen-pounds-per-person dinner, for example.

A friend of Langtry's in San Francisco had sent her a newspaper clipping from the August 30, 1891, edition of the *San Francisco Chronicle,* in which Gen. John T. Cutting, a member of the U.S. House of Representatives, praised the Savoy. Langtry had given the article to Ritz:

I maintain that for service, there is no hotel in the United States to compare with the Hotel Savoy in London. There is no rush nor excitement when you arrive. You are courteously escorted by an attendant to your apartment, not by an officious bellboy who wants to wear his whiskbroom out on your clothes in the expectation of a tip. You open your trunk and lay out your crumpled clothes and go to your breakfast. Every wish seems to be almost anticipated, and you don't feel like being obliged to lay down a fee for attendance. You return in the early evening to dress for dinner, and your dress suit is there freshly pressed and ironed for use. In the morning your day suit is similarly fit for wear.

You couldn't have your wants better attended to if you were at home . . .

Ritz was filled with pride when he read the piece. To be recognized in America! And for the very things that he strived to achieve, that he had driven his staff to understand: the guest's wishes anticipated as if by magic; the feeling of being at home. He couldn't have hoped for a more flattering review of the Savoy if he'd written one himself. He planned to quote it extensively in an upcoming advertising brochure.

Yes, the service at the Savoy had improved greatly, but now Ritz had a new problem: Les Grandes Cocottes, as they were known in Paris — courtesans, women of "doubtful reputation and uncertain revenue," as his wife, Marie, referred to them. These were no common prostitutes; some of them were in fact celebrated for their great beauty and their aristocratic lovers. They were notorious and darkly glamorous, moving easily between the worlds of the theater (some of them were dancers and actresses) and high society. They were the height of fashion. It was only natural that they would flock to the Savoy, and Ritz welcomed them. But then there were the other, less glamorous courtesans, wearing large hats and noticeable quantities of makeup, women whose presence Ritz considered a threat to the hotel's good name and reputation. They had begun to appear in the lobby and restaurant with increasing frequency.

It was tricky. On the one hand, the Savoy thrived by attracting all of cosmopolitan London to a room where they could see and be seen, and who better to *see* than a dissolute Continental prince escorting a hauntingly beautiful French chorus girl? On the other hand, Ritz had made great efforts to induce "respectable" society women to entertain and be entertained at the Savoy, and those efforts were undermined by the appearance of too many prostitutes, however high class.

Ritz's solution was to declare that formal evening dress was de rigueur in the dining room at the Savoy. Furthermore, no unaccompanied women would be admitted, nor any woman wearing a hat. (An extravagant hat worn in the evening, Ritz had discovered, was a sign of trouble.)

Problem solved. Rather than policing private behavior, or attempting to divine the identities and backgrounds of his guests, he would rely on a simple dress code. This was, in a way, a hallmark of the fin de siècle moment, and it was new. In the same way that the Savoy had opened its doors to the nouveau riche (who would never be admitted to the best gentlemen's clubs, for example, but who were regulars at the hotel), it now did to elements of decadent, bohemian London (but only those who wore the right clothes).

Indeed, there was an element of decadence in the Savoy's brand of luxury — it was this decadence that made it modern, the sense that pleasure was to be celebrated. This could be seen in Escoffier's cooking, and in the peacocking, theatrical crowds in the dining room.

"You can lay down the law now," Liane de Pougy said to Ritz with an amused smile when she heard of the new rules, "for you have reached the height of your career in your profession — as I have in mine!" De Pougy was a young and well-known courtesan and Folies Bergère dancer, and they both laughed at this joke.

"Alas," he replied, "I am afraid with far less pleasure and far more trouble than you have experienced, mademoiselle!"

The social dynamics of the Savoy dining room were a reflection of London's West End nightlife scene, especially in the theaters and music halls. At the Empire Theatre of Varieties, the Alhambra Theatre, and the

Palace Theatre, all on nearby Leicester Square, the entertainment was titillating, and drew audiences from all parts of society. Writing in *Harper's New Monthly Magazine* in 1891, the journalist Frederick Anstey described the scene at the Empire:

You pass through wide, airy corridors and down stairs, to find yourself in a magnificent theatre, and the stall to which you are shown is wide and luxuriously fitted. Smoking is universal, and a large proportion of the audience promenade the outer circles, or stand in groups before the long refreshment bars, which are a prominent feature on every tier. Most of the men are in evening dress, and in the boxes are some ladies, also in evening costume, many of whom belonging to what is called good society. The women in the other parts of the house are generally pretty obvious members of a class which, so long as it behaves itself with propriety in the building, it would, whatever fanatics may say to the contrary, be neither desirable nor possible to exclude. The most noticeable characteristic of the audience is perhaps the very slight attention it pays to whatever is going on upon the stage. In the upper parts of the house the conversation renders it impossible to hear distinctly anything being said or sung, though the same remark does not apply to the stalls, where the occupants, if not enthusiastic are at least languidly attentive.

The Empire was managed by an old friend and protégé of D'Oyly Carte's named George Edwardes, who for the past few years, since the late 1880s, had been putting on spectacular ballets. There were two shows a night, each lasting for about half an hour and involving dozens of dancers wearing revealing, brightly colored costumes.

The music halls were popular among the literary set, who reveled in the seedy thrills of late-night London and wrote about their experiences (or talked about them over dinner at the Savoy the next day). The poet and critic Arthur Symons, who in the mid-1890s published *London Nights,* a collection of erotic verse devoted to the showgirls and dancers he loved, explained: "Those burning nights were so vivid, so essentially part of my vivid and burning existence, I was so inextricably mixed up with crowds of ballet girls, the hurried or lazy throng, the ballet girls as they came one after the other with much jostling, with much jolly laughter out of the stage door on to the pavement . . .

that particular, strange, original, bewildering, perplexing, exciting, passionately-colored, whirlwind of a world in which like a scented whirlwind I existed."

The Palace Theatre featured performances called "Living Pictures," just as popular as the ballets, in which women dressed in skintight, flesh-colored silk and posed as nude figures from famous paintings. These tableaux vivants were dramatically lit and accompanied by music.

The performances at the theaters were provocative, and soon attracted the attention of the National Vigilance Association, which lobbied against public vice and immorality, and tried to shut down the theaters. They were mostly unsuccessful. Laura Ormiston Chant, a prominent suffragist and writer, inspected the Empire Theatre and complained in a letter to the *Daily Telegraph* about the numerous unaccompanied women who were "painted" and who "accosted young gentlemen who were strangers to them and paid little attention to the performance." The Vigilance group also objected to the revealing costumes worn by the dancers at the Empire and by the tableau vivant models at the Palace. After a hearing at the London County Council, the Palace agreed to be more careful about the performers' costumes, and the Empire, after being closed for a few days, reopened with a canvas screen separating the bar area from the promenade that was meant to keep alcoholic drinks out of the theater proper. The audience immediately tore the screen to shreds, cheering loudly.

At the Savoy, meanwhile, there were no seminude dancers, but the atmosphere was dazzling, and business was booming. The numbers D'Oyly Carte had cited at the shareholders meeting, showing income increasing month after month, continued to rise.

As an experiment, a French company had been invited to install what it called "Theatrophones" in the lobby of the hotel, allowing customers to pay sixpence to hear five minutes of the opera being performed next door at the Savoy Theatre. Coins fed into the machine produced music (via two receivers, one for each ear) that could be heard with "purity and clearness" according to the London *Times*. It was the same technology Ritz had seen demonstrated at the Paris Exposition a few years earlier. Electronic communication in general was becoming more common. For callers in London, it was now possible to reach the Savoy to make a reservation by telephone;

the hotel's number was 2830.

"England will soon be fit to live in!" said the French comic actor Benoît-Constant Coquelin to Ritz. "You have revolutionized hotels, you have revolutionized the habits of society. But alas, you can't change England! The law is no respecter of persons — particularly of actors! And nothing would convince the English that it is not wicked to dine in public on Sundays. They are resigned, I tell you, to their cold joint and gloom on Sundays. More — they like it; they make a virtue of it! *O tempora! O mores! O Paris! I am homesick!*"

But Coquelin was wrong: Ritz had begun a campaign to change the law, enlisting the Savoy board members and every important contact he could muster to apply pressure. He spoke with members of Parliament and with newspapermen when they came to the restaurant; he buttonholed Lord and Lady Dudley, Lord and Lady de Grey, Lord and Lady Randolph Churchill; he strategized with Henri Blowitz, the influential foreign correspondent for the *Times*. Blowitz was a tiny man with a very large head and extravagant whiskers. He knew everyone.

"We might," he said, "if we work things properly, get some slight alteration in the law . . . or a re-interpretation; I don't know."

They did succeed, and the result was that dinner at the Savoy was now legal on Sunday, which soon enough became the most popular and fashionable night of the week at the restaurant. Lady de Grey and the Duchess of Devonshire led the way.

It was at one such Sunday dinner that Ritz found himself talking with Hwfa Williams, who had arranged for Johann Strauss and his orchestra to travel from Vienna and perform in London that season. Strauss gave public concerts and was also in high demand for private events.

"Why not bring him here?" Ritz asked.

"Do you know what that man charges?" Williams replied. It was an exorbitant sum, but Ritz didn't blink.

"It would be well worth it," he said. "Music would induce many people to linger over their dinners . . . and ask the sommelier what that would mean!"

Strauss's waltzes and other light music could soon be heard at the Savoy, adding a new dimension to the dining experience. The restaurant was more than ever a kind of theater, and the diners were the audience.

Just as Ritz had predicted, the crowds lingered happily, and just as Williams had warned, the orchestra was fantastically expensive. But Ritz didn't worry about that now.

In the Savoy kitchens, Escoffier was experimenting with new recipes, new flavors and sensations. The borscht he had served at the infamous fifteen-pounds-per-person dinner, for example, was a hit — the soup was now one of the most popular items on the menu.

He was expanding the English palate. For a grand dinner at which the Prince of Wales himself was to be in attendance, Escoffier decided to present a dish he called *Cuisses de Nymphes à l'Aurore,* or "Thighs of Nymphs at Dawn." This was a cold, poached dish, served with a golden *chaud-froid* (a cream-based sauce with aspic that set when it cooled) and presented on elegant platters on blocks of ice.

"Nymphs at Dawn! Lovely name and lovely dish. But what is it?" asked members of the prince's party. "Is it a small bird? Or what?"

It fell to Ritz, presiding in the dining room that evening, to explain. Escoffier was in the kitchen of course, safely hidden away, and Ritz was on the spot, suddenly terrified that serving the "nymphs" had been a serious mistake. The English had long scorned the eating of frogs, and this was Escoffier's attempt to sneak them onto the menu. (He knew that the prince himself loved frogs, snails, and other French delicacies, and he figured the "nymphs" would be popular, as long as no one knew what they were.)

Ritz's heart was pounding, but he betrayed no anxiety and replied coolly: Oh no, not a small bird, he said. They are frogs' legs — very French, of course. Monsieur Escoffier has poached them in a court bouillon, and the sauce is flavored with paprika and tarragon.

The reaction was pure shock, but the prince himself only laughed. He was so amused, in fact, that he ordered *Nymphes à l'Aurore* again when he came to dinner at the Savoy a few days later. "This was not a novel dish for him," said Escoffier later. "He was too much of a gourmet and a friend of France to disapprove of my culinary hoax."

As for the others, the ones who seemed so shocked: "Messieurs les Anglais," Escoffier said, "my friends, allow me to say that the French are not the only 'frog-eaters' anymore!"

Soon the nymphs had achieved a kind of notoriety — not only the frogs' legs themselves but the name that Escoffier had bestowed upon them.

He had always had a knack for this sort of thing. Even as a teenager, working in the kitchen at his uncle's Restaurant Français in Nice, Escoffier had written the menus: "I started looking for words that sounded gentle and pleasing to the ear while expressing a connection with the food being proposed. All well-presented menus should be evocative, and increase the desire to partake of a skillfully prepared and presented meal."

The menu was a kind of poem, Escoffier believed — teasing, seducing, promising pleasure. A poem of anticipation. The list of dishes had power, and never more so than when Escoffier invented something new, and *named* it: *La timbale Grimaldi, les filets de sole Walewska, les cailles Carmen, la poularde Adelina Patti . . .* Starting in the mid-1880s at the Grand Hotel in Monte Carlo, he'd begun naming many of his culinary inventions for aristocratic and historic or literary figures, but he soon found that flattering his contemporary celebrity guests in this way was a brilliant kind of advertising. A dish named for an opera star, after all, attached that star's glamour to the recipe prepared in his or her honor, and to the restaurant, too.

And, of course, to Escoffier himself: he was sought out by high-profile guests, who

171

wanted to consult with him about their dinner menus, to make special requests, to flirt with the chef and talk about food. Escoffier had found a new kind of semi-celebrity, and he liked it. He had always resented the idea of the chef as servant, toiling away invisibly in the kitchen, and now reveled in the recognition of his artistry.

When the beautiful Hungarian ballerina known only as Katinka stayed at the Grand in the winter of 1885/86, they had struck up a friendship that revolved around food. Katinka was devoted to Hungarian cooking, and to its characteristic paprika, and Escoffier was always interested in learning new recipes. "I frequently had the occasion to talk to this wonderful dancer, and she enjoyed telling me of the food of her native country, which was of particular interest to me," Escoffier would later write, rather formally.

"I love crayfish, but I hate having to peel their shells off at the table," she said to him. "Could you serve them without their shells?"

Of course he could. As it happened, Katinka was having dinner the following night with a Russian aristocrat, Prince Kochubey, and two other Russians. Escoffier prepared a menu that included caviar, blinis, and vodka, and a dish he called *Le Rêve de Katinka,* or "Katinka's Dream." This was a light mousse made of fresh whiting, egg whites, and cream surrounded by crayfish sautéed with butter and sliced truffles, and served with a paprika cream sauce.

The crayfish, needless to say, were served without their shells.

Katinka came to the kitchen the next day to thank Escoffier for the wonderful meal. The prince had loved it, too, she said, and was planning another dinner soon. "But I know that he loves that fine amphibian you call a frog, and as I know that you always have beautiful ones, could you add a few frog's legs to the shrimp?"

Of course he could, he replied.

Nothing gave him more pleasure than moments like this: the great dancer, so delicate and ethereal, visiting his kitchen and laughing with him about frogs' legs and crayfish. The same thing was now happening in London, but more so. Escoffier was in demand. When he walked into the dining room at the Savoy to greet a prominent guest, to stop at a table to ask if the meal had been satisfactory, he was recognized and celebrated.

Escoffier hadn't expected to like London. He didn't speak English, and the English didn't understand food. What he found instead was that his very Frenchness had become his calling card, and that the English were indeed learning how to eat. He was already well known among the aristocratic set who came to Monte Carlo and Lucerne, but now he discovered wider acclaim. The dishes he invented in London were finding an international audience.

When the novelist Emile Zola came to London for the first time in the early 1890s, he stayed at the Savoy and spent hours reminiscing with Escoffier about the food of his childhood in Provence, and exclaiming at the chef's way with grilled sardines. Zola also loved *Blanquette de veau à la Provençal* with saffron noodles, and he had a special fondness for polenta with thinly sliced white truffles from Piedmont.

They would talk about pot-au-feu with stuffed cabbage and other rustic dishes of southern France. The mutton! The garlic! The cassoulet with tomato, eggplant, zucchini, and bell peppers!

Escoffier was honored by Zola's attention, even though the man's visceral passion for food (and for talking about food) was so different from his own cerebral, artistic manner. Which was ironic, of course, given that Zola was the writer and he was the chef. Then again, maybe not: Escoffier sought to bring calm and creativity to the chaotic restaurant kitchen, while Zola was intent on bringing passion and social realism to the novel.

And another irony, not lost on Escoffier, was the fact that Zola was staying at the luxurious Savoy to begin with: the author had come to London to observe the conditions of the working class, to see the vast slums of the world's biggest city. So it was perhaps "paradoxical," Escoffier thought, that Zola had chosen the Savoy, whose luxury shielded its guests from London's harsher realities.

Zola loved London — the scale of it, the energy, the constant movement on the Thames. Perhaps he would set a novel here, he said, though that would require more research. "I may place some French characters in a London framework, and perhaps give a few English silhouettes in the second rank," he said. "To go into the psychology of a strange people is, however, another thing. That would need not months but years of residence."

Escoffier was less concerned with the psychology of the English than with serving them authentic French dishes while also expanding his repertoire. Many of his

recipes required specialized ingredients —
not just vast quantities of truffles, or the
odd specially requested item (like those
edelweiss flowers for the Swiss
mountaineering-club dinner), but also all
kinds of cured meats, cheeses, and certain
fresh vegetables, including asparagus imported from the Continent. Escoffier had
long-standing relationships with many suppliers from his years in Monte Carlo and
Lucerne, and he now turned to them for
help procuring what he needed. He also
invested in a small fruit-preservation company in Switzerland, a move that allowed
him to import canned tomatoes for the
Savoy. (The company soon ran into trouble
when the tomato crop failed, but Escoffier
maintained a lifelong interest in food preser-
vation.)

Escoffier had established himself as London's premier French chef, an icon of correct and meticulous taste. Still, his business
dealings were sometimes necessarily messy:
in many cases, he was dealing directly with
his suppliers (and paying bribes when
necessary), and then asking Ritz for reim-
bursement from the Savoy. He'd been doing business with some of these purveyors
for years, and they expected to deal with
him directly. The accounting may have been

imprecise and under the table, but the results were what mattered. And as long as the restaurant business was booming, Ritz and Escoffier had no trouble with these arrangements. Ritz signed off on large shipments of Escoffier's tomatoes, for example, not paying too much attention to the price, or to Escoffier's possible conflict of interest as both the buyer and the seller. The two men had known and trusted each other for too long to worry about the price of tomatoes.

But someone *was* paying attention, keeping an eye on the books, and on Escoffier's and Ritz's dealings with the hotel's many vendors, and on the line-item costs for everything in the Savoy's budget. Helen D'Oyly Carte was suspicious by nature, and found much to interest her as she watched, ever so slightly resentfully, as Escoffier and Ritz made the Savoy a stunning success.

8
EXPANSION PLANS AND
NEW PRESSURES

In late 1891, the Savoy Hotel company bought a plot of land in Rome, near the Baths of Diocletian. This was to be the luxury hotel that Rome so desperately needed: Americans were coming to Europe in droves on transatlantic ocean liners, and in Rome there were no hotels at the level of the Savoy to serve them. The Marquis di Rudini, the Italian premier, had traveled to London on a state visit in the spring, and encouraged Ritz (whom he knew from years before, when he stayed at the Grand Hotel National in Lucerne) to set up shop in Rome. "We need a new Savoy, a new Grand National, in Rome," he said. And so it came to be.

The previous owner of the site, a Mr. Cavallini, had begun construction of a building and then run out of money; he was introduced to Ritz by an old friend, Franz Josef Bucher, another Swiss hotelier Ritz knew from his days in Lucerne. (Bucher ran the Bürgenstock and had spearheaded the building, a few years earlier, of a funicular railway running from Lake Lucerne up to the resort.) Cavallini was desperate to sell. The site was magnificent, right in the center of Rome, on a small hill, the Viminale. The hotel would be close to Termini, the central train station built in the mid-1870s, the point of arrival in Rome for more and more visitors.

Ritz was sure the board of directors of the Savoy would be interested. The board wanted to expand, and had every faith in him as hotelier. But he was merely an employee — a situation that was beginning to rankle. He had engineered the Savoy's success after its rocky start, and yes, he was well paid, but his authority would always be superseded by that of D'Oyly Carte and the other owners.

Was this his chance to put himself on more equal footing? If the Savoy's Rome project came to be, he was determined to own a piece of it. And if the Savoy said no, then he might find investors of his own to launch the hotel . . .

He explained his situation to Cavallini: he was in Rome as a representative of the Savoy, but he also worked independently.

One way or another, he said, he would find the investors they needed; he asked Cavallini for two letters of intent to sell the half-built hotel: one addressed to the Savoy and the other to him personally. The second letter he kept secret: it stated simply that if Ritz were to arrange the financing, he would receive a payment of £2,000, a significant sum.

The Savoy agreed to the deal, and met Ritz's demands for ownership. They formed a new company, the London and Foreign Hotel Syndicate, to develop and run the Rome hotel, which they named the Grand. Ritz and D'Oyly Carte held the majority of shares, along with some of the early Savoy shareholders, including Michael Gunn and Arthur Sullivan. Yet Ritz also argued that his key deputies be given ownership, too: they were not putting up capital, but their expertise was crucial. And so Escoffier and Echenard, Ritz's number two, were also issued shares in the new company.

It was a moment of triumph for Ritz, though mostly a symbolic one, as the shares meant nothing unless the hotel was a success. He also collected his £2,000 from a grateful Cavallini. He felt no guilt at taking this payment — after all, he had put the deal together. Still, he told no one about it, except for Marie.

Ritz was put in charge of the entire project as managing director, overseeing the construction, staffing, and launch of the new hotel, and adding Rome to his list of regular travel stops. He convinced his old friend Alphonse Pfyffer, one of the sons of the family that owned the National in Lucerne, to come to Rome as general manager of the hotel. Escoffier would organize and staff the kitchen and restaurant. Echenard would take charge of the Savoy whenever Ritz was absent, as he always did.

On his first visit to Rome, Ritz was filled with awe and a surprising melancholy. The city was so lovely, and there was so much history here, yet he knew so little of it. His lack of formal education was something he kept quite well hidden, but at times like this his shame would reveal itself.

"All this beauty, all this magnificence," he said to Marie. "And to think I never even knew about it before! How ignorant I am! How ignorant!"

When he and a local dignitary, Princess Mirafiori, toured the Vatican, admiring the Sistine Chapel, he had stared at the ceiling in awe. "Michelangelo had a glimpse of another world," he said, sounding appropriately respectful. It was stunning. But when they entered the immense, soaring St. Peter's Basilica, he had blurted out, "What a magnificent banqueting room this would make!"

Princess Mirafiori only smiled, as the words echoed in his head: a banqueting room! Ritz was mortified. How could he have said something so perfectly inane? A historic church, its dome designed by Michelangelo, a most holy site, and all he could think about was catering a dinner in it?

It was Marie who put an end to the self-recriminations, and forced Ritz to laugh at himself, as she always did. It was amusing, he had to agree. He started telling the story of his tour of St. Peter's (and his silly remark) at dinner parties, and everyone laughed and laughed.

Still, he wanted to know more.

As they rode its streets in a carriage, he asked Pfyffer, whom he'd known since they were young men, to tell him as much of the history of the city as he could remember. What was this building here, and that ruin, and that church? And the great men of Roman history: Caesar, Augustus, Cicero — what were their stories?

But I'm not an encyclopedia! Pfyffer protested.

"Why are you not?" Ritz replied, suddenly furious. "If I had had your opportunities, I should *know*!"

Pfyffer was well born and well educated — his ancestors, the Pfyffers von Altishofen, had been members of the noble class in Switzerland going back to the sixteenth century, serving as commanders of the Swiss Guard at the Vatican. Alphonse Pfyffer and his younger brother, Hans, had always looked up to Ritz when he managed their family hotel. Only a few years older than the two brothers, Ritz was worldly and independent. He'd lived in Paris. He had his own money. He understood women. He had once offered the Prince of Wales a light for his after-dinner cigar. He had waited on Sarah Bernhardt. Nevertheless, the Pfyffers also poked fun at Ritz for his ignorance about art, history, and literature.

It didn't bother Ritz then, in his twenties; he was too busy making his way in the world — scrambling, hustling, working. Now he was older. Working just as hard of course, and more successfully than ever, but the gaps in his knowledge seemed more consequential now, reminding him that however much he looked the part, it was a part he was playing. He was the elegant and culti-vated César Ritz, mastermind of luxury, but he couldn't escape the feeling that he might be revealed, at any moment, to be an impostor, nothing more than a servant.

The truth, he feared, was detectable in the size of his hands and feet. They were large, peasant-size hands and feet, he was convinced, and he did everything possible to keep them hidden.

He wore his shoes a half size too small. This was painful, of course, but preferable to ridicule.

He also put great effort into caring for his hands and nails, spending as much time on them, Marie laughed, "as a vain woman."

It was easy enough to look the part, to play the dandy. But his sense of his own flaws remained. He was, in some ways, in his own mind, a fake.

This was, it seemed, the modern condition. You couldn't always be sure who anyone really was.

There had been an incident at the Savoy soon after the hotel opened, when an American named W. S. Reese checked in and soon began receiving multiple packages from a Hanover Square tailor, Mr. Nelson: morning walking suits, frock coats, topcoats, an entire wardrobe. Reese was from Alabama, he said, the son of one of the largest iron-ore manufacturers in the United States, and was visiting London to find investors to expand the business. He was in his mid-twenties, fair-haired, and quite short.

When Reese called on Nelson, he presented a visiting card from the U.S. consul in London, Gen. John New, upon which New had written a note of introduction, attesting that Reese was a man of character. General New was a good client of the tailor's, so that was all it took: soon Reese and his companion, another young American, were being fitted for their clothes. They had a long discussion about the relative merits of astrakhan versus sealskin topcoats, and went with the fine wool.

All the details of the story only came to light when the enormous £200 bill for the clothes went unpaid, and Nelson came looking for his clients at the Savoy. He asked for Reese at the front desk.

The Americans, it turned out, had checked out the week before, gone to Liverpool to board a steamer bound for New York. The Savoy porters had loaded their heavy trunks into a cab. They were gone.

Nelson went to the U.S consul's office and was shown in to see General New. Yes, of course, the general said, he remembered Mr. Reese, and had written the note of introduction. Nelson felt a surge of relief.

He had been momentarily worried, he said, because Reese had emphasized repeatedly that there was nothing more abhorrent to him than an overdue bill, and to please send the bill with the clothes, which Nelson had done. It was surely just a misunderstanding, then.

What did he look like, this Mr. Reese? asked General New.

"He was a very short man —" Nelson said, and was immediately interrupted.

"That is not the man at all," said General New. The Reese he'd met was six foot two and large: "He could fill a hansom without even trying."

How the swindlers had gotten their hands on General New's card and note would remain a mystery. The newspapers had a field day. One series of headlines read:

TWO TRICKY AMERICANS

*

AN ENGLISH TAILOR YIELDS TO THE CHARMS OF A SMOOTH STRANGER

*

PERSONATING A WEALTHY IRON MAN

*

TRUSTING A GENTLEMAN FOR £200 UPON THE STRENGTH OF A RECOMMENDATION GIVEN TO ANOTHER MAN

Ritz felt a pang of recognition when he thought of the "tricky Americans" and their fashionable new suits. He was no thief, obviously, and had no sympathy for them. Just the opposite: their existence infuriated him. And yet he, too, wore conspicuously fashionable suits and presented himself as a paragon of discretion and taste. He was not wealthy, yet he presided over a world of luxury at the Savoy. He was steeped in the byways and pecking orders of the aristocracy, even as he stood apart from it entirely, in shoes a half size too small.

Yes, they were a sign of the times, the swindlers: their coveting of wealth, their savvy manipulations of class and identity, their easy mobility. Indeed, the Savoy was an emblem of all these things, so it made perfect sense that Reese and his partner in crime had made themselves at home there. They dressed the part. At the Savoy, everyone dressed the part.

Indeed, the Savoy brand of luxury was traveling — Rudini had been right to encourage Ritz to come to Rome. The city was full of visitors (the English, the Germans, the Americans), and new hotels were opening all over. The Hotel Eden, on Via Ludovisi, owned by the Munichborn hotelier Francesco Nistelweck, was only a few years old. The Hotel Hassler was soon set to open at the top of the Spanish Steps — it was owned by Alberto Hassler, who was Swiss. Rome was much smaller than London, and had an easygoing, resort-like atmosphere. The weather was balmy. The hotel men all knew each other; indeed, Hassler's daughter Berta was married to Nistelweck.

The Grand would be as modern as the Savoy: electricity throughout the entire building, a bathroom for every suite of rooms. English plumbers were imported to oversee the installation of the pipes. Italian gardeners filled the courtyard with lush and exotic plantings and flowers. This was becoming a Ritz trademark: "Do palms grow in your hotels, Ritz? They seem to!" the Prince of Wales had remarked upon arriving at the Hôtel de Provence when it first opened in 1889. Ritz had placed potted trees along the hotel's main corridor. In Rome, they would fill an entire square.

Ritz asked his wife, Marie, to take charge of the interior decoration. "Your taste is good," he told her, "so go ahead and choose colors and fabrics at once. I trust you."

Marie was soon immersed in the world of linen manufacturers, pillow merchants, and designers of electric chandeliers. She studied furniture catalogues and met with carpet salesmen. She visited textile workshops and collected fabric swatches.

She may have had good taste, as her husband said, but mostly she had a twenty-four-year-old's innate sense of what was outdated and fusty, and what felt modern. Most of what she saw was hideous: garish pseudo-Japanese wall hangings; completely useless furniture (a small bamboo table with a built-in oil lamp and lace-trimmed shade, for example); and metal chandeliers and lamps in the form of Greek statuary. She did her best to choose the "least awful" options.

The previous summer, 1891, Marie had given birth to a baby boy, Charles, and the young family was now living in a four-room suite at the Savoy. After she put Charles to bed at night, she and César would eat dinner and talk about work. She loved being his partner in this way, planning and strategizing.

One recurring concern, beyond the difficulty in finding decent furniture, was Helen D'Oyly Carte's quiet hostility. She was perfectly polite, but Marie could tell she resented being displaced in her role at the hotel. After all, before Ritz arrived, Helen had overseen the design and furnishing of the Savoy. Not only had Ritz rolled back many of those choices (removing wallpaper, heavy drapery, and many of the objets d'art she had bought for the hotel lobby and other public spaces), but now he'd put Marie in charge of decorating the Rome property.

But the real problem was money. Helen disapproved of many of Ritz's decisions, mostly because they were expensive.

The Strauss orchestra, for example, had cost an arm and a leg.

And now that Sunday evenings were so busy (after the law was changed), Ritz had decided the restaurant needed to bake its own bread, as getting fresh loaves on Sundays was impossible. He'd imported a Viennese baker for the job — also expensive.

At a board meeting in early 1892, Ritz was confronted about his spending, and he momentarily lost his temper.

What exactly do you think I'm trying to do? he shouted. I am running the hotel as best I can, and I will not stand here and listen to your ignorant criticism!

Ritz stormed out of the meeting, but he soon regretted it, and sent a note to D'Oyly Carte apologizing for "having lost control of myself in a moment of excitement, a thing which will not occur again."

The pressure was getting to him. He was stretched too thin.

Over the course of 1892 and into 1893, the strain only got worse. The Rome hotel was behind schedule. Was any hotel ever opened on time? Ritz didn't think so. Watching the Italian construction workers unpacking large sandwiches and opening large bottles of red wine on their lengthy, leisurely lunch breaks, it was possible to imagine they would never finish at all.

"These foreigners haven't the ghost of an idea of time," one of the English plumbers complained. "They say 'yes, the work will be done on time.' But what time, is what I want to know. Next month, or next year?"

Ritz was in perpetual motion, traveling from London to Baden-Baden to Cannes to Rome and back again. The winter season was his time to focus on his own affairs in Germany and Provence, but now the Rome hotel opening had to take precedence. Alphonse Pfyffer was in Rome full time, but Ritz's presence and authority were frequently required. When the construction workers threatened to strike, for example, Ritz took the next train to Rome. When the carpeting that Marie had ordered failed to arrive, when the courtyard garden failed to materialize, when the furniture being custom-made for the hotel failed to get built, it was Ritz who put things right.

He soon found he was spending most of his time away from the Savoy on the Rome project, and neglecting his small hotels and restaurant. After all the negotiating with D'Oyly Carte about keeping his independence, maintaining his small properties even as he took over at the Savoy, he was now too busy to pay attention to everything.

What to do?

He and Marie were in their apartment at the Savoy. It was a rare moment of calm: early evening, before dinner. Ritz was tired. He was always tired. He had taken off his shoes and was holding Charles in his arms; the baby was quiet. Marie sat across from them on the couch. She was worried: her husband seemed worn down. She was used to his periodic dark moods — he had been particularly gloomy after his blowup at the Savoy board meeting — but now he just seemed exhausted.

We should sell the Provence and the Minerva, she said, and the restaurant, too.

Ritz looked at his wife. He'd been contemplating the same thing. Sell the small hotels, focus on London and Rome. It was the rational choice. The Savoy and the Grand were large, state-of-the-art luxury hotels, internationally known. Ritz's reputation had reached new heights at the Savoy, and in Rome he was opening what would be, he was sure, the best hotel in the city.

Still, he felt a stab of shame, of dismay, at the thought of abandoning his own hotels, especially the Provence.

Baden-Baden: fine. He had no qualms, really, about selling the Restaurant de la Conversation and the Hotel Minerva. Business was business. He had done well with both but now did not have the time to run them properly.

But the Hôtel de Provence in Cannes was different. It was more than a business. He had a sentimental attachment to the place. The Provence was where he and Marie first lived as a married couple; it represented his independence, the end of his many years as an employee in Lucerne and in Monte Carlo. The Provence was *his* and his alone. It was almost impossible to explain to Marie what that meant to him, how deep that feeling went. She had grown up in a family of hoteliers, but for Ritz, owning his own hotel was the signal achievement of his life, marking his escape from his past.

Ritz's parents were long dead. They were farmers, and he loved them, but he had found his way in the world far from the rural Alps of his childhood. When he and Marie got married, in January 1888, only a single brother, Josef, had come from Switzerland to the wedding in Cannes. Josef had stared in wonder at the people gathered in the church. Otto Kah had been there — he was Ritz's first and most important investor, the German who'd helped him win the restaurant concession in Baden-Baden and who had also been his backer in the Hôtel de Provence. Hans and Alphonse Pfyffer were at the wedding — his old friends, the sons of his former employer. And Marie's parents, aunts, and uncles, hoteliers all.

It was a momentous occasion. The organist played a wedding march and then Charles Gounod's "Ave Maria." This was Ritz's favorite song, one that he often asked Marie to play for him on the piano. The music filled him with longing. Not far away, the Hôtel de Provence, which he had just purchased, was being renovated and readied for opening. César and Marie were on their way.

And now?

"It means giving up my liberty," he said to Marie. Selling the Provence felt to César like going backward. "It means tying myself forever to the Savoy company. Do I want to do that?"

Not true, she argued, not at all. Ritz was already recognized as one of the premier hoteliers in Europe, if not the world. He was very much in demand — indeed, he received inquiries from hotel companies on a regular basis, asking him to consult on, or manage, or advise, or one way or another to give his blessing to their projects. There would be no shortage of opportunities for Ritz, she was sure.

Marie was right. As hard as it was, they would sell the Provence.

Ritz began to cry a little. He was looking down at his son's hands and feet. Charles's hands and feet were tiny, and he held them gently in his own hands.

"Thank God he will have small hands," he said to Marie. "He has inherited his hands from you, not me. He will not suffer as I have because of peasant hands!"

Marie always made light of César's shame and vanity, and his too-small shoes, but now her eyes filled with tears.

Yes, they would sell the Hôtel de Provence, Ritz said again, but he would fight twice as hard for his independence, for Marie, for Charles. He would not resign himself to being D'Oyly Carte's employee. He would own his own hotels again, in London, in Rome, maybe even in Paris. It was destiny.

■ ■ ■ ■

PART 4
SCANDAL,
1894–1898

■ ■ ■ ■

9

THE PRINCE OF WALES VS.
THE DUC D'ORLÉANS

Even with Ritz's attention now focused entirely on the Savoy, friction and complications were perhaps inevitable. Ritz's outsize ambition, his insistence on his independence, was always bound to cause trouble, blurring the line between loyalty and self-interest. But, for a while, it all seemed to work.

After he'd sold his Provence and Baden-Baden properties, Ritz devoted himself single-mindedly to the Savoy, and to launching the Rome Grand. He was the ever-present impresario, scrutinizing every detail, overseeing every gala dinner. The Rome hotel had opened in January 1894, and was an immediate and enormous success, drawing throngs of curious aristocrats and dignitaries to the opening night party — there were cardinals, lords, and princes; representatives from the Vatican, the Quirinal, the city government. The Grand was the new center of the city's elite social life, just as the Savoy was in London. And just as in London, the city was changing. Marie Ritz recalled:

> To the Rome of the antiquarian, of the pilgrim of the arts, of the diplomat, was added another Rome — that of the *monde qui s'amuse.* It had its headquarters at the Grand Hotel, this new, cosmopolitan, lighthearted Rome; its own hierarchy, composed of the flower of Italian society, visiting diplomats, American millionaires, aristocratic tourists of every race, the gilded caravan of nomads wandering from capital to resort, from resort to capital. César Ritz was their ruler.

Prince Colonna, the mayor of Rome, toasted Ritz at the opening night gala as "the new César, returned to conquer Rome."

Ritz was riding high, running the two best hotels in Europe. A new, conquering César, indeed. No one appreciated the hyperbolic compliment more than Ritz, with his great reverence for all the history he didn't know.

At the Savoy, the dinners and parties were more extravagant than ever, reaching a fever pitch as the fin de siècle drew closer. Ritz and Escoffier managed to outdo themselves again and again.

In May 1895, Prince Philippe, the Duc d'Orléans, exiled claimant to the French throne, called on Ritz at the Savoy. His younger sister Princess Hélène was to marry Prince Emanuele, the Duke of Aosta, an Italian royal, in June. It would be the highlight of the social season, the prince said. Surely Ritz had heard about the wedding plans.

Yes, of course, Ritz replied.

The Duc d'Orléans and Princess Hélène had a long history in England, having been raised in exile in Twickenham, in southwest London. Princess Hélène and Prince Eddy, the eldest son of the Prince of Wales, had fallen in love and planned to marry in 1890, but the match had been thwarted for political reasons. Prince Eddy died of the flu two years later, at the age of twenty-eight. Now Princess Hélène's engagement to the Duke of Aosta, considered one of Europe's most eligible bachelors, had once again put her in the spotlight. The wedding would bring a parade of English and international royalty to the London celebration.

The ceremony was to be held at St. Raphael's Catholic Church, in Kingston upon Thames in southwest London.

The Duc ran through the guest list, which included representatives of all the royal families in Europe: the Prince and Princess of Wales and two of their daughters, Princesses Victoria and Maude; the Duke and Duchess of York; Prince and Princess Henry of Battenberg; the Duke and Duchess of Connaught; the Duchess of Saxe-Coburg and Gotha, who was married to Prince Alfred, the Prince of Wales's younger brother; the Prince of Naples, Crown Prince of Italy; Prince Antonio and Princess Eulalia of Spain; the Duke of Oporto, representing the King of Portugal; and numerous French aristocrats, including the Duchess of Montpensier; Prince and Princess de Joinville; the Duc d'Aumale; the Duc de Nemours; and the Duc de Luynes.

Ritz listened, rapt — entranced — as the Duc spoke, the names working their usual magic. Ritz had a weakness for royalty, and it was indeed an impressive guest list. The marriage of Princess Hélène and the Duke of Aosta, the joining of two royal families, would bring all of European royalty to London. Royals were expected to marry other royals, their alliances serving political as well as social purposes, so of course they all knew each other. (Indeed, Victor Emmanuel, the Crown Prince of Italy, had been widely discussed as a possible match for Princess Hélène, but nothing came of it. He would also be attending the wedding, naturally.)

Official mourning in Russia and France, following the deaths the previous year of the Russian czar Alexander III and the French president Marie François Sadi Carnot (assassinated by an Italian anarchist), had recently been lifted. There was pent-up desire for a celebration and a grand party — a most spectacular dinner.

At the Savoy, of course.

Well, said the Duc, he should not have waited this long to inquire, but what with the complicated wedding arrangements and the politics and all the royal guests . . . His voice trailed off. You understand, he said.

Yes, of course, Ritz replied.

The date in question was Tuesday, June 25, the young aristocrat said — only a few weeks hence, but surely enough time for Ritz and his team to prepare a royal feast. It would be an intimate affair, the Duc said — just sixty-four guests. He was counting on Ritz, he said emphatically. And he wanted the best Escoffier had to offer. He would leave all the details to them — in fact, he himself was leaving town shortly, traveling to Spain on a hunting expedition, and would return in time for the wedding.

The Duc d'Orléans was in his mid-twenties. He was tall, blond, and athletic, with a full but well-trimmed beard and an overconfident bearing. He was regal; he had been known to keep tiger cubs as pets and to walk them in public. His father, Philippe, the Comte de Paris, had died the previous year, after years spent hoping for a monarchist restoration that never came. Now the Duc was in line for the French throne, should such a restoration ever happen. (There was no sign that it would.)

Ritz opened the reservation book. There was a problem.

The best banqueting rooms were already booked on June 25, he said, for a regimental dinner hosted by the Cornish Club —

The Duc interrupted him, smiling. The royal wedding dinner was a rare event, he said, an important event. It would be remembered for years to come. And the Cornish Club, well, it was the Cornish Club. Fine gentlemen, of course, but royalty must take precedence.

The Duc was used to getting his way. He was perfectly polite, but he addressed himself to Ritz as he would a servant. There was a certain tone, an undertow of impatience, that aristocrats tended to adopt in such conversations. Ritz was used to it, and indeed he was supremely talented at striking just the right posture of serene, compliant servitude in response.

But of course, Ritz was no servant, and it was at moments like this that he felt most acutely the contradictions of his position. He was eager to please, to a fault, but at the same time keenly aware of his power. The Savoy was his domain.

The Cornish Club, he explained, had arranged for the Prince of Wales to preside at its dinner. Ritz could therefore not move the group to one of the smaller rooms. It was the Prince of Wales, after all.

The Duc d'Orléans understood, of course, but he didn't like it one bit. He and the Prince despised each other. Who knew why. ("Two such perfect princes, such perfect gourmets, such perfect gentlemen! What a pity they did not get on well together," said Ritz's friend Olivier, the headwaiter at the Amphitryon Club, who had served both men for years.) The Prince of Wales would be attending the wedding, it seemed, but not the wedding dinner. And now the Cornish Club dinner he *was* attending had thrown a wrench into the Duc's plans.

It is unfortunate, said Ritz, but with such short notice . . .

The Duc stood to leave. "Too bad," he said. "Well, I must see what the Hotel Bristol can do for me."

As soon as the Duc left, Ritz was overcome with anguish. Despair. It was ridiculous to feel so deeply about a lost dinner reservation, no matter how distinguished the guests. But for Ritz, it felt like an existential failure, and he turned the problem over in his mind in a state of increasing torment. There must be a solution. And if he could find one, the triumph would be significant: to host the Prince of Wales *and* the Duc d'Orléans at simultaneous dinners, with all Europe's royalty in attendance, at the height of the London season . . .

He called Echenard, his second in command, into his office, and together they studied the reservation book. It was hopeless. Both the wedding and the Cornish Club dinners were large affairs: sixty-four guests expected for the former, fifty for the latter. They did not have room to accommodate the wedding dinner. Echenard shook his head sadly.

And it was at this moment that Ritz had an idea: the basement. One of the large rooms was empty and mostly unused. There was a billiard table down there but not much else.

Echenard laughed.

It was an absolutely absurd idea. A wedding dinner in the basement? It would be stiflingly hot, and damp, too. The windows were too small. There was no air. The room was ugly.

But Ritz could see it, his set designer's imagination already filling the subterranean room with flowers and palm trees. They would bring in masons to enlarge the tiny windows and the doorway. They would cool the room with large blocks of ice. It could work.

The next day, Ritz went to see the Duc in person, at Orléans House in Twickenham, where he described his plans for the event. Unfortunately, the Duc's mother, the Comtesse de Paris, was also present, and she was immediately skeptical. The cellar, she said? "Not to be thought of!" But the Duc was intrigued. The Bristol, where he had also made inquiries, was a good hotel in Mayfair, but it was not the Savoy. And he had faith in Ritz. The truth was, he liked the idea of stealing a bit of the Prince of Wales's thunder with a high-profile dinner at the same time and in the same hotel.

"Go ahead," he said.

So they did. Over the next few weeks, Ritz

oversaw the renovation of the basement room, hiring carpenters and masons to enlarge the door and windows, and painters to whitewash the walls. He bought tables and chairs, and a number of large mirrors to brighten the room. The billiard table was too big to move anywhere else, so he planned to surround it with potted palm trees and ferns. Enormous blocks of ice, brought in to cool the space, would also be hidden behind trees and plants. There would be flowers everywhere: white lilies (the fleur-de-lis being a traditional symbol of French royalty) and pale pink La France roses on every table.

More than ever before, Ritz was in command. He ran the Savoy with no interference from D'Oyly Carte or the board of directors, who were pleased to see the hotel accumulating ever-higher profits and the company's shares trading at ever-higher prices, and paying a dividend. Ritz was indispensable: he had just signed a new contract awarding him, in addition to his generous £1,200 annual salary, a sliding scale commission on the company's profits. As long as the Savoy directors and shareholders were collecting dividends of more than 5 percent of profits, Ritz would collect his share, too. This was a way of rewarding him for the success of the hotel without giving him actual ownership.

Ritz had tried to convince the board, during his most recent contract negotiations, to assign him the unissued shares in the company, valued at nearly six thousand pounds. He had been rebuffed. Instead, he was offered the commission on profits, as well as various stipends for overseeing the other hotels in the Savoy portfolio, including the Rome Grand and now also Claridge's in London, which the company had bought the previous year and was currently rebuilding. In 1895 the Savoy earned record profits, and after taking his fees and commissions, Ritz had never made so much money in one year in his entire life.

It wasn't just Ritz: Escoffier and the other key members of Ritz's staff were also well paid, and collected fees from the hotels for which they consulted. The Frankfurter Hof, for example, had brought in Ritz and his team to advise and manage the hotel. The newly formed Egyptian Hotels Ltd. had hired Ritz as an "Advisory Expert to the Board," and Lorenz Adlon, the German restaurateur, asked him for advice about the hotel he planned to open in Berlin, the Continental. All these arrangements were entirely separate from the Savoy.

It was just as Marie had predicted: Ritz's focus on the Savoy had only increased his prominence. "César was excessively busy with his Rome and London affairs and any number of new ventures which took up every scrap of his time," she wrote:

From all over Europe, he was besieged with requests to start hotels and run them, if only for a few months, just long enough to give them the prestige of his name, which was now enormous. America offered him fantastic sums as an inducement to cross the Atlantic and teach innkeeping *de luxe* to the New World.

Ritz said no to the America trip. He had enough on his plate.

Among the Savoy's board of directors, though, there were quiet murmurings of disapproval at Ritz's independent business dealings, his sometimes arrogant autonomy, his high pay. He and his team "received the emoluments of Prime Ministers," one of the board members declared, in wonder. Had they heard that Ritz had installed new windows and doors in the basement, without consulting anyone at all? Not that the board would have disapproved — the royal wedding was the event of the season — and the truth was, what did it matter? The money was flowing. But still. Ritz could have asked.

D'Oyly Carte, for his part, was glad to have the Savoy running profitably, and he left Ritz to his own devices. He had gotten old, suddenly, it seemed, though he was only fifty-one. Heart trouble, the doctor said; poor circulation. In any case, he felt weak sometimes, suffering through periods when he was confined to bed, his feet and ankles swollen with dropsy. Helen took charge of their business affairs when this happened — she had always been the one to look after the details, so it wasn't much of a change — and Richard was back on his feet soon enough.

Ritz, meanwhile, forged ahead. June 25 was fast approaching. There had been many great dinners and parties at the Savoy since it opened six years earlier, but these two felt momentous. The entire staff was on edge.

For Escoffier, the simultaneous dinners would require two different elaborate menus. He consulted his files: he had cooked for the Duc d'Orléans and for the Prince of Wales many times, and knew what they liked and didn't. The Cornish Club dinner menu, for example, would include spit-roasted saddle of lamb, piles of tiny fried whitebait fish, and, as a savory at the end of the meal, soft roe on toast — all favorites of the Prince of Wales. For the wedding dinner, Escoffier designed and named a peach dessert in honor of the bride: *Pêches Princesse Louise d'Orléans,* served on a layer of strawberry mousse.

It would be a true test of his kitchen to produce and serve so many dishes at once. There would be some overlap among the menus, but each would be a unique expression of Escoffier's artistry, a procession of dishes in the classical style, meant to flow naturally from one to the next. After talking with his various suppliers, he knew he could procure a good supply of quail, trout, chicken breast, and lamb, so he planned to use those ingredients in both menus; other, rarer items, including lobster, turtle, ortolans, and soft roe, would appear on only one.

Each menu consisted of ten courses, and each would begin with cantaloupe.

For the Cornish Club dinner:

MELON CANTALOUP
Cantaloupe

❁

TORTUE CLAIRE SAINT-GERMAIN
Turtle soup

❀

TRUITE SAUMONÉE ROYALE
Poached trout

❀

WHITEBAIT À LA DIABLE
Deep-fried whitebait

❀

MOUSSE DE JAMBON AU VELOUTÉ
Ham mousse with cream sauce

❀

EPINARDS AU BEURRE
Spinach in butter

❀

SELLE D'AGNEAU À LA BROCHE
Spit-roasted saddle of lamb

❀

HARICOTS VERTS À L'ANGLAISE
Green beans

❀

POMMES DE TERRE À LA CRÈME
Potatoes in cream

❀

SUPRÊMES DE VOLAILLE EN GELÉE
À L'ALSACIENNE
Poached chicken breast in herbed jelly

❀

CAILLES SOUVAROW
Quail stuffed with foie gras

SALADE DE BLANC DE ROMAINE
Hearts of romaine salad

ASPERGES D'ARGENTEUIL
Purple asparagus

BISCUIT GLACÉ À L'ANANAS
Ice cream with pineapple

FRAISES AU MARASCHINO
Strawberries with maraschino liqueur

LAITANCES
Soft roe on toast

CAFÉ TURC
Turkish coffee

For the Aosta-Orléans royal wedding dinner, at the *table d'honneur:*

MELON CANTALOUP
Cantaloupe

FRONTIGNAN
Sweet wine

CONSOMMÉ EN GELÉE
Jellied consommé

VELOUTÉ DE CHAMPIGNONS À L'ITALIENNE
Italian cream of mushroom soup

TRUITE SAUMONÉE POCHÉE AU VIN D'ASTI ACCOMPAGNÉE DE PAUPIETTES DE SOLE À LA MONTPENSIER
Salmon trout poached in Moscato wine with stuffed paupiettes of sole with truffles

SELLE DE MOUTON PRÉ SALÉ À LA PIEMONTAISE
Saddle of salt meadow mutton

PETITS POIS À LA FRANÇAISE
Green peas stewed with lettuce

POMMES NOISETTES
Potato balls cooked in butter

SUPRÊMES DE VOLAILLE ROYALE ALLIANCE
Poached chicken breasts

POINTES D'ASPERGES À LA CRÈME
Asparagus tips in cream

SORBETS AU CLICQUOT ROSÉ
Sorbet of Clicquot rosé champagne

CAILLES AUX FEUILLES DE VIGNE
Quail with grape leaves

BROCHETTES D'ORTOLANS
Ortolan brochettes

SALADE VICTORIA
Lobster and asparagus salad

COEURS D'ARTICHAUTS À LA MOELLE
Artichoke hearts with marrow sauce

SOUFFLÉ D'ÉCREVISSES À LA FLORENTINE
Crayfish soufflé with sliced truffles

PÊCHES PRINCESSE LOUISE D'ORLÉANS DRESSÉES SUR MOUSSE À LA FRAISE
Poached peaches with strawberry mousse

FRIANDISES
Various sweets

LES PLUS BEAUX FRUITS
The most beautiful fruit

CAFÉ MODE ORIENTALE
Oriental coffee

FINES LIQUEURS DE FRANCE
French liqueurs

The guests at the wedding reception would be served most of the same dishes as those at the head table, minus some of the rarer delicacies, such as the ortolans. Instead of the delicate crayfish soufflé, the guests would have a lobster aspic. Everyone would be served the *Pêches Princesse Louise d'Orléans,* of course, but only at the head table would it be served with the strawberry mousse. Both the wedding party and the Cornish Club would be eating asparagus at the same time, but in different preparations. The trout would be poached in wine for the wedding dinner but pan-fried for the Cornish Club, and so on. There would be many calibrations, details, substitutions, and variations to look after and coordinate, all on a strict and unforgiving timetable, and all while the full complement of regular customers was being served in the dining room, which was completely booked.

Escoffier distributed the menus to his team in the days before the event and went over the evening's plans with his *chefs de*

217

partie. As much as possible would need to be prepared in advance, so they went over each dish and mapped out a strategy. The restaurant kitchen at the height of the dinner rush was a kind of battlefield — Escoffier the general overseeing his battalions of cooks. This particular Tuesday would be no different, only more intense than ever, with the addition of the sixty-four-person wedding party in the basement and the multitudes of high-profile royal guests.

Escoffier himself oversaw the orders that went out to Hudson Brothers and Bellamy's, the two grocers that supplied the majority of the restaurant's meat, eggs, fish, and produce. Just like Ritz at the hotel, Escoffier had taken complete control of the restaurant and all its dealings with vendors, who knew just what he wanted and how he wanted it. What Escoffier couldn't get from the local grocers he bought from his continental suppliers. In all these cases, he had negotiated significant discounts for the hotel, usually 5 percent, and he also collected an additional, personal 5 percent commission on all orders, which he was given in cash when he visited the shops and warehouses. The personal commission was a fair reward, he figured, for the discounts he'd achieved for the Savoy. After all: the very reason the Savoy was such an important customer for all its food suppliers — the restaurant ordered vast quantities of the highest-quality ingredients on a weekly basis — and was thus able to demand discounts, was Escoffier himself! He had made the restaurant an astounding success. The fact that he was also working with Ritz on various consulting jobs for other hotels only further enhanced his standing with specialty-food suppliers and other vendors, who hoped to be hired for future projects and expansions. Another token of the food suppliers' gratitude: the plentiful gifts and samples of their wares, which Escoffier shared with his staff.

The Savoy was the most successful restaurant in England, and everyone wanted a piece of it.

But Escoffier did not sit on his laurels. Indeed, he was as resolutely devoted to his work as ever. And so he pored over the menus and supply lists, thinking through every detail. The wedding party would drink champagne throughout the meal, while the Cornish Club had requested wine. Escoffier showed the menu to Echenard, who was in charge of the wine cellars, and asked him to compose a list of pairings suitable for a dinner hosted by the Prince of Wales.

TO START:
Amontillado, a dry sherry

WITH THE SOUP:
Milk punch

WITH THE FISH AND THE MOUSSE:
Bernkasteler Doctor, 1874, a white Riesling

WITH THE LAMB:
Château Brown Cantenac, 1888, a red Bordeaux

WITH THE CHICKEN:
Pommery Brut, 1884, a champagne

WITH THE QUAIL:
Château Léoville Poyferré (cachet du Château), a red Bordeaux, 1878

WITH THE ASPARAGUS:
Moët Cuvée, 1884, a champagne

WITH DESSERT AND THE SAVORY:
Grande Fine, 1865, cognac
Croft Old Port, 1858
Curaçao Marnier, extra dry

They looked at the wines. The Bern-kasteler Doctor was a renowned Riesling from the Moselle Valley in Germany, perfect for the trout, Echenard said; and the two Bordeaux wines, the Brown Cantenac and the Léoville Poyferré, were of superior vintages.

The kitchen was already in high gear, intense and purposeful. Rows of large salmon trout were being cleaned and then poached in wine. Ortolans were arranged on skewers for roasting. Quail were stuffed with large-dice foie gras and then wrapped in bacon and lined up in large terrines. The *chef entremétier,* in charge of vegetables, was making consommé and trimming and parboiling artichokes and asparagus. The *chef garde-manger,* overseeing the pantry, made soufflés, mousses, and aspics, pushing ham and béchamel sauce through a fine sieve, decorating fish-jelly molds with truffle, lobster, egg whites, capers, and tarragon. The *chef pâtissier* made pastries, whisking eggs and poaching dozens of peaches.

The smells were wonderful. Even after all these years, Escoffier still found this preparatory period of concentration and calm in the kitchen to be a source of deep, elemental comfort. It took him back to his childhood: watching his grandmother make his favorite ragout (he had carefully recorded all her recipes, and still used them); learning from a neighborhood confectioner how to make preserved fruit; toasting slices of bread on the hearth of his maternal grandfather's fireplace when he was ten, and then spreading strong, fresh *brousse* cheese (a local favorite) on top and eating them with a half glass of sweet wine . . .

The kitchen was calm, but soon enough the mood would shift, with waiters, servers, and busboys rushing in and out with plates and platters, terrines and trolleys, glasses and silverware, and the clatter and din of the meal service would be upon them.

At 8:00 p.m. the guests began to arrive, their carriages lining up in the courtyard. Royal couples swept grandly into the lobby, ebullient and celebratory; the men of the Cornish Club struck a more sober pose. All were greeted by Ritz himself, who directed them to the wedding dinner downstairs or the banqueting room for the club's gathering. The Prince and Princess of Wales arrived together and then parted ways; with her husband at the dinner upstairs, it fell to Princess Alexandra to preside at the head table at the wedding party.

Ritz was outwardly calm, dressed in his

usual dark suit with a white carnation in his lapel, but he was wound up, jittery. Such a large gathering of royalty in a public restaurant was unprecedented, he thought, and he was beset with last-minute doubts about the wisdom of his basement renovation scheme. What if it was too hot? Or too humid? What if the decorative façade of flowers, palm trees, and mirrors failed to convince anyone? If the aristocratic guests sneered in dismay as they were led downstairs: Dinner in the cellar? *Really?*

The Duc d'Orléans arrived in a wheelchair. He'd fallen off his horse during the Spanish hunting expedition outside Seville and banged up his knee.

I'm a temporary invalid, he said to Ritz cheerfully, as he was rolled into the hotel by a servant. It took two men to maneuver him down the stairs to the wedding dinner, at which point Princess Alexandra herself took charge, pushing the wheelchair into the room, much to everyone's delight. The Duc had been unable to walk down the aisle at the wedding to give his sister away (his duty as head of the House of Orléans and pretender to the French throne), and he had asked his uncle, the Duc de Chartres, to do the honors.

The evening was long, and Ritz was everywhere at the same time — welcoming guests in the dining room, passing by the banqueting room as the Cornish Club's first course was being served, heading downstairs to the wedding dinner as the champagne was poured.

All his anxiety about the basement proved unwarranted: the rooms were stunning — cool and full of plants and flowers, lights hidden among the palm fronds. The effect was of an enchanted garden, lush and glamorous, perfectly suited to the colorful gowns worn by the ladies and the fairy-tale narrative of the day. A number of the princes and dukes wore elaborate ceremonial military uniforms, with braided fourragères strung under their epaulettes and brass buttons down the front of their coats.

Upstairs, the men talked politics: Lord Rosebery had resigned as prime minister not three days earlier. His administration had lasted a mere fifteen months. Downstairs, the wedding guests discussed the many marvelous gifts the couple had received, displayed at Orléans House that morning: a bracelet of diamonds from the queen; a mercury wand of diamonds and rubies from the Prince and Princess of Wales; a crown studded with enormous diamonds from King Umberto and Queen

Margherita of Italy; and from Princess Louise, the Prince of Wales's younger sister, a fan made of white ostrich feathers mounted with tortoiseshell.

But it wasn't long before everyone, at both private dinners and in the restaurant too, found themselves talking about Oscar Wilde. A few weeks earlier, in late May, Wilde had been sentenced to prison for crimes he'd allegedly committed at the Savoy, and the thought of the literary star and flamboyant dandy's scandalous behavior occurring right there in the hotel made for irresistibly titillating conversation. The press had covered the case feverishly, just as it did all scandals with well-known protagonists. In recent years, there'd been the Parnell Affair (an Irish nationalist politician accused of sleeping with the wife of a supporter), the Baccarat Case (a friend of the Prince of Wales accused of cheating at cards), and the ongoing Dreyfus Affair in Paris (a French-Jewish soldier accused of being a spy for Germany).

The Wilde case had its origins in a libel suit brought by the writer against the Marquis of Queensberry, the father of Wilde's lover, who had publicly accused Wilde of being a homosexual — a "ponce and a sodomite." Wilde had lost that case, but even worse, the evidence presented by the other side had exposed his reckless hedonism. He and his lover, Lord Alfred Douglas, were as well known in the netherworld of young male prostitutes and grifters as they were in the salons of bohemian London. After Wilde lost the libel case, he found himself facing charges of "gross indecency," with the prosecution using as evidence his many friendships and suspected liaisons with young men, and a homophobic onslaught of questions about the sexual subtexts of his plays and letters. Both the libel and criminal trials were covered obsessively in the press, for Wilde was not only famous, he was also a brilliant witness when he took the stand:

"What is the 'Love that dare not speak its name'?" demanded the prosecutor, with a sneer, referring to a line from a poem recently published by Douglas, his lover.

"It is that deep, spiritual affection that is as pure as it is perfect. It dictates and pervades great works of art like those of Shakespeare and Michelangelo," Wilde replied.

It is in this century misunderstood, so much misunderstood that it may be described as the "Love that dare not speak its name," and on account of it I am placed

226

where I am now. It is beautiful, it is fine, it is the noblest form of affection. There is nothing unnatural about it. It is intellectual, and it repeatedly exists between an elder and a younger man, when the elder man has intellect, and the younger man has all the joy, hope, and glamour of life before him. That it should be so the world does not understand. The world mocks at it and sometimes puts one in the pillory for it.

The crowd had applauded loudly, though there were a few boos and hisses. Wilde's friend Max Beerbohm wrote in a letter describing the scene, "Here was this man, who had been for a month in prison and loaded with insults and crushed and buffeted, perfectly self-possessed, dominating the Old Bailey with his fine presence and musical voice. He has never had so great a triumph."

Nevertheless, Wilde lost, and was sentenced to two years' hard labor.

The Savoy's connection to the case was much discussed: Wilde and Douglas had checked into the hotel in early March 1893 and stayed for the month. They had lived like kings, racking up an enormous bill, and received numerous guests in their adjoining rooms.

Ritz remembered the episode well — for one thing, because Wilde had failed to pay the bill for more than a year, and for another, because Wilde and Douglas had entertained quite extravagantly in the restaurant, usually with very young men, ordering turtle soup and ortolans and bottle after bottle of champagne.

Among the staff, the hotel pageboys in particular, Wilde was notorious for his large tips, and his lecherous advances. His favorite was fourteen-year-old Herbert "Chips" Tankard — "Hello! Here's my Herbert," Wilde would say when the teenager entered the room, proceeding, on at least one occasion, to lean down, open the boy's pants, and begin to kiss him. Tankard was shocked, needless to say. He was later questioned by lawyers for the Marquis of Queensberry, as were various chambermaids and the Savoy housekeeper, about the men seen sleeping in Wilde's bed when they came to light the fire in the mornings, and about the stains on his sheets.

It was all very scandalous. Ritz was mortified — not about the sex, but about the breach of privacy and trust the case represented. He was a man of absolute discretion. A hotel contained many secrets, and a hotel manager, he had learned long ago, must keep those secrets close. "The hotelier who cannot learn to keep his own counsel had better choose another *métier*," he would often say. The Savoy had failed Wilde in this regard, through no fault of its own, and now the man was in prison. (The Marquis of Queensberry himself had come to see Ritz before the trial, demanding to know if it was true that Wilde and his son had been banned from the hotel for their "disgusting conduct." Absolutely not, said Ritz.)

Wilde had belonged at the Savoy. He was a gourmand, an aesthete, a lover of beauty and luxury and pleasure, all the things the hotel embodied. His anti-Victorian decadence made sense there, and indeed, it was that sense of liberating, fin de siècle exhilaration that attracted all of London to the hotel, including the high-society diners that night.

As the dinner service drew to a close, guests drinking coffee, the Princess of Wales called Ritz over. Ritz had been standing discreetly at the door as the waiters poured snifters of cognac.

Princess Alexandra was soft-spoken and reserved — she suffered from deafness — but she had known Ritz for years, having stayed at his hotels in the South of France, and now she was extravagant in her praise of the dinner and the décor. She took particular note of the flowers, which were set in vases made of carved ice. Quite clever, she said — cooling and beautiful. She planned to try the same thing at Marlborough House one day. She was beaming, and Ritz was flattered. Now he wondered if he might ask a favor — a small thing, but it would mean so much to him: would she sign a menu for him, to commemorate the evening?

Of course, she replied happily, taking the menu and Ritz's fountain pen and writing her name in the top left-hand corner: "Alix." She passed the menu and the pen around the table, and the page soon filled as princes, princesses, dukes, and duchesses scrawled their names with flourishes and underscores, and then, when there was no more room, turned it over and continued on the back. This went on for some minutes, as Ritz circled the table, thanking the guests, receiving their compliments, singing the praises of his incomparable chef, Auguste Escoffier, who, just then, entered the room in his chef's whites. He did not normally wear them, but this was a special occasion, and the guests raised their glasses to the two men, Escoffier and Ritz, and to the newlywed couple.

Ritz was filled with pride. He would keep the menu as a souvenir, a prized possession. It was an emblem of all he had achieved as a hotelier. He couldn't help but think of his parents: if only they could see him now, how far he'd come. To be here in this room, surrounded by royalty — to be *respected* by royalty. His large, manicured hands (his godforsaken peasant hands) held the signed menu and trembled.

10
RITZ MAKES A MOVE

Alfred Beit, the South African gold and diamond magnate who was a regular at the Savoy, would regale Ritz with stories of his exploits, always encouraging him to think big. There was a dearth of great hotels the world over, Beit said. Why, with the right backing, a man of Ritz's quality could open a luxury hotel in every capital in Europe — and in Africa, too. Johannesburg, for example, where Beit and the other mining investors had made their fortunes, was sorely in need of a grand hotel. And what about Cairo? Everyone was going to Cairo these days. And New York City, of course. And Madrid, and Paris, and London, too. Yes, London could always use another luxury hotel, and so what if that meant competing with the Savoy?

It was exhilarating to imagine the possibilities, the conversations fueling Ritz's ambitious dreams and his persistent sense that he was undervalued by the Savoy.

What had started as idle talk soon became more than that. Ritz's contract with D'Oyly Carte had always left him free to pursue his own business dealings, as long they took place abroad. He had made sure of that. The Savoy was running like a Swiss clock; now was the time to expand his portfolio, to reassert himself. His dealings over the past year with other hoteliers and hotel companies in Europe had only galvanized his determination. He was far and away the most respected hotel manager in Europe, yet he did not have a hotel of his own.

In early 1896, Ritz began approaching some of the wealthy businessmen who frequented the Savoy about the idea of forming a new company. It would be called the Ritz Hotel Syndicate Ltd. Some of these potential investors were shareholders in the Savoy, and they knew firsthand how talented Ritz was, that he'd been instrumental in making the hotel a success. Ritz's arrangement with D'Oyly Carte, they knew, allowed him his independence. He worked at the Savoy for only six months of the year.

Ritz hosted a series of small lunches and dinners in the restaurant's small private dining rooms, at which he described his plans to open luxury hotels in numerous cities.

Beit was an early supporter, as were the Neumann brothers, Ludwig and Sigismund. Sigismund, like Beit, had made his fortune in the mining business in South Africa; his brother was a stockbroker at Leopold Hirsch and Company. This would turn out to be a fruitful connection, for soon some of the other partners at the bank, including the Russian baron Jacques de Gunzbourg and Leopold Hirsch himself, also invested in the new company. So did iron and steel magnate Robert Crawshay (a principal Savoy shareholder); Calouste Gulbenkian, a British-Armenian oil trader; Sir Joseph Duveen, a Dutch importer and antiques dealer; and A. G. Brand of Lazard Bank in London. Two Savoy insiders, Lord de Grey and Henry Higgins, were also investors.

They were a colorful and uniquely modern cast of characters, most of them Jewish, many of them immigrants or sons of immigrants, all of them exceedingly wealthy. The principal investors in the Savoy company had included a single Jewish financier, Arthur Weguelin. But Ritz's company was backed almost entirely by self-made men, members of an emerging financial and Jewish establishment, a group that was increasingly active and visible in English public life.

In every way, it made sense that it was the nouveau riche who formed the core of Ritz's investor group. They had a taste for extravagance and luxury, and yet they also understood luxury as a business. They were charmed by Ritz, yes, but they also believed he would make them money.

Not that they needed more money: Beit, for example, had built himself one of the grandest private residences in London, Aldford House, on Park Lane. The walls of the vaulted billiard room were covered in silk brocade, and the house contained an enormous winter garden, complete with palm trees, ferns, and a fountain. Barney Barnato, the millionaire who carried loose diamonds in his pocket, had also bought a plot of land on Park Lane, and was building an even grander Renaissance-style mansion with a vast marble staircase beneath a glass dome, a conservatory and winter garden, two billiard rooms, and a ballroom. The construction was ongoing.

The nouveau riche spent their money ostentatiously, and craved acceptance in high society. Attitudes were changing, but snide condescension was still the prevailing aristocratic sentiment when it came to "new money." When Lady Randolph Churchill, a leading society hostess, met Col. John

North, the so-called Nitrate King (he'd made a fortune sewing up the Peruvian nitrate industry), her description of him as a "rough diamond" was typical:

> He had a large place near London, which was furnished regardless of expense, where he kept open house and entertained in a most lavish manner the hordes of hangers-on and sycophants by whom — like all rich men of that type — he was invariably surrounded. Dining with us once I was much amused at the description he gave me of his picture gallery. That very day he had bought a "grand picture" for which he had given the large sum of £8,000. I asked who it was by; that he could not remember, nor even the subject. "But," he added, "it is twelve feet by eight!"

Ritz was selling shares in his company, but he was also selling an idea: that luxury and good taste belonged to anyone who could afford them.

Sometimes one on one, sometimes in larger groups, Ritz met with his possible investors and described his plans for the company as they ate Escoffier's elegant dishes and drank especially good wine — Ritz did everything he could to win them

236

over, and his most convincing argument was his hospitality. Escoffier was very much a part of the plans — if they got the Ritz Hotel Syndicate off the ground, it was understood that he would be in charge of the hotel kitchens and an owner of the company. At the end of the meal, Ritz would always generously sign the check, waving off his guests as they reached for the bill. Dinner was on him; it was his company he wanted them to invest in.

Eighteen ninety-six was a difficult year for Helen D'Oyly Carte. Her husband's health had not improved; he was increasingly weak, leaving her to run the business. He was ready to retire, he said. Helen's focus was mostly on the theater: Gilbert, Sullivan, and Richard D'Oyly Carte had made up after their dispute about expenses — the "Carpet Quarrel," as it was dubbed in the press. D'Oyly Carte conceded that he'd made some mistakes in his accounting, and Sullivan had written to Gilbert: "Let us meet and shake hands. We can dispel the clouds hanging over us by setting up a counter-irritant in the form of a cloud of smoke." They continued to work together, and their latest musical, *The Grand Duke,* had opened in March, to generally dismal reviews.

The hotel was in Ritz's hands, and he ran it with aplomb. The previous year, 1895, had seen record profits, and the shareholders were pleased. Still, Helen took note of Ritz's extracurricular business dealings: the many meetings with bankers and various flamboyant gold and diamond millionaires.

She had been suspicious of Ritz from the very beginning. She didn't trust him; she didn't like him. She had always thought he was profligate, heedless with money that wasn't his.

But it was about more than money: it was Ritz's style that rubbed Helen the wrong way. His imperiousness, his Swiss rectitude, his obsequiousness. (Was it even possible to be imperious and obsequious at the same time?) He told people what to do and exactly how to do it, and he also told people what they wanted to hear, and in the most gracious way.

He was slippery. She found his Swiss accent irritating.

It was also true, if she was being entirely honest, that Ritz had diminished her role at the Savoy, and that she resented this. During the early years, first when the hotel was in the planning stages and then when it was under construction, her husband had asked her to oversee the décor and to help supervise the staff. After the grand opening, she had occupied a suite of rooms just off the lobby, but she soon had to give them up to Ritz, Echenard, Agostini, and the rest of Ritz's minions, when they arrived in the spring of 1890.

She had buried her resentment as Ritz and his team worked hard to make the Savoy a success. And she and Richard were too busy with their ever-expanding theater empire (multiple traveling shows, American tours) to worry about the hotel when it was doing so well. The numbers got better every year and the stock price was rising.

Recently, though, something had changed: Ritz seemed more scattered than ever before. Yes, he'd always been a whirlwind of energy and activity, a man whose attentions were forever shifting. But he was always present, engaged. He solved problems. Now he seemed absent more often than not, consulting for hotels all across Europe, traveling all the time, even during the busy London season. Ritz had sold his own hotels, which should have helped but hadn't.

Perhaps it was Richard's illness that liberated Ritz. D'Oyly Carte was sidelined for long stretches, which only seemed to fuel Ritz's sense that the Savoy was his own property. He was acting more like a hotel owner than a hotel manager.

While it didn't really matter as long as the hotel was running smoothly, Helen was watchful, and more so now that Richard was ill. It was her duty, she felt, to look after their business, to ensure they not be swindled. Not that Ritz and his staff were swindlers, but they were taking advantage of their positions, no doubt about that.

For example: Ritz's laundry.

It was a small thing, ridiculous, really; too small to mention. But she had noticed that Ritz was charging his family washing to the Savoy, at a rate of three pounds a week. He and his family had recently moved to a house in Hampstead, though they still kept an apartment at the Savoy. All the laundry from both places was being billed to the hotel.

And then there were the carriages: whenever Ritz needed transportation, which was often, he arranged it through the Savoy jobmaster and charged the fees to the hotel. Again, it was a small thing but, as with the laundry, a sign to Helen that Ritz was treating the Savoy as his own.

Maybe he was entitled to free laundry, and to order taxis willy-nilly at the Savoy's expense — after all, he was the general manager, architect of the hotel's success —

but the secretive bamboozlement was unbecoming, Helen felt.

And was there more to it than these minor expenses?

One Sunday afternoon in the fall of 1896, Helen noticed a deliveryman bringing a large box of food supplies out of the hotel and loading it into his carriage. This was unusual, she thought. Normally such deliveries came *into* the hotel, not *from* it. When she asked the man about the box, he said it was for Mr. Ritz himself — the deliveryman was bringing it to Hampstead, just as he did every Sunday. And the other box was for Mr. Echenard — he was delivering that, too, as usual.

Helen only nodded, but she was incensed.

The idea of Marie Ritz, César's young wife, receiving her groceries free of charge, delivered and paid for by the Savoy, while Helen worried herself sick over the health of her husband, the man who rightfully owned the hotel and who was being hoodwinked . . . It was infuriating. She would never have even thought to supply her own kitchen with food from the Savoy. And not only Ritz but his deputy, Echenard, too, both of them extremely well paid, both of them stealing. Yes, stealing is what is was, she was sure; that was not too strong a word for it.

Helen confronted Ritz immediately, but he only laughed his charming laugh and said there was a truly simple explanation: the Savoy was such a valued client of the various grocers and specialty food shops that these tradesmen insisted on providing Escoffier, Ritz, and Echenard with gifts now and then. It was nothing.

Helen didn't quite believe him, but what could she say? She let the matter drop. Why was she concerning herself with the minutiae of the hotel business when she had a play struggling to fill seats in the theater — what would replace *The Grand Duke* if they ended its run? Another revival of *The Mikado, again*? — and her bedridden husband to attend to?

And then the strangest thing happened: a few weeks later, Helen received an anonymous note.

It was scrawled on nine foolscap-size pages and folded into an envelope. The handwriting was hard to read, and the note was not addressed to anyone in particular, so it took Helen a moment to decipher what exactly she had in her hands.

The note was an indictment, an exposé: everything that was wrong with the Savoy, every unfairness, every swindle, every instance of corruption, from top to bottom. On the last page was the bold, ominous signature:

ONE WHO KNOWS

Helen soon concluded that the document had most likely been written by a disgruntled waiter. Many of the complaints had to do with the *tronc,* the communal fund in which all tips were collected every day and then divided among the staff. (Most of the waiters were paid no salary, and therefore lived entirely from the *tronc.*) But of course, not all tips made their way into this fund. The headwaiter, for example, had the privilege of supplying fresh fruit for the restaurant and then collecting two pence for each *table d'hôte* meal and three pence for every banqueting guest directly from the restaurant's receipts, regardless of whether the fruit was eaten. This was one of the perquisites of being headwaiter. Waiters, meanwhile, supplied flowers for the tables upon request, adding a charge to diners' bills for the service. The fees charged for flowers went into the *tronc.* This was all aboveboard, a way of paying the staff a bit more — except that the waiters frequently charged guests for flowers they hadn't ordered. Indeed, a number of guests had written letters to the restaurant to complain about this practice.

Waiters also received a 20 percent commission from the restaurant on cigar sales, fees that were not added to the *tronc*. On busy nights at the restaurant, waiters would also collect money from guests in exchange for a table — one pound per table on weeknights, two pounds on Sundays.

Guests who were particularly generous with their tips, the anonymous writer claimed, could expect to be granted credit by the restaurant, which allowed them to sign for their checks. In a few cases, the credit was so generous that guests were known to sign for cash, using the restaurant as a de facto bank. But as long as the tips continued to flow, the bills were never collected.

Helen was shocked. And also delighted, for everything she had always suspected about Ritz was proving to be true. All the confirmation she could have dreamt of for her instinctive mistrust of the man could be found in the anonymous screed:

Ritz, Echenard and Escoffier are all masters and they have no power over one

244

another. The Savoy Hotel is like a house without any master. Escoffier has climbed to such a height that nobody dare approach him, not even Ritz, when it is a question of the supply of food to the kitchens; in fact he does what he likes, and does it how he likes and when he likes. Mssrs. Ritz and Echenard seem afraid of Escoffier.

Helen had never noticed that Ritz and Escoffier were anything other than close confidants, and doubted that either was afraid of the other — they'd been partners for many, many years. She did believe, however, that Ritz let Escoffier do as he wished. Indeed, the most damning charge in the entire letter, if it was true, was that Escoffier was taking kickbacks on all the food orders coming into the Savoy:

There is no doubt, however, that the Chef at the Savoy does insist upon and extort commission all round. This is notorious.

The letter described the cashier at Bellamy's, one of the hotel's main grocers, complaining about how difficult it was to "allow 5% off the Savoy account, give 5% to the chef and supply Ritz and Echenard's private homes for nothing."

Helen planned to take the letter to her husband, and to the board of directors. Something needed to be done.

11
A Secret Investigation

The mood in London in late 1896 and early 1897 was exuberant, even giddy. The century was coming to a close. History felt tangible; so much was changing so fast. The city seemed, if such a thing was possible, even more cosmopolitan and glamorous than it had even just a few years earlier. The Savoy had never been busier.

There were increasing numbers of American heiresses in London, marrying into titled families, changing the tenor of society. They were fantastically wealthy, and sought the prestige of an aristocratic title; certain titled families, meanwhile, were desperate for money.

Perhaps the most prominent example was the recent marriage, in November 1895, of Consuelo Vanderbilt, an heiress to the unfathomably vast American Vanderbilt railroad fortune, and Charles Spencer-Churchill, the Duke of Marlborough. She was eighteen, beautiful, and had no interest in marrying the duke, but her mother, Alva, had insisted — and her mother could be persuasive. The duke, twenty-three, meanwhile, was most eligible, but short of the income needed to keep his grand estate, Blenheim Palace, in Oxfordshire, or to underwrite his political ambitions. He was a nephew of Lord Randolph Churchill, and a cousin of Winston.

The courtship had been covered both breathlessly and skeptically in the American press. The duke had come to Newport, Rhode Island, at the invitation of the Vanderbilts, and his proposal had been announced in September 1895. "It was a famous victory," declared the *World,* a New York City paper, casting the engagement in military terms, and providing a tally of the young bride's various measurements and statistics:

Age: Eighteen years
Chin: Pointed, indicating vivacity
Color of hair: Black
Color of eyes: Dark brown
Eyebrows: Delicately arched
Nose: Rather slightly retroussé
Weight: One hundred and sixteen and
one half pounds

Foot: Slender, with arched instep
Size of shoe: Number three. AA last
Length of foot: Eight and one half inches
Length of hand: Six inches
Waist measure: Twenty inches
Marriage settlement: $10,000,000
Ultimate fortune: $25,000,000 (estimated)

"Why Do Women Crave Titles? Are They by Nature Imperialists and Enemies of Democracy?" was the headline a month later, also in the *World.* Joseph Pulitzer was the publisher of that paper and a critic of what he called "our vulgar moneyed aristocrats" buying "European gingerbread titles" for their daughters.

The financial arrangements of the marriage of Consuelo Vanderbilt and Charles Spencer-Churchill were subject to much speculation in the press. The Vanderbilt family was possibly the wealthiest in America; how large a dowry would be paid to the duke? The $10 million figure printed in the *World* was wrong; in fact, he was given $2.5 million in shares of the Vanderbilt's Beech Creek Railway Company in Pennsylvania, which paid out 4 percent a year, or $100,000. This was guaranteed regardless of whether the couple remained married.

Consuelo's father, William Vanderbilt, with an eye to his daughter's independence, also arranged for her to receive a guaranteed $100,000 annual payment of her own.

These were enormous amounts of money. Consuelo's jewelry was much remarked upon as she made her London debut that summer of 1896, attending balls and parties — she was "the rage of the season and everybody makes a fuss of her," according to Mary Leiter, an American heiress. Leiter's father was the cofounder, with Marshall Field, of the Chicago department store Field and Leiter, and she herself had married into the English aristocracy. Her husband was George Curzon, a prominent Conservative British politician and son of the Fourth Baron Scarsdale. They'd been married the previous year in Washington, DC; her marriage settlement, like Consuelo's, had run into the millions of dollars.

"Everyone raves about Consuelo," Leiter wrote in letters to friends back in the States. Leiter was a bit older, twenty-five, and welcomed Consuelo as if she were a younger sister. "She is very sweet in her great position, and shyly takes her rank directly after royalty. She looks very stately in her marvelous jewels, and she looks pretty and has old lace which makes my mouth water. I never saw pearls the size of nuts."

Frederick Townsend Martin, the progressive American writer, described how some older members of society looked down on the newly arrived Americans, "but this did not last long, for nothing could have successfully withstood these charming invaders, whose luxury and extravagance were almost bewildering."

The American woman starts her social progress unhampered by caste and tradition. She takes people as she finds them — not on the valuation of their ancestors; she is a person of spirit, she has her own ideas, and she is worldly to the tips of her fingers. She realizes her own value; she knows what she wants in exchange for it, and she makes up her mind that once she has obtained her ambition she will play her part to perfection. The heiress makes no secret of her admiration for a title; she knows that her money will work wonders, and often some neglected stately home has looked in pride again under her benign influence.

These daughters of Liberty are generous. They spend their money lavishly, but they spend it with discrimination, and, if their manner of doing so is occasionally a little blatant, surely, as the saying has it, much can be forgiven those who give much. They believe in the value of advertisement, they like to see society paragraphs about their jewels and their gowns; and they love to know that all the world, at the expenditure of a penny, may read about their vast improvements on their husband's estates. To them it represents business, *not* snobbishness, and they regard a position in the peerage much as other people look upon an investment, for in both cases the idea is that they will become paying concerns.

The American women in London may have been seen as glamorously outré, but they were not alone: the "New Woman" of the 1880s had blossomed in the 1890s, and could be seen riding bicycles and wearing "rational garments," including long skirts that were buttoned around each leg, forming pants. Still bolder women wore bloomers while bicycling, which extended below the knee. *The Queen* magazine approved, explaining that the bloomers were "so full that they lack all indecorous suggestion."

Bicycling had become immensely popular, and was, for women, a brazen sign of freedom and mobility. In good weather, between two and three thousand people would gather in Hyde Park to ride back and forth between the Achilles statue and the Gunpowder Magazine during the permitted cycling hours (9:00 a.m. to 12:00 p.m.). Marie and César Ritz would often go the park to watch, joining the crowds along the Serpentine Lake. On Sundays mornings, it seemed as if all of fashionable London was gathered in the park.

The private dinners at the Savoy were ever more extravagant. Escoffier had designed an entire menu in red, in honor of the roulette-table winnings of a group of young Englishmen; they had collected 350,000 francs in Monte Carlo betting on the red number 9. The menus and chairs were red, the table was covered with red rose petals, and dishes included a consommé of red partridge, foie gras in paprika gelée, lamb with red bean puree, and many other similarly hued items. The host of the dinner, Woolf Joel, was presented with a live red mullet fish swimming in a tank before it was taken away to be cooked. The cost of the dinner was ten pounds per person, according to the *Daily Mail,* which reported on the meal. Alfred Beit, meanwhile, hosted a Venetian-themed dinner, for which the Savoy courtyard was flooded with water and guests were served in gondolas while Italian opera singers performed barcarolles. The food was all Italian of course.

Sarah Bernhardt held forth in the Savoy dining room, fashionable as always, wearing a small live lizard attached to a fine chain that was pinned to her dress. It darted about listlessly on her breast. Elisabeth de Gramont, a French aristocrat and descendant of King Henri IV, was seen smoking cigarette after cigarette one night while her husband, the Duc de Clermont-Tonnerre, talked and talked. Everyone was shocked and delighted. Some even stood to watch the amazing event: a woman smoking in public!

Still, as much as the old strictures were changing, society continued to be ruled by etiquette and manners. The Americans and the nouveau riche took to carrying slim manuals in their pockets (*vade mecums,* Latin for "go with me"), which told them when to bow, whom to greet and when, and other details of decorum. The new social mobility could be awkward, and the Prince of Wales, in particular, took protocol and prerogatives seriously.

"I remember what happened to an American girl who offended him," recalled writer

Frederick Townsend Martin in his memoir of the period:

At a smart bazaar, the winner of a lucky lottery ticket had the privilege of asking three wishes from the Prince of Wales, and fate favored a young lady from the States.

"What is your first wish?" asked HRH.

"Oh, sir, it is to have your photograph."

The prince beamed. "Granted," he said. And the next?"

"I would like you to bring me the photograph in person."

HRH hesitated, frowned, and, recovering from his surprise, answered, "That shall be done, now what is the last?"

Never was the truth of the saying so apparent that "Fools rush in where angels fear to tread." The young lady disregarded the warning looks from those around her. "The third wish, sir, is that you will present me to the Princess of Wales."

The prince looked at her coldly. "Granted," he said, and walked away without a word. The silly girl realized that she had sinned against society, which never forgives fools. She made a hasty exit, and the waves of the social sea closed over her forever.

The young American had crossed a line: it was one thing to flatter or flirt with the prince, quite another to ask for such a formal introduction. The breach of social protocol would not be forgotten.

Indeed, the "waves of the social sea" could be unforgiving. The nouveau riche were tolerated but still not embraced. The coming social season in London would be dominated by commemorations of Queen Victoria's sixty-year reign, the Diamond Jubilee. There would be numerous galas and dinners, and visiting royalty. There would be costume balls and opera suppers. The event everyone was talking about, though, was the Duchess of Devonshire's costume ball. Consuelo Vanderbilt and other wealthy American women who had married into English society were of course invited. Vulgar industrialists, businessmen, and diamond and gold tradesmen and their wives (the nouveau riche of the sort caricatured in George du Maurier's *Punch* cartoons) were not.

And so Barney Barnato, diamond millionaire, was racing to finish building his enormous house on Park Lane before the Jubilee celebrations in June, and planned to host a party there. After all, he figured, even if he would not be attending the duchess's ball, many of London's social elite would be curious to see his new mansion.

The Savoy kept Ritz busy, as did his plans for the Ritz Hotel Syndicate. He was looking for a building in Paris. This was the dream: to open his own hotel in the capital where he had started his career as a waiter. The most beautiful city in the world, and one sorely lacking in luxury accommodation, Paris was the perfect place to launch the first Ritz hotel.

The very idea of a hotel called "Ritz" filled him with pride and trepidation. To bring such attention to himself was gauche, he knew, yet he felt elated at the prospect. He had redefined luxury over the past decade (with the help of Escoffier, of course), and his name meant something. He had earned the right to put it on a hotel, hadn't he?

It was two of his investors, the Neumann brothers, who found the site for the hotel. They were in Paris buying antiques and had come across a building just put up for sale by a banking company, Crédit Mobilier, adjacent to the Ministry of Justice on the Place Vendôme. Ritz immediately went to Paris to see the property. The building was relatively small, which appealed to him. The location was excellent.

A perfect square lined with elegant townhouses, the Place Vendôme was a nexus of Parisian luxury shopping: the shirtmaker Charvet, jewelers Chaumet and Boucheron, couturiers Jean-Philippe and Gaston Worth (sons of Charles Frederick Worth), the perfumer Guerlain, and many others had shops on the square or on the Rue de la Paix, which bisected the square on the north side. The Rue de la Paix had been home to the best jewelers in the city going back decades. Worth was where Marie Ritz had always bought her dresses — indeed, the Place Vendôme was where the wealthy and fashionable from all over France and beyond came to shop, and it was exactly these people whom Ritz hoped to welcome in his new hotel.

At the other end of the Place Vendôme, at numbers 3 and 5, was the Hotel Bristol, long considered the best in Paris. The Prince of Wales stayed there when he came to Paris.

That would have to change, thought Ritz.

As he entered the building, he knew immediately that it was the one. It had the right scale. There was a beautiful curving staircase, just as he had envisioned.

Ritz wanted his hotel to feel like a home; an elegant home, to be sure — the home of a gentleman, a nobleman, a prince — but not a grand, impersonal palace. Beautifully decorated, breathtakingly luxurious, but above all, intimate.

Number 15 Place Vendôme was perfect. It was also expensive.

Some of Ritz's investors were dubious. The building was too small, they said. How would they make any money? As they hesitated and delayed, Ritz was determined to obtain alternative financing. He didn't want to lose the Place Vendôme building, and knew that if he could buy a little time, he would be able to convince his backers that he was right.

An eight-day option on the property would cost thousands of pounds. Ritz was scrambling, calling on possible investors in Paris, when he remembered his friend Louis-Alexandre Marnier Lapostolle. He was the inventor of an orange cognac liqueur called Curaçao Marnier, which Ritz had immediately ordered for the Savoy. More important, Ritz had proposed a new name for the product: Grand Marnier, "a grand name for a grand liqueur." At the time, everything was being called "petit" — "le petit journal," "le petit café," "le Petit Palais." Grand Marnier went brashly against this convention, and was hugely successful.

Marnier Lapostolle had always been grateful, and now, without hesitation, he wrote Ritz a check for the amount of the eight-day option.

Back in London, the Ritz Hotel Syndicate quickly spun off a new company that would own the Paris hotel; it was named the Ritz Hotel Development Company Ltd., with starting capital of £120,500. This was less than the £200,000 the Savoy had raised eight years earlier, but it was enough to build a hotel. Ritz was the managing director; he took no salary but was allocated deferred shares amounting to a quarter of the company. Escoffier and Echenard were also granted shares.

They were owners now. They had a building in Paris. The Ritz hotel, the dream, would soon be a reality.

When the board of directors of the Savoy met in September 1897, they confronted an unpleasant turn of events: the restaurant was busier than ever before, and yet the monthly income numbers were dropping. The restaurant was barely making money. The numbers did not add up.

For the first half of the year, the gross kitchen profits had dropped to 24.5 percent, down more than 10 percent, and the numbers were worsening, even as the gross receipts were increasing.

They studied the numbers in silence.

How was such a thing possible? Richard D'Oyly Carte exclaimed.

They were meeting at D'Oyly Carte's Adelphi Terrace house just off the Embankment, not far from the hotel. It was a grand home, which he had wired for electricity while building the Savoy. He had also installed an elevator, the first ever in a private home in London. This turned out to be extremely useful, for he was now confined to a wheelchair. "I am not allowed to walk," he said. "I have to be wheeled or carried everywhere." D'Oyly Carte was not well, but his quick-tempered intelligence had not dissipated.

They all looked at the accounting numbers some more.

Isn't it obvious? Helen said. She had been lobbying the board to investigate Ritz and Escoffier since late the previous year, to no avail. But these new accounting figures were a shock.

Ritz and Escoffier, she said, were corrupt. Had the others not read the anonymous note she'd received? From top to bottom, from waiters and headwaiters all the way up to Echenard, Ritz, and Escoffier — everyone had a hand in the till: the waiters charging customers for flowers they had not ordered; the headwaiters accepting bribes in exchange for restaurant reservations; Escoffier taking commissions on food orders; Ritz and Echenard supplying their homes with groceries from the Savoy kitchen.

And they all knew that Ritz was conducting outside business at the hotel, Helen said, lining up investors for his hotel development company. Who was paying for all those lunches and dinners? And who had been extended credit to sign for their bills at the restaurant? Were those bills ever paid?

The board of directors had all seen the anonymous note, and were perfectly aware of the mostly trivial accusations it contained. The truth was this was how restaurants operated: employees skimmed and hustled for tips. And it was to be expected that Ritz and Escoffier would live well from the success of the hotel and restaurant. What did a few groceries matter? D'Oyly Carte had resisted taking action, despite Helen's entreaties, for the better part of a year.

Now, however, looking at the accounts, he realized they had to act. D'Oyly Carte's son, Rupert, and Arthur Sullivan, also present at the meeting, agreed. The board voted to launch an investigation. It would be conducted in secret: they must be discreet. Deloitte, Dever, Griffiths, and Company, the Savoy's auditing firm, would take charge, and report back to the board's Committee of Investigation.

A few days later the auditors were given the letter from "One Who Knows." It would be the starting point of the inquiry. They would look at all the books, all the restaurant receipts, and take a complete inventory. They would hire private investigators to follow Ritz and Escoffier as they went about their daily business.

The investigation was under way.

12
CALAMITY

Escoffier lived alone in a small rented apartment not far from the Savoy. He was a man of steady habits: He walked to the hotel every morning, stopping by the Hudson Brothers grocery on the Strand to see what was fresh that day. He attended the morning meeting of the Savoy staff, presided over by Ritz. He consulted with Echenard about the day's lunch and dinner reservations, and planned menus for upcoming private dinners and events.

He continued to invent new dishes, often, as was his habit, inspired by celebrity guests. The previous year, for example, Nellie Melba, the Australian opera diva, had performed Wagner's *Lohengrin* at Covent Garden, and he'd designed a dessert in her honor, based on the mythical swan that appeared in the first act. He called it *Pêches Melba:* peaches on vanilla ice cream, covered with a puree of sugared raspberry and served in a bowl set in a block of ice carved in the shape of a swan.

Melba had loved the dessert, and Escoffier continued to serve it, though it wasn't on the menu. He kept his recipes on notecards and was increasingly interested in organizing them in a systematic way, and perhaps writing a book. This was something he'd been talking about for years. All the way back in 1883, Escoffier had been one of the founders of a magazine called *L'Art Culinaire,* to which he regularly contributed articles on cooking. Also around this same time, when he was working for Ritz at the Grand Hotel in Monte Carlo in the mid-1880s, he had befriended Urbain Dubois, a frequent guest at the hotel. Dubois was older, a renowned chef, and the coauthor of the seminal French cookbook *La Cuisine Classique,* published in 1856. They traded recipes — Dubois was working on a new book, to be called *La Cuisine d'Aujourd'hui.* Escoffier told Dubois about his own idea for a book, and later described his reaction in a letter to a friend:

During that period, I told him about my idea to write a little pocket dictionary, an aide-memoire for the use of the kitchen people and the waiters in restaurants, so that arguments would no longer occur between the two sides as to the name and composition of dishes. It would also permit kitchen staff to know the makeup of garnishes and for waiters to be able to respond to clients' questions. All this would facilitate service and good relations between dining room and kitchen. Monsieur Dubois, who was interested very much in my idea because of his new book, was in favor.

Still, despite the encouragement of both Dubois and his friend and editor at *L'Art Culinaire,* Philéas Gilbert, nothing had come of it. And indeed, the idea of a comprehensive reference book and culinary dictionary had been taken up by someone else, a waiter named Pierre Dagouret — Escoffier did not know him — who had recently published, to great success, a pocket reference called *Le Petit Dagouret.*

In the meantime, Escoffier was writing a series of articles for *L'Art Culinaire* under the title *"L'École des Menus: Étude et Composition des Menus Modernes à la Maison, à l'Hôtel, et au Restaurant"* ("The School of Menus: The Study and Composition of Modern Menus at Home, at the Hotel, and at the Restaurant"). He was now thinking more ambitiously about menu design, and about a possible book of his recipes. He had invented so many dishes (the *Pêches Melba,* for example); he should codify them in some way.

Even as he ran the Savoy kitchen, Escoffier was also pursuing entrepreneurial ventures. His canned-tomato importing business had come to nothing, but more recently he had been approached by a group of investors about making bottled sauces. They were in the process of establishing a company called Escoffier's Food Preparations Syndicate Ltd.

And so, in the fall of 1897, Escoffier made his way about the city, meeting with investors and food purveyors; putting in long hours in the Savoy restaurant; thinking about writing a cookbook; and talking with Ritz about their plans for the Paris hotel, where Escoffier would be organizing and staffing the kitchen.

He did not know he was being followed.

One of the first people the Deloitte, Dever, Griffiths, and Co. detective tracked down was a man named Charles Liddell.

The detective had seen Escoffier meet with Liddell, and he had proceeded to arrange a meeting of his own. Liddell was a salesman. They met in the first-class waiting room of the Broad Street railway station. Posing as a businessman, the detective soon discovered that Liddell was acting as a liaison to various wine and cigar companies on Escoffier's behalf. They were marking up prices substantially, reselling the goods to the Savoy, and splitting the profits.

The detective then visited the Savoy's main food suppliers, Bellamy's and Hudson Brothers, and found that, just as "One Who Knows" had claimed, Escoffier was indeed collecting a commission on all orders.

Robert Price, the manager at Hudson Brothers, told the detective that this had always been true, at least as long as he'd been there. "The 5 percent paid to Mr. Escoffier was common knowledge in the shop," he said. His predecessor in the position, he said, had taken him around to all the hotels and restaurants the grocer supplied and told him who got kickbacks: "When we got to the Savoy hotel, he introduced me to Escoffier. He said 'He has commission' or 'He is a commission man.' I cannot remember the exact words."

How exactly did Escoffier collect these commissions? the detective asked.

"He did not actually ask for the commission," Price replied. "But he came and hung about and talked in a way that I knew exactly what he had come for."

The suppliers were also sending "large presents consisting of packages of goods" to Ritz's and Echenard's private homes.

As the detective probed the details of the arrangement — the discounts, the commissions, the free groceries — he stumbled on something much more significant. How did it make sense for the suppliers to offer such extensive discounts? How were they making any profit doing business with the Savoy?

He was talking with Henry Mann when he discovered the truth. Mann was the head of the egg department at Hudson Brothers. He was a beleaguered employee, and eager to talk.

"By the instructions of Mr. Robert Price," he explained — Price was his superior — "the eggs supplied to the Savoy Hotel were always delivered short."

This was how Hudson Brothers covered the cost of the discounts and commissions: by underdelivering and overcharging.

"For instance, if seven hundred eggs were ordered," Mann continued, "about four hundred fifty to five hundred would be delivered."

It wasn't just eggs. It was everything.

"I know from talk I heard in the shop that

everything was delivered short to the Savoy Hotel," Mann said. "For instance, the hams were delivered underweight. I weighed them sometimes and weighed short."

Of course, Escoffier was well aware that the groceries were being delivered short, Mann explained to the investigator. The staff at the restaurant had surely noticed by now that, week after week, the number of eggs ordered did not match the number delivered. Or that hams and other meats were underweight. Escoffier had never said a word, and neither had anyone else. It was business as usual.

The scheme resulted in a stunning 30 to 40 percent shortfall in the deliveries to the Savoy. When the detective reported his findings to the auditors at Deloitte, Dever, Griffiths, and Company, they had a word for it: *fraud.*

Ritz was also being followed.

In the summer of 1897, he and Marie had moved from Hampstead to a house farther out in the country, in Golders Green. Marie had given birth to their second son, René, in 1896, and they needed more room. She had always disliked the Hampstead house — it was furnished, and embodied "the stuffiest kind of English taste," she said. In Golders Green they had a large garden and more open space. Ritz went on long walks to Primrose Hill to clear his mind.

He was overworked. The London season had been relentless, and his plans for Paris were all-consuming. He had been making numerous trips to Paris to oversee the renovation of the building on the Place Vendôme. His physician, Dr. Cole, had recommended rest and relaxation. Ritz needed to recuperate properly, spend time outside in the fresh air.

On Sundays mornings, he would go horseback riding or walk the family dogs — a pair of Newfoundlands. He played with his sons. In the afternoons, Escoffier and Echenard would come to visit, and Marie served them tea outside on the lawn. They would discuss work and plans for the week ahead. Agostini, the Savoy cashier, was also a frequent weekend guest, as was Bernard Strauss, a wine merchant.

The Savoy had been reviewed by Lt. Col. Nathaniel Newnham-Davis, the gastronomic correspondent for the *Pall Mall Gazette.* Newnham-Davis was an amateur actor and had written for many newspapers over the years. He had served in the army, never married, and now wrote a column for which he escorted various society ladies (never named) to London's best restaurants, and described the meal.

Ritz, Escoffier, and Echenard gathered around the table and read the review. Soon enough they were laughing with delight, both at the positive review and its slightly comical descriptions of themselves. Newnham-Davis described his difficulty getting a table when calling the Savoy restaurant's newly installed telephone:

"No. 35,466, if you please"; and being switched on to the Savoy, and having asked for a table, I received the answer I expected, having applied so late, that every one was taken, but that the management would do what they could to find space for me in a supplementary room. This meant dining in one of the smaller dining rooms, and as at the Savoy the view of one's neighbors and their wives is no unimportant part of the Sunday dinner, I asked if M. Echenard, the manager, was in the hotel, and if he was, would he come to the telephone and speak to me.

M. Echenard was in the hotel, and as soon as I had secured his ear I made an appeal to him that would have melted the heart of any tyrant.

"If it is possible, it shall be done," said M. Echenard.

Newnham-Davis then came to the hotel to order the dinner:

In the office on the ground floor, an office crowded up with books and papers, I found M. Echenard — who, with his little moustache with the ends turned upwards and carefully trimmed beard, always has something of the look of the Spanish señores that Velasquez used to paint.

The ordering of the dinner came next, and to take on one's self the responsibility of this with such a chef as Maître Escoffier in the kitchen is no small matter.

Hors-d'oeuvres, of course, and then I suggested *Bortsch* as the soup, for of all the restaurants where they make this excellent Russian dish the Savoy takes the palm.

Timbales de filets de sole à la Savoy, hinted M. Echenard, and though I didn't quite know what that was, it sounded well, and went down on the slip of paper. I wanted a *mousse* for the entree, for I know there are no such *mousses* to be got elsewhere as the Maître can make; and then M. Echenard suggested *Poulet de grain Polonaise,* and as he described the method of cooking, and how the juices of the liver soaked into the bird, and essence of the chicken permeated the liver, I gave up my first idea of the celebrated *Canard en chemise.* That was my idea of a little dinner, but M. Echenard insisted on the finishing touches being administered by a *Parfait de foie gras,* English asparagus, and *Pêches glacées vanille.*

The dinner was a triumph, Newnham-Davis wrote. He went on at great length, describing the crowd in the dining room:

There was on this particular evening in our immediate vicinity, a lady who once won celebrity on the stage, which she left to take a title; there was an Indian prince, the first swallow of the dusky, jeweled flight that comes each summer to our shores; there was the manager of one of the best known of our comedy theatres, with whom was dining one of the most beautiful of our actresses and her husband; there was a lady who has the notoriety of having nearly ruined the heir to the throne of one of the kingdoms of Europe, and whose brown diamonds are the envy of all the connoisseurs of the world; there was a

274

party of South African stockbrokers, who from their appearance did not suggest wealth, but whose united incomes would make the revenues of half a dozen Balkan principalities.

And so on. Ritz was described standing with "his hands clasped nervously, almost, with his short whiskers and carefully clipped moustache," going from table to table "with a carefully graduated scale of acknowledgement of the patrons."

They were all amused by the article, and by their small measure of fame. They had conquered London, just as Ritz had said they would seven years earlier. The Savoy was a symbol of a changing London.

Indeed, in many ways, the summer of 1897 felt like a turning point. The eclectic, heterogeneous variety of guests in the Savoy dining room celebrated in Newnham-Davis's review (the actors and aristocrats, the foreign princes and notorious ladies and wealthy stockbrokers) stood in vivid contrast to the exclusive, high-society crowds of the queen's Diamond Jubilee, a series of dinners and balls that had about them a tinge of cast-in-amber nostalgia. Or was it just decadence? For the costume ball at Devonshire House, for example, the social event of the season, guests had spent weeks and months deciding on their costumes. Who would dress as which historical figure? Who would design the various jewel-encrusted dresses? It was not unusual for the women to spend £1,000 and more on their costumes, an astonishing amount. The Countess of Warwick came (with only the slightest hint of irony) as Marie Antoinette; Lady Randolph Churchill came as the Byzantine empress Theodora; the hostess, the Duchess of Devonshire, was dressed as Zenobia, Queen of Palmyra. There were knights in armor, court jesters, Watteau-style shepherdesses, and at least three Cleopatras. A photographer had been hired to take pictures of the guests against painted backdrops. The waiters were dressed as Egyptian footmen.

If the extravagant Devonshire House ball was the grand finale of an extravagant season, it also felt like the last hurrah of the old social order. The unselfconscious celebration of aristocratic wealth and privilege seemed out of step with the speed and mobility of the fin de siècle period.

Lady Randolph Churchill would later recall the slower pace and formality of the late Victorian period, the 1870s, '80s, and '90s:

The writing of ceremonious notes, the leaving of cards, not to speak of *visites de digestion,* which even young men were supposed to pay, took up most afternoons. There was little or none of that extraordinary restlessness and craving for something new which is a feature of today, necessarily causing manners to deteriorate, and certainly curtailing the amenities of social life. A nod replaces the ceremonious bow, a familiar handshake the elaborate courtesy.

That was all disappearing, and the Savoy had helped it disappear.

The contrast between the rarified, indulgent world of the aristocracy and the teeming, striving city and its sometimes desperate poverty could be striking. Consuelo Vanderbilt, the new Duchess of Marlborough, described leaving the Devonshire House ball that July this way:

The fancy dress ball at Devonshire House was a fitting climax to a brilliant season. The ball lasted to the early hours of the morning, and the sun was rising as I walked though Green Park to Spencer House, where we then lived. On the grass lay the dregs of humanity. Human beings too dispirited or sunk to find work or favor, they sprawled in sodden stupor, pitiful representatives of the submerged tenth. In my billowing period dress, I must have seemed to them a vision of wealth and youth, and I thought soberly that they must hate me. But they only looked, and some even had a compliment to enliven my progress.

But Ritz could feel the world was changing. Yes, there were the Upper Ten Thousand, the social elite at their costume balls; and yes, there was the "submerged tenth," the indigent and poor; but there was also a new and dynamic cosmopolitanism, a new social mobility, the thrilling possibility of success. The fact that someone like him, César Ritz, could *own* a hotel — could name a hotel after himself — was proof of that.

The detective following Ritz, observing him at home and at the Savoy, confirmed that he was indeed receiving substantial packages of food, both directly from the hotel kitchen and from the Hudson Brothers grocery. But the investigation soon turned to more serious matters: wine and liquor.

The Deloitte, Dever, Griffiths, and Company auditors went through all of the hotel and restaurant accounts, and all of the inventory. They found that, for the first six months of 1897, £37,549 worth of wine had been sold. But when they added up all the receipts, they totaled only £34,073, meaning that £3,476 worth of wine had gone missing. That was a lot of wine — thousands of bottles unaccounted, not paid for.

Ritz was a generous host: he'd been giving away food and wine freely to favored guests; sending bottles of champagne, on the house, to opera stars, politicians, and princesses. All of his friends had credit at the restaurant, and some of them ran up enormous bills they then never paid. In some cases, there was an actual quid pro quo, the investigators found: Ritz had given credit to certain railway executives, and had been given free rail passes in return. His personal stockbroker had signed for lunch and dinner bills totaling £281 and never paid; so had his personal doctor. The total credit outstanding in June of 1897, accumulated over the years, was £13,000.

Yet it was Ritz's extensive entertaining of his financial backers in the Ritz Hotel Syndicate that would prove to be most galling to Richard D'Oyly Carte. The cost of the lunches and dinners with Alfred Beit, the Neumann brothers, Robert Crawshay, and many others was dwarfed by the cost of all the unpaid wine, the freely given credit, and Escoffier's underweight food deliveries. But Ritz's brazen disloyalty was impossible to stomach.

In early 1898 the investigation became more invasive — the stakes got higher. Escoffier arrived at the Savoy one morning to find himself locked out of his own office while the auditors went through his records.

He was outraged. If he hadn't been bound by his contract, he said, he would have quit right then and there.

When the auditors confronted him about the many food suppliers he did business with directly, buying goods himself and then reselling them to the Savoy, he said that those foreign companies had longstanding relationships with him and knew he was credit-worthy, but they were unfamiliar with the Savoy. It was true that he'd been doing business in France and Switzerland for years, but given the stature of the Savoy now, the argument was preposterous.

Ritz was also questioned by the auditors, and was likewise indignant at the intimations of impropriety. Why was his staff being questioned when he wasn't present? The accusations were absurd, he said. The profit numbers were down, it was true, but that was because competition had forced the Savoy to reduce the prices of many wines. Staff salaries, meanwhile, had gone up — other hotels were trying to poach his waiters, he said, and he'd been forced to pay them more. But the drastic drop in profits could not be explained away so easily: in 1897 the Savoy profits had fallen by £11,000, to £15,585, down more than 40 percent.

On Monday, March 7, 1898, Ritz, Escoffier, and Echenard were summoned to D'Oyly Carte's Adelphi Terrace residence. They walked the few blocks from the hotel impatiently, expecting further questions about the restaurant accounts. The audit had gone on for months already, and must be coming to an end. The London season would soon be upon them. They had work to do.

They were shown into a drawing room. D'Oyly Carte's house was flamboyant and theatrical, with gilded ceilings and painted moldings and carvings on the walls. The mood in the room, however, was dark and sober.

D'Oyly Carte sat in his wheelchair grimly, Helen standing beside him with her arms crossed. The company secretary, Charles

Munro, was there, as were the Hon. Charles Russell, who had overseen the investigation for the Savoy, and other members of the board of directors.

D'Oyly Carte got right to the point: Ritz and Escoffier, he said, had "forgot they were servants, and assumed the attitude of masters and proprietors." It was clear, he continued, speaking to Ritz directly, that "you have latterly been simply using the Savoy as a place to live in, a pied à terre, an office, from which to carry on your other schemes."

Ritz stood silently.

Russell now read from a sheet of paper, as if listing criminal charges: "The Savoy, with its luxurious suites for the reception and entertainment of subscribers to schemes, formed an ideal machinery for company promoting," he said, referring to the Ritz Hotel Syndicate, "whilst the adjoining restaurant, full of rich and good-natured clients won over by the suave attentions which Mssrs. Ritz and Echenard from their positions could give them, formed a happy hunting ground for subscribers which left nothing to be desired."

The investigation, "conducted practically day by day, has been a very laborious task and has occupied many months. The directors have ascertained the principal causes of the deficiencies." It revealed, he said, that Escoffier had been accepting bribes, and that food ordered for the hotel kitchen was routinely delivered significantly underweight. And then there was "the astounding disappearance of over £3,400 of wine and spirits in the first six months of 1897"; furthermore, "wine and spirits consumed in the same period by the managers, staff, and employees amounting to £3,000."

The board had consulted Sir Edward Carson, the preeminent lawyer, D'Oyly Carte said. After reading the auditor's report, he advised them in no uncertain terms: "It is the imperative duty of the directors to dismiss the manager and the chef."

It was D'Oyly Carte who handed each of them his official note of dismissal.

By a resolution passed this morning you have been dismissed from the service of the Hotel for, among other serious reasons, gross negligence and breaches of duty and mismanagement. I am also directed to request that you will be good enough to leave the Hotel at once.

Escoffier, Echenard, and Ritz had been fired.

■ ■ ■ ■

PART 5
PARIS, 1898–1899

■ ■ ■ ■

13
A NEW BEGINNING

Ritz was in shock. He understood intellectually what had happened, but it didn't seem quite real. As he and Escoffier walked into the Savoy lobby, he felt weightless and strangely carefree — untethered. The hotel was humming with quiet activity, guests checking in and checking out, footmen carrying luggage to waiting taxis, an assistant arranging flowers in vases. Everything was in perfect order; nothing had changed.

But everything had changed. All the details that normally consumed Ritz's attention — Who exactly was that American couple at the check-in desk, and what room would they be given? How fresh were the flowers in those vases? What time were guests arriving for the private banquet that evening, and did they have enough champagne for the occasion, and was it properly chilled? — all these questions were now inconsequential. It was as if his entire reason for being, his purpose, had evaporated. Ritz was a hotelier without a hotel.

He, Echenard, and Escoffier had to leave the Savoy immediately, the board of directors had made clear: that very day. Ritz would need to pack up his office. But where to go?

There was no time to talk to his backers in the Ritz Hotel Syndicate, no time to contact all the suppliers and vendors he was hiring for the Paris hotel, all of whom normally reached him at the Savoy. Most important of all, he would not be able to tell his regular clientele, at the hotel and the restaurant, where he was going or what had happened. There would be no smooth transition.

This was deliberate, Ritz realized. D'Oyly Carte did not want him to make any arrangements, to be able to explain himself. Ritz was meant to be humiliated.

But Ritz was not humiliated. He was furious. After all he'd done for the Savoy, this was his thanks? To be cast out under a cloud of suspicion and false allegations? It was outrageous.

Everything he'd done had been for the betterment of the Savoy. *Of course* he'd sent bottles of champagne on the house to important guests dining in the restaurant.

Of course he'd signed for checks and extended credit sometimes. That was his job as the manager, the host, the personification of the hotel and its generosity. All those who'd been given credit would certainly be paying their bills; it was insulting to suggest otherwise. And as for his dealings with backers of the Ritz Hotel Syndicate: he'd been perfectly aboveboard from the outset. D'Oyly Carte had always understood that Ritz maintained his independence, and would be involved in outside projects. Indeed, from the very beginning, this freedom had been written into his contract with the Savoy. For D'Oyly Carte to be holding it against him now was nothing less than a betrayal.

As for accusations against Escoffier, that he had been taking kickbacks from his suppliers, Ritz was sure the chef was only doing what was best for the restaurant. Of course Escoffier had good relations with his vendors — the Savoy was the best restaurant in London! It was only natural that the various grocers and specialty food importers had bestowed gifts upon him. (And had supplied Ritz's home with groceries — that was also true.) Ritz did not enjoy thinking too hard about the particulars: Escoffier demanding cash payments from the Hudson

Brothers grocery; deliveries to the restaurant coming in underweight on a regular basis. Ritz figured business was business, which was to say, there were skids that needed to be greased, payments that needed to be made, payments that there was no harm in receiving. In his heart, though, he knew the truth: that Escoffier had taken advantage of his situation, just as he himself had. They had made the Savoy a resounding success. They deserved their share of the rewards. It was only fair.

Indeed, it was just as D'Oyly Carte had said: he and Escoffier had "forgot they were servants, and assumed the attitude of masters and proprietors." The words echoed in his head, even now. The idea that they should be seen as servants was the cruelest of insults. César Ritz, Auguste Escoffier, *servants*?

When he thought back to the meeting that morning, and the sight of D'Oyly Carte in his wheelchair, his swollen legs covered with a blanket, and the other members of the board gathered in the room sanctimoniously reciting trumped-up charges against him and Escoffier, it was Helen's small, tight smile that bothered him the most. She'd had it in for him since the very beginning. And now she'd had her way.

He would not stand for it, he decided right then and there. He was going to fight back.

Ritz, Escoffier, and Echenard gathered the senior staff in Ritz's office and told them the news: Agostini, the cashier; Henry Ellès and François Rinjoux, managers of the restaurant; William Autour, hotel manager; the men who'd been there since the beginning. Ritz did the talking. He was sorry, he said, about this unexpected turn of events. He had let them down.

The men immediately declared their allegiance to Ritz. They would all resign in protest. The idea of staying on at the Savoy after their leaders had been dismissed was unthinkable. They would follow Ritz and Escoffier wherever they went.

Among the managers, the mood was somber. In the kitchen, meanwhile, events quickly spun out of control.

As Escoffier announced the news to the cooks, some of them shouted in anger and threw pots to the floor. Escoffier's serene kitchen was suddenly in chaos, all hot emotion and fury. Just as with Ritz at the hotel, the kitchen staff all determined to quit, on the spot. They would walk out right now, during dinner.

Escoffier urged calm; they were professionals, as he'd always said. They must complete the dinner service. He could well remember the scene that greeted him on his first day at the Savoy: the kitchen trashed by the outgoing chef and his team, spoiled food all over the floor. He would not leave his kitchen, whatever the circumstances, in such a state. He was Auguste Escoffier, after all. All he had done to civilize the working conditions of the restaurant kitchen would not be undone now.

D'Oyly Carte, meanwhile, called the police. He, too, remembered the damage Monsieur Charpentier had wrought on his way out the door in the spring of 1890. Notifying the authorities was a precautionary measure. He knew the staff of the Savoy would take the side of the men he'd fired: it was tribal.

And so the Savoy that Monday night was in a state of barely functioning chaos. The managers were gone, replaced by a few temporary workers borrowed from other hotels. In the kitchen, angry *chefs de partie* turned out passable versions of Escoffier's dishes, while the waiters gossiped anxiously. A group of policemen gathered by the service entrance to the kitchen, looking for any sign of trouble; and in the lobby loitered members of the press, alerted to the drama by rival hotels.

One of the reporters spotted Ritz as he was leaving the hotel and asked him why he and Escoffier had been fired. I haven't the faintest idea, Ritz declared, maintaining his dignity but not breaking his stride. He was going to see an old friend, E. Neuschwander, the manager of the Charing Cross Hotel. He needed a place to stay, somewhere to set up shop temporarily, to make plans, receive visitors.

They'd come full circle, it seemed, Ritz and Escoffier: the Charing Cross Hotel was the very place Escoffier had gone for help on the day they'd arrived in London and found the Savoy kitchen bereft of supplies. Escoffier's old friend Louis Peyre had given him what he needed. Now it was Ritz's friend Neuschwander, the manager at the same hotel, who offered to help, putting him up in the best room he had available.

It was from the Charing Cross Hotel that Ritz sent word to Marie about their new and unfortunate circumstances. She was out in the country, in Golders Green, with the two small children. They would be moving soon, he said: to Paris. There was no reason to stay in London for the season. Marie should begin closing up the house.

The next day, Ritz called an emergency

meeting of the board of directors of the Ritz Hotel Syndicate. He explained what had happened at the Savoy as best he could. He was as shocked as they were, he said. (The Ritz syndicate and the Savoy company shared some investors but did not have board members in common. The news of Ritz's and Escoffier's dismissal therefore came as a total surprise.) Clearly, D'Oyly Carte had grown uncomfortable with Ritz's independence — the coming launch of the Paris hotel, for example, and all the syndicate's other ambitious plans. Ritz was perfectly within his rights to launch his own hotel company, he said, but D'Oyly Carte had found a pretext upon which to dismiss him, claiming that he and Escoffier had caused the restaurant's profits to decline. It was ridiculous.

The newspapers were already full of speculation, with headlines including "A Kitchen Revolt at the Savoy"; "Savoy Hotel Sensation"; and "The Savoy Hotel Mystery." The *Star* reported on the commotion:

During the last 24-hours the Savoy Hotel has been the scene of disturbances which in a South American Republic would be dignified by the name of revolution. Three managers have been dismissed and 16

294

fiery French and Swiss cooks (some of them took their long knives and placed themselves in a position of defiance) have been bundled out by a strong force of the Metropolitan police.

The *Daily Mail* had more details. Ritz was shocked to see that the Savoy was going public about the affair, making oblique but unmistakable accusations against him:

"Under New Management; Startling Changes at the Savoy Hotel" was the headline.

The familiar public-house window bill, "Under entirely new management," may not appear among the luxurious surroundings of the Savoy Hotel. But it might, with perfect accuracy.

Startling changes have been made in the staff. After a special meeting of the directors of the company, held on Monday, M. Ritz and M. Echenard, the joint managers of the establishment, received letters, in consequence of which they retired from their positions and left the premises.

At the same time, M. Escoffier, the famous chef of the hotel, vacated his artistic throne, and a studio full of his French and Swiss subordinates threw down their stew-pans and left the place. In anticipation of possible trouble the directors sent to Bow-street for police protection.

What it is all about no one who has an explanation to offer seems to know, and no one who is in a position to know will offer any explanation.

The various officials of the company will say nothing. M. Ritz himself, seen by a "Daily Mail" reporter, says he has no idea what it is all about . . .

That there has for some time past been trouble on a large scale at the Savoy Hotel is indicated clearly in an official communication which has just been made by the directors to the shareholders.

"A matter of great importance became apparent to the directors in the autumn, and that was, that there was a much less percentage of profit on the sale of food and wine than in previous years . . . The directors have ascertained the principal causes of the deficiencies. They further have ascertained that other abuses have sprung up prejudicial to the business in many ways, and calculated to alienate customers."

The Savoy had all but accused him of theft in the morning newspaper.

As a formality, Ritz offered to resign from the board of his own company. His name — Escoffier's, too — was being slandered, and he planned to defend himself. He hoped the board of his own company would stand by him, which of course they did, recording a vote of full confidence in Ritz and, more important, agreeing to take his entire team on the payroll while they waited for the Paris hotel to open. It was only a matter of a few months — the new hotel was nearing completion. Escoffier, Echenard, Agostini, Ellès, Rinjoux, and Autour all joined the Ritz Hotel Development Company.

Now Ritz went to see his lawyer. He planned to sue the Savoy. Escoffier and Echenard would join him in the lawsuit: they had all been fired improperly, and he meant for the world to know it. All three of them had signed contracts with the hotel, which D'Oyly Carte had violated. And all the evidence the Savoy had collected was dubious, Ritz felt. He and Escoffier had been running the hotel the same way for years. Why now the sudden investigation?

He instructed his lawyers to bring the case. The *Daily Mail* reported the following day: "The Savoy Expulsions: From the Hotel Kitchen to the Law Courts."

The mysterious proceedings at the Savoy Hotel prior to and following the expulsion of a portion of the staff by the directors are, it appears, to be unfolded in the Law Courts.

We are informed that Mssrs. Ritz, Echenard and Escoffier, the late managers and chef of the hotel, yesterday instructed their solicitors to commence actions against the company for wrongful dismissal and breach of contract.

The writs in the actions were served upon the company's solicitors in the course of the afternoon.

In his suite at the Charing Cross Hotel, Ritz received an outpouring of support from his loyal friends and clients: notes, phone calls, visits. Marie was sent large bouquets of roses. The Duchess of Devonshire, Robert Crawshay, Alfred Beit, the Neumann brothers, Lillie Langtry, and Nellie Melba all made their allegiance known.

Lady de Grey came in person to pay her regards, and to bring word from Ritz's most important client of all, the Prince of Wales. He had canceled an upcoming party at the Savoy. "Where Ritz goes, I go," he had declared.

Never had Ritz been so glad to hear a bit

of good news. It was the best endorsement he'd ever received.

"In times such as these one learns to know one's friends," Marie said to Ritz. And enemies. Marie would later recall the indignities administered by Helen D'Oyly Carte: "She was in a great hurry to rid our apartment at the Savoy of all our personal belongings. Indeed, she practically threw them out into the street, sending precious pieces of Saxe and Sèvres, fragile Venetian glass and Roman pottery, to us packed anyhow, helter-skelter, in cardboard boxes. The whole thing was incredible."

Two years earlier, in 1896, soon after buying the building at 15 Place Vendôme, Ritz had hired the architect Charles Mewès to reconceive it as a hotel. The structure had been built in 1705 by the Duc de Gramont, the façade designed by Jules Hardouin-Mansart, Louis XIV's chief architect. Indeed, Hardouin-Mansart had designed the entire square, the mansard roofs of the iconic Parisian buildings done in the style named after his great-uncle François Mansart, also an architect. The original idea was that Louis XIV deserved a square built in his honor, just as the Place des Vosges and the Place Dauphine honored his father,

Louis XIII, and his grandfather Henri IV, respectively. But the plans for Place Louis-le-Grand, as it was called, stalled for many years, partially built, and eventually the land was sold to the City of Paris. The Hardouin-Mansart façades were constructed around the square, and then sold in sections to wealthy families, who built mansions behind them.

The Place Vendôme was a wide and austere square — there were no trees — in the middle of which stood the Vendôme column, with its statue of Napoléon on top. (There had been many statues of military leaders on the column over the years.) Ritz had seen the original column torn down in the spring of 1871 by the Paris Commune, who saw it as a symbol of war. He had been working as a waiter during the Siege of Paris, but made his way back to Switzerland soon after. The column had been rebuilt a few years later.

Mewès and Ritz would not be altering the structure of the building or its façade in any way but, rather, would reconfigure the interior rooms, adding modern plumbing and electricity throughout.

"My hotel must be the last word in modernity," Ritz told Mewès. "Mine will be the first modern hotel in Paris; and it must be hygienic, efficient, and beautiful."

Beyond the desire that it be state of the art, Ritz did not have strong opinions about the design or décor of the building. He did not consider himself to be educated or sophisticated enough to talk about such matters. He was a philistine. "I know nothing, really, of periods of architecture and furniture," he said to Mewès. "You shall teach me."

Of course, the truth was Ritz knew what he wanted. Though he had no knowledge of the finer distinctions between Regency and Louis XIV styles, or any other school or era, he had a very clear sense of what his hotel must *feel* like, and just how luxurious it should be.

There would be a small, intimate lobby, as in a private home. The mere one hundred guest rooms would be tall and perfectly proportioned, with very large and beautiful bathrooms attached to each one. This was crucial — if there was one thing Ritz had learned from D'Oyly Carte, it was the central importance of bathrooms. The Hotel Bristol, also located on the Place Vendôme, had a single bathroom per floor; when the Prince of Wales stayed there and required a bath, a carriage would arrive to deliver the so-called bath-at-home service, and large tanks of hot water would be carried upstairs, along with a large bathtub, to be positioned in the middle of the prince's bedroom. This was extravagant, of course — he was royalty. More common were the flat baths, found in every bedroom, which servants would prepare for their employers.

Times were changing, though: people did not travel with servants the way they once did, and the Ritz would not have servants' quarters in the manner of older hotels like the Bristol.

There would be a garden, a quiet retreat in the city. There would be no wallpaper, no plush fabrics — no velvet collecting dust — and no knickknacks or other unnecessary ornaments. There would be electric lights and telephones. The hotel must be easy to clean. Hygienic, as he said repeatedly. Modern.

The key point for Ritz, and what would distinguish his establishment from any other newly built luxury hotel, was that it have "the atmosphere of a gentleman's town house — a house in which several distinguished generations had lived, entertained, and enjoyed themselves."

"It can be done," Mewès replied. "And we shall do it!"

Mewès was a large man, charismatic and

erudite. He was younger than Ritz, forty years old, with close-cropped hair, a goatee, and a moustache. He was from Strasbourg, born to a Jewish family, and had trained with the renowned architect Jean-Louis Pascal, who had designed the National Library of France in Paris.

During their many visits to Paris over the course of 1897, Mewès went about educating Ritz and Marie as best he could about design, taking both of them on excursions to museums and art galleries, and to carpet and furniture manufacturers.

He had much work to do to convince Ritz that his classical aesthetic would work for the hotel — Ritz's first instinct was to buy contemporary furnishings. How could the dining room be furnished in the style of Louis XIV or Regency, as Mewès proposed? They would never find the furniture.

"We cannot hope to furnish the hotel rooms with authentic pieces," said Ritz. "And I loathe imitations. I want things throughout to be genuine and first class."

True enough, said Mewès, but high-quality reproductions were not the same as cheap imitations. "Our furniture shall be perfectly copied from the best of the various periods."

And so they determined that the décor of

the hotel would be a mix of periods and styles. Mewès would ensure that everything worked together: the gardens would be seventeenth-century Louis XIV, as would the adjacent "Square Room"; the dining room would be early 1800s English Regency; the stairway and many of the suites would be eighteenth-century Louis XV; the "Royal Suite" would be done in early 1800s French Empire style. The cumulative effect, however, was just what Ritz was after: a sense that the hotel had been furnished piece by piece, room by room, over generations.

It was an illusion that would work only if executed with great care, and as it turned out, Mewès, Ritz, and Marie were all perfectly suited to the task. Mewès was a classicist, with great respect for history. Marie later described him talking in an "almost exalted voice of the purity and integrity of line and structure that had characterized the work of eighteenth-century architects and craftsmen. He said that it would be for him a positive joy to design rooms and furnishings to harmonize with that harmonious exterior."

Ritz was a perfectionist, and determined that every detail be just right. He was the ideal architectural client: he knew the effect he wanted, and was therefore decisive — there was nothing worse, Mewès knew, than a vacillating client — and yet he was also open to suggestions and eager to learn. Marie, for her part, was a veteran shopper: as she had for the launch of the Grand in Rome, she took charge of the linens and carpets, corresponding with pillow manufacturers, milliners, and fabric merchants.

Marie was an aficionado of fabrics — "I have always had a passion for linen," she told Mewès, laughing. Growing up in a hotel, she had been taught by her mother, for example, that "linen needs repose": it should be stored in a warm place between launderings, so that the fibers could "relax." For this reason, there needed to be four sets of sheets for every bed at the hotel. She took her husband shopping at Rouff's and the Grand Maison de Blanc, both in Paris. At Rouff's, Ritz announced to the salesmen, "My wife knows all about linen!" They bought the best they could find.

"The best is not too good," Ritz would say. This was his philosophy about everything at the new hotel. It would be superlative in every way.

14
THE COOKBOOK

Escoffier suddenly had time on his hands. Packing up his office at the Savoy, going through all his papers and recipes, his careful records of every menu he'd ever served to his regular customers over many years, his notes for his occasional column for *L'Art Culinaire,* he decided to revisit the idea of compiling a recipe book.

It was an overwhelming prospect: to attempt to condense the entirety of his kitchen knowledge into a single volume. At first, he thought he might limit himself to describing only his new recipes, his signature dishes, his modern innovations. That was the original idea and impetus for the project. But the more he thought about it, the more he realized that for the book to be actually useful, he would need to start from the beginning. The art of cooking was always changing, but the essentials remained the same. Every one of his culinary inventions stood upon the foundations of his training: the stocks, sauces, and methods of classical French cooking.

He did not want the book to be "a luxurious work of art or curiosity that would be relegated to library shelves," he told his editor at *L'Art Culinaire,* Philéas Gilbert. It should instead be "a work tool more than a book, a constant companion that chefs would always keep at their side." A book for working professionals.

He would divide the book into two parts: First, "Fundamental Elements," a basic and comprehensive guide to everything from compound butters and aspics to marinades and garnishes to cooking operations like poaching, braising, and frying. The second part would consist of recipes, thousands of them, divided into sections by ingredient and kind: hors d'oeuvres, eggs, soups, fish, meat, poultry and game, roasts, salads, vegetables, savories, desserts, ices and sherbets, drinks and refreshments, and fruit stews and jams.

The first task was to organize all his recipes. He made lists, and then expanded the lists, and then expanded them some more. It was a Herculean task. There were key recipes he had written down over the years, as guides for the kitchen staff. But there were also numerous variations on each, and variations on the variations. Take game birds, for example:

1. The various pheasants, grey and red partridges, the Tetras Californias.
2. The hazel-hen, grouse, prairie fowls, ganga, sand-grouse.
3. The various wild ducks and teals.
4. The woodcocks and snipes.
5. The various plovers, lapwings, sandpipers, water-rails, water-hens.
6. The quails, land-rails, Virginia quails.
7. The various thrushes, Corsican blackbirds.
8. The various larks.
9. The warblers.
10. The ortolans.

He had dozens of recipes for the pheasants alone, both classic preparations and his own variations, and he described each one as succinctly as possible: *Faison à la mode d'Alcantara* was stuffed with duck's foie gras and quartered truffles, marinated for three days in port wine, and then cooked *en casserole* with more truffles. *Faison à l'Angoumoise* was stuffed with pork fat, truffles, and chestnuts; wrapped in bacon; roasted; and served with a truffled Périgueux sauce. *Faison à la choucroûte* was braised and served on sauerkraut. *Faison à la Normande* was roasted in a terrine with finely chopped apples and a bit of cream. And there were more: *Faison à la Bohémienne, Faison Kotschoubey, Faison Demidoff, Faison à la régence, Soufflé de faison, Faison Souvaroff,* thirty-five pheasant recipes in all, including a series of cold dishes — aspics and terrines.

Escoffier tried to make each recipe as clear as possible, giving essential measurements and cooking times but only the barest of instruction on technique, since that would all be covered in the "Fundamental Elements" section. Every recipe would be numbered, allowing him to refer to his instructions for poaching chicken, say, when discussing a recipe for poaching pheasant. There would be a glossary at the back of the book to explain the culinary terms — *brandade, chiffonade, papillote, paupiette, poêle, profiterolles, salpicon,* and so on.

Most of the recipes were quite simple — stuffing and roasting or sautéing the birds, preparing a sauce and garnish — but he did not shy away from describing far more elaborate preparations. The *Faison à la Sainte-Alliance,* for example, went like this:

Bone 2 woodcocks, and put their livers and intestines aside.

Chop up their meat, together with 1/4 its weight of poached and cooled beef-marrow, and as much fresh fat bacon; salt, pepper, and herbs. Add to this hash 6 oz. raw peeled and quartered truffles, slightly cooked in butter.

Stuff the pheasant with this preparation; truss it; wrap it in slices of bacon, and keep it in the cool for 24 hours, that the aroma of the truffles may be concentrated.

Roast the pheasant on the spit, or, if in the oven, set it on a somewhat high stand in a baking-pan. Cut a large croûton from a sandwich-loaf, and fry it in clarified butter.

Pound the woodcocks' livers and intestines with an equal weight of grated fresh fat bacon, the well-washed filets of an anchovy, 1 oz. butter, and 1/2 oz. raw truffle. When this force-meat is very smooth and all its ingredients thoroughly mixed, spread it over the fried croûton.

When the pheasant is 2/3 cooked, set this coated croûton under the bird in such wise as to allow the juices escaping from the latter to drop upon the croûton. Complete the cooking, and dish the pheasant on the croûton. Surround with slices of bitter orange, and send the gravy separately.

When serving, accompany each piece of pheasant with a slice of orange and a small slice of coated croûton.

This was a dish fit for a king, and as Escoffier walked through the many steps and wrote them down, he thought back on all the grand dinners he had presented over the years, at galas and royal affairs, and on the dishes he had invented for celebrated guests, the opera singers and princesses and courtesans. The book would be a tool for other chefs, but it was also, in the writing, a kind of memoir.

He remembered every dish as if he'd prepared it yesterday: the *Cuisses de Nymphes à l'Aurore,* the frogs' legs he'd made at the Savoy for the Prince of Wales and served disguised with this mythological name; the *Selle d'agneau de lait de Pauillac,* the saddle of suckling Pauillac lamb he'd made for the prince years earlier, in Monte Carlo; the Provençal stews and braises he'd cooked for Emile Zola; the *Mousse de merlan aux écrevisse* he'd made for the Hungarian ballerina Katinka.

Escoffier sat at his desk surrounded by pieces of paper, each one a recipe, arranging them in piles and making notes for yet more recipes. After leaving London, he'd come to Paris to help Ritz with the preparations at the new hotel, but mostly he devoted himself to the recipes. He was methodical by nature; the work was calming, meditative.

The disaster at the Savoy had caught him entirely off guard. He had accepted the situation with equanimity, declared his innocence, and packed his bags (and cartons of recipes, menus, and notes). But he was thoroughly shaken, his pride wounded. How could they do this to him, insult him in this way, after everything he'd done to make the Savoy a success? It was painful to contemplate.

True, he had accepted gifts from his suppliers. And yes, he had accepted commissions, too, and overlooked deliveries that were short and underweight. But none of this was unusual in his experience. Suppliers offering commissions was nothing new. He had been doing his job. The success of the Savoy restaurant spoke for itself.

Escoffier had achieved fame in London, but fame was fleeting, he knew, and now he was a chef without a restaurant. It was the strangest thing: he was home, returned to France, but felt as if he'd been exiled.

And so for him the book was more than a

record of his recipes: it was a way to lay claim to his reputation, to document the changes and advances he had brought to modern restaurant cooking, to establish his place in the pantheon of chefs who'd come before him. Marie-Antoine Carême, of course, was the godfather of grand French cooking; no one had engineered the spectacular, monumental displays of food de rigueur in the early nineteenth century better than he. In the 1850s, Urbain Dubois and Emile Bernard had helped popularize *service à la russe,* in which dishes were brought to the table sequentially rather than all at once. Dubois and Bernard had published their important cookbook, *La Cuisine Classique,* in 1856, laying out all the advantages of serving dinner this way (food arriving from the kitchen still properly hot, for example), and had set down key recipes and methods. Dubois himself had been one of the first to encourage Escoffier to write a cookbook, when they met years ago.

Now it was Escoffier's turn. There had been many cookbooks written in recent years, but they were primarily aimed at home cooks. They had decorative black-and-white engravings and often included instructions for running a household. Escoffier aimed to do something different: to write a book for professionals that would not only be comprehensive, but also express the essence of modern cooking. It would contain his recipes but also encompass his philosophy of cooking. It would be a book only he could write.

Escoffier had not revolutionized French food: Many of his dishes were versions of classic preparations, after all. The flavors were familiar; *Truite meunière* was *Truite meunière*. But he had altered the formulas, the equations, in some fundamental way. Partly this was a result of his having drastically streamlined the work of the chefs in his kitchens. The division of labor and the increased specialization, precision, and speed at the heart of his *brigade de cuisine* system meant that recipes and the presentation of dishes were far less complicated than before. Both Carême and Dubois had spent their careers working in private, often royal kitchens (Carême for Napoléon and Talleyrand, Dubois for Prince Orlov of Russia and the Prussian Hohenzollern dynasty), whereas Escoffier had always worked in restaurants, where the pressure was relentless and where juggling simultaneous orders from hundreds of guests required a new level of organizational and cooking sophistication, and an embrace of simplicity.

Carême's recipe for *chaud-froid* of poultry, for example, placed great emphasis on the decoration of the dish, poached chicken pieces served cold with a creamy sauce and truffles:

This entree should be raised high, and on the top of it place a fine truffle dressed in champagne, but not peeled, on which put a fine double cock's comb. Afterwards mix a tablespoonful of lukewarm aspic jelly with your sauce, which will thicken it a little, but at the same time make it very sleek, then pour it regularly over the surface . . .

The dish was then surrounded with chopped jelly.

Escoffier's version of this classic dish proposes a simpler presentation:

Old method of dishing: Formerly, chaud-froids were dished on a cushion of bread or rice, placed in the middle of a border of jelly; and, between each piece, cock's combs and mushrooms, covered with chaud-froid sauce or jelly, were set.

They were also dished on stearine tazzas, made in special molds; but these methods, however much they may have been honoured by old cookery, are generally scouted at the present day.

The method of dishing detailed hereafter is steadily ousting them; it allows of serving much more delicate and more agreeable chaud-froids in the simplest possible way, and was inaugurated at my suggestion at the Savoy Hotel.

Modern method of dishing: Set the decorated pieces, coated with chaud-froid sauce, side by side on a layer of aspic jelly, lying on the bottom of a deep square dish. Cover them with the same aspic, which should be half melted, and leave to set. When about to serve, incrust the dish in a block of carved ice or surround it with the latter fragmented.

This procedure allows of using less gelatinous products in the preparation of this aspic, and the latter is therefore more delicate, mellow, and melting.

The emphasis for Escoffier was on the taste of the food itself, and he dispensed entirely with wax pedestals and other inedible ornamentation. (The poached cock's combs, for example, were technically edible but essentially decorative.)

Escoffier's cooking was responsive to changing contemporary taste. He always joked that his best cooking was inspired by women — the secret to his success, he would say, "is that most of my dishes were created for the ladies!" They had a finer palate, he was convinced; a woman was his ideal customer.

Escoffier's cooking was light and delicate in comparison to what preceded it; the portions were smaller, the ingredients fresh, the sauces pure and less overwhelming. As he contemplated how cooking had changed, and how *he* had changed *cooking,* he wrote:

The number of dishes set before the diners being considerably reduced, and the dishes themselves having been deprived of all the advantages which their sumptuous decorations formerly lent them, they must recover, by means of perfection and delicacy, sufficient in the way of quality to compensate for their diminished bulk and reduced splendor. They must be faultless in regard to quality; they must be savory and light. The choice of raw material, therefore, is a matter demanding vast experience on the part of the chef; for the old French adage which says that *La sauce fait passer le poisson* ["the sauce helps the fish go down"] has long since ceased to be true, and if one does not wish to court disapprobation — often well-earned — the fish should not be in the slightest degree inferior to its accompanying sauce.

He made another list, of fish. It was by no means complete; he would limit himself to popular and available varieties:

1. Salmon
2. Trout
3. Sole
4. Lobster
5. Crayfish
6. Oysters
7. Cod
8. John Dory
9. Haddock
10. Mackerel
11. Whiting
12. Char
13. Red Mullets

He looked at the list, and then began another, "Ways of cooking fish": there was boiling, frying, frying in butter *à la meunière,* poaching, braising, grilling, and cooking au gratin. The possibilities were numerous: he could think of two dozen salmon recipes off the top of his head — including *Saumon Chambord, Saumon Lucullus, Sau-*

mon Royale, Saumon Valois . . . And then there were mousselines of salmon, cold salmon *à la Norvégienne,* salmon salad mayonnaise, and so on.

As he worked, Escoffier found that the vastness and encyclopedic nature of the task appealed to him. He sat at his desk like a scholar. He had not been in school since he was a child, age thirteen, and now here he was writing a book, a treatise.

He turned his attention to cold salmon. It should always be cooked whole or in large pieces, he wrote. "Pieces cooked separately may seem better or may be more sightly, but their meat is drier than that of the salmon cooked whole. And what is lost in appearance with the very large pieces is more than compensated by their extra quality." This was a common problem, he found: chefs choosing visual perfection over taste. "In dishing cold salmon," he continued, "the skin may be removed and the filets bared, so that the fish may be more easily decorated, but the real gourmet will always prefer the salmon served in its natural silver vestment."

Writing recipes was mostly an exercise in scientific clarity and step-by-step precision. Still, Escoffier would allow his own prejudices and preferences to shine through.

Obviously, the silver skin of the salmon *could* be removed before serving, but just as obviously, it *shouldn't* be. And as to decoration, he wrote, "I am not partial to the decorating of salmon with softened butter, colored or not, laid on by means of the piping bag. Apart from the fact that this method of decoration is rarely artistic, the butter used combines badly with the cold sauces and the meat of the salmon on the diner's plate. Very green tarragon leaves, chervil, lobster coral, etc., afford a more natural and more delicate means of ornamentation."

Escoffier wrote late into the night.

15
THE PERFECT HOTEL

In late March 1898, César and Marie Ritz moved into an apartment on the top floor of the unfinished hotel on the Place Vendôme. The building was a construction site. There were painters, electricians, carpenters, masons, plasterworkers, and gilders all over the place during the day, all hard at work.

They hadn't planned to be living in the hotel, needless to say, with two small children, before construction was complete. But it made sense: the renovation was far enough along to make the building habitable, and Ritz was obsessed. Their fourth-floor rooms overlooked the Place Vendôme.

This was his hotel: the Hôtel Ritz, the one he had always dreamed about. Every lesson he had ever learned in his years as a hotelier would be brought to bear; every compromise he had ever been forced to make would be avenged.

Every detail would be perfect.

Ritz was obsessed with lighting. He had done his best to soften the electric lights at the Savoy, but there was only so much he could do. Now, however, he would design every lamp and ceiling fixture exactly the way he wanted it.

Indirect light the was the key: no bare bulb should ever be visible. This despite the fact that current fashion dictated just the opposite: "The last word in artistic lighting," Marie noted, was "a bronze nymph holding up a cluster of naked electric-light bulbs in lieu of flowers." Whatever one thought of such statues — they were awful, in Marie's opinion — the light they produced was harsh and unforgiving.

For the Paris hotel, Ritz had installed overhead lights hidden in alabaster bowls hung from the ceiling by silk cords. In the main dining room, large urns, also alabaster, concealed lights that lit up the ceiling. The small table lamps would have lightshades, of course, but what color exactly? What shade would be most flattering to the complexion of a woman eating dinner at the restaurant? This was, for Ritz, a most crucial question. The comfort and ease of women in the restaurant was paramount, and "nothing helps them to look their best so much as the proper lighting," he said. The better everyone felt they looked, the better for business.

He and Marie began a series of experiments in the dining room: she would sit quietly while he and one of the electricians patiently tried out different shades, materials, and colors, over and over, for hours.

Marie enjoyed these sessions. They were a calming, intimate respite from the rest of the day. They did their experiments in the evening, as the sun was going down. You look beautiful, Mimi! Ritz would say as he studied the light. It should not be too yellow; nor too orange or too red; not too white or too blue, too hot or too cold. It was quite remarkable what a difference the slight color shifts made — as they worked, Marie went from sallow to ashen to flushed and back again.

She had never seen her husband so intent and relentless as he was in the weeks and months after leaving the Savoy. Ritz was pushing himself to the limit to get his hotel opened on schedule, that summer, and to make it perfect. He had always been a perfectionist, but this was different. Everything was riding on the success of the Hôtel Ritz. His pride, his self-confidence, his very spirit depended on it, Marie understood.

And there were moments when he was overwhelmed by doubt. A black mood would descend. I'm getting old, he would say. This was a constant refrain. He was so full of energy and ambition, yet also prone to melancholy. When the Prince of Wales's youngest daughter, Princess Maud, was married in the summer of 1896, just as Ritz was struggling to arrange financing for the Paris hotel, he said to Marie sadly, "When I first saw the Prince of Wales [his daughter] was just a baby! Mimi, I am getting old!"

"Do not talk about getting old until you are fifty, at least!" Marie replied lightly.

"I have only four more years to go — or less!" Ritz replied. "And what have I accomplished? Nothing!"

The drama and despair soon passed, subsumed as always by Ritz's work. Still, Marie worried. Now, as the hotel neared completion, he was working harder than ever. The previous summer, during the queen's Diamond Jubilee and at the height of the London season, Ritz had been exhausted, and his doctor told him to rest. Now he was back at it.

There would be no doubt, when he was done, just what he had accomplished. The Hôtel Ritz would bear his name for a reason.

The evening sessions with Marie and the

lampshades eventually yielded a solution: a pleated lampshade, white, with a silk inner lining that was pale apricot-pink. The resulting light was warming but not too bright and, Ritz exclaimed, "reduced the appearance of a woman by ten years!"

The perfectly flattering lampshades were but one of the many details Ritz agonized over. The closets and cupboards in the bedrooms: Were there enough of them? Were they positioned correctly? Was there enough hanging space for a woman's dresses? Should the dressing table be in the bathroom or in the bedroom?

He and Mewès consulted Marie, who was asked to speak as a "an average woman." The first thing she noticed was that there was no special drawer for false hair — "all the false curls, buns, rolls, and 'rats' " and other accessories that were so fashionable at the moment required significant space. Mewès was dismissive, but Ritz took the suggestion absolutely seriously. The drawer was added.

Marie also proposed installing a light just above the wardrobe, so that dresses could be seen properly.

Ritz had also commissioned a special reversible seat cushion for the hotel's armchairs: cane on one side, plush on the other.

Cane was popular, but it tended to leave impressions on the velvet and silk dresses women wore. Now the cushion could be flipped over to avoid this fate.

A detail, yes, but it was just such details that would mark the difference between the Hôtel Ritz and other, larger luxury hotels, the Savoy and Rome Grand included. The Ritz would stand apart. All of the furniture, glass, silver, and china were being specially fabricated for the hotel based on Ritz's preferences and Mewès's designs.

In the restaurant dining room, for example, Ritz had solved the problem of handbags: he asked for small brass hooks to be attached to the arms of half the chairs so that women could hang their handbags while they ate rather than hold them in their laps or place them on the floor. Again, a tiny detail, a solution to a problem no one had ever even put into words, but one that Ritz, in his obsessive way, had noted and now acted upon. It had always been his philosophy (repeatedly explained to all his employees) to anticipate a guest's wishes before the guest did. Now, as he was designing his own hotel, that carefully intuitive sort of thinking informed every decision.

But as concerned as Ritz was with all the details, and they were endless, it was a larger effect he was after. A sense of comfort and luxury.

Every night before bed, César and Marie would walk through the hotel. It was their version of an evening constitutional, except instead of open air and birdsong, there was sawdust and echoing rooms. "Ritz was always pleased," Marie remembered, "but never satisfied."

That wall was too bare — a tapestry was needed. This room had too many shadows — a few more lamps should be installed. Here the view was too lovely to be excluded — a thinner net must be used at the window. The light in this room was too cold — the pale blue curtains needed a warm tint for lining: pale rose or apricot. That table had unequal legs; this drawer did not work smoothly; here was a lock which was defective.

Ritz took detailed notes, which he would give to Mewès the following morning, and who would then make all the necessary fixes. The progress was either painstakingly slow or shockingly fast — some of the painters seemed to spend days working on a single patch of ceiling, while the carpenters could open up a wall and frame a new doorway in a matter of hours. He could feel the hotel coming together in fits and starts, and the haphazard progress didn't bother him. The goal was to open the hotel in June, only a few months hence, but he and Marie had been through this before, in Rome. Marie could still remember the final rush of preparations there, the last-minute furniture and carpet deliveries, and how impossibly unfinished the hotel seemed to be until the very moment it was finished. Of course, the Rome hotel opening had been delayed more than once. But the Ritz would be different.

Every night, the process began again: César and Marie would go on their evening walk, Ritz checking on the day's progress and taking more notes for Mewès. "Was there ever a house built with so much loving care to every detail?" Marie wondered. "I much doubt it."

Escoffier designed the kitchens at the Hôtel Ritz exactly the way he wanted them. It was the first time he'd controlled every aspect of his workspace and equipment, from the placement of the ovens and the organization of the various stations to the design of the plates and serving dishes.

The ovens were hulking and beautiful, black enamel and chrome, fired with wood and coke. Escoffier was a traditionalist: to roast a chicken or leg of lamb properly required the direct heat and flames of real fire. Yes, there was electricity in the kitchen — bright lights had been installed just above all the stoves and food preparation areas — but that was it. The newly popular electric oven had no place here. And there was only a single gas burner — "for the Fire Eternal," Escoffier told Ritz, to heat the enormous pot of simmering stock, the essential base of so much of his cooking.

All the pots and pans were copper or cast iron. Escoffier did not care for the aluminum pans and utensils now being imported from America; they were of inferior quality. Ritz had commissioned Christofle, the famed French silversmith company, to make all the silverware for the new hotel. Escoffier took the lead, telling the artisans just what he desired. In particular, he wanted a collection of rectangular silver serving platters and covers.

He had been dreaming of these serving dishes since childhood, ever since his time as a teenager working at his uncle's restaurant in Nice. His uncle had bought a collection of ten silver serving platters and covers from an English lord who lived in Nice. Escoffier studied the beautiful, tarnished silver intently. He could still remember the luxurious, cool weight of the dishes in his hands. "If I ever open a restaurant of my own," he said to himself, "this is the type of platter that I will have."

He requested one important modification, however, to the traditional design: the handles on the tops of the covers should be removed and the covers instead be fitted with two small handles, one on each side. This meant that, first of all, the platter covers could be easily stacked. Second, and more important, the covers could be turned over and themselves be used as serving dishes for cold entrees.

The men at Christofle were delighted. They named the platters *les plats Escoffier,* after their inventor.

Yes, he was an inventor. He'd been thinking about this recently as he worked on his cookbook: so much had changed during his lifetime — new ingredients, new flavors, new techniques — yet good cooking remained rooted in tradition and quality.

The *Potage bortsch,* for example, so popular at the Savoy (and extravagantly praised by Lieutenant Colonel Newnham-Davis in his column in the *Pall Mall Gazette:* "About the *Bortsch* soup there could be no two questions, and the cream stirred into the hot, strong liquid makes it, in my humble opinion, the best soup in the world") was new to England but traditional in Russia. Escoffier's preparation depended upon the slow, four-hour cooking of grated beets, fennel, and breast of beef in a large quantity of consommé. It was the quality of that consommé that was paramount. Indeed, he would make the recipe for simple consommé the very first one in his book. For it was things like this that needed to be done right, and that were the basis of all good cooking.

Too many chefs were bastardizing the proper methods, taking shortcuts, their ignorance in technique and training leading to mediocre cooking. Part of the problem was a hunger for the new. "Novelty by hook or by crook!" Escoffier wrote in his book. "It is an exceedingly common mania among people of inordinate wealth to exact incessantly new or so-called new dishes."

What feats of ingenuity have we not been forced to perform, at times, in order to meet our customers' wishes? Those only who have had charge of a large, modern kitchen can tell the tale. Personally, I have ceased counting the nights spent in the attempt to discover new combinations, when, completely broken with the fatigue of a heavy day, my body ought to have been at rest.

And ingenuity was not even properly rewarded! "The painter, sculptor, writer, and musician are protected by law. So are inventors. But the chef has absolutely no redress for plagiarism on his work," Escoffier wrote. His successful recipes would always be copied.

Now that he was laying claim to his legacy and publishing all of his culinary knowledge, including recipes for the dishes that had made him famous, he took pains to counter what he called the "frantic love of novelty" with a proper understanding of the elementary preparations.

It all started with stocks — the "Fonds de Cuisine": "Stock is everything in cooking," Escoffier wrote, "at least in French cooking. Without it, nothing can be done." The secret to excellent stocks was not only to use the best, freshest ingredients, but also to cook them judiciously. "In cooking, care is half the battle."

The simplest consommé, for him, was a work of art. It contained only humble ingredients (beef shin, lean beef, fowl carcasses, onion, carrots, turnips, leeks, celery, and parsnips), but his instructions were detailed, and emphasized the importance of skimming all impurities from the surface of the liquid as it cooked. Once this was done, it could be set on low heat for four or five hours.

Escoffier read over his recipe, all the while thinking: even if one were to follow the detailed instructions precisely as written, there was every chance the stock would be imperfect. Why? And now he wrote an addendum to the recipe, titled:

REMARKS UPON THE DIFFERENT CAUSES WHICH COMBINE TO INFLUENCE THE QUALITY OF A CONSOMMÉ

Obviously, one concern was the meat. It needed to come from comparatively older animals, "whose flesh is well set and rich in flavor," he wrote. "This is a *sine qua non.*" But it was not always easy to find well-aged meat, as he knew from his time at the Savoy. In England, cattle were killed at around three or four years old, far too young to make a decent stock.

The solution was to make a kind of pre-stock, stewing the beef bones for at least twelve hours with some vegetables, so that their gelatinous element would be released into the water. This liquid could then be strained, and used instead of water in the standard consommé recipe.

It sounded complicated and time consuming, but the slow concentration of flavors was the only way to avoid "flat and insipid consommé," which Escoffier knew was all too common. Insipid stock would yield insipid sauces, and it was downhill from there. Best not to take shortcuts.

The weeks leading up to the grand opening of the Hôtel Ritz were frantic. Ritz and Escoffier had assembled what they considered to be the best hotel and restaurant staff in Europe. They poached freely from the Savoy and the Rome Grand: Jacques Kramer, who'd worked at the Savoy, would run the restaurant; Mr. Branchini, from the Grand, would be in charge of reception. Dozens of waiters also came from London and Rome to join the staff. Agostini, as always, was the cashier; and Henry Ellès was to be the hotel's general manager day to day. Escoffier had hired dozens of cooks, and a capable deputy, Georges Gimon, who had worked at numerous restaurants and as the *chef de cuisine* at the Russian embassy in Madrid. Ritz and Echenard would look after the business as a whole — the Ritz Hotel

Syndicate planned to open Ritz hotels in other cities, but first came Paris.

The staff was ready, but the hotel was not. There were no tables and chairs in the restaurant, for example. New furnishings were arriving and being installed every day.

The furniture Ritz and Mewès wanted for the hotel's public areas, exacting reproductions of late seventeenth- and eighteenth-century designs, was expensive — prohibitively expensive, and they were already over budget. But the two men devised a solution that was simple and brilliant, and could only have worked at the Ritz. They asked the furniture manufacturers and merchants to give them the furniture for free, with the understanding that the hotel would sell any item in the lobby to any guest who inquired. Or they would refer the guest to the manufacturer or merchant directly. Knowing just the kind of clientele Ritz would attract to the hotel, the furniture suppliers readily agreed.

It was a similar money-saving impulse that led Ritz to another seemingly strange idea: to solicit advertisements for the deluxe brochure he planned to publish to promote the new hotel. The "booklet," as he referred to it, to be called *The History of the Place Vendôme,* would be a lavishly produced

335

celebration of the hotel and its Paris neighborhood and would be given for free to the hotel's first guests. The cost of printing and binding a few hundred copies of the brochure came to one hundred francs a piece — far too much. And so Ritz approached all the suppliers of the art objects and decorative items found in the hotel and asked if they would like to advertise in the back pages of the booklet. He also visited the luxury shops in the neighborhood: Cartier, Worth, Charvet, all businesses that scorned advertising, on principle, as beneath their dignity. Nevertheless, they agreed to buy ads, and instead of costing money, the promotional booklet made a profit. As with the furniture manufacturers who supplied the lobby, these luxury retailers realized that a Ritz hotel guest might well be a client of theirs, too. Ritz policed the design of all the advertisements, making sure they suited the luxurious atmosphere the booklet presented and that the hotel promised.

Indeed, the hotel was beautiful. Mewès's elegant intermingling of period styles and Ritz's fanatical attention to detail had produced stunning interiors, full of grand gestures and subtle colors — the white marble staircase with a black wrought-iron balustrade and brass handrail, the Oriental carpets, the tapestries, the small pneumatic Swiss clock found in every room, the Baroque gold-plated light switches that turned like keys.

Ritz's investors came to Paris to see the hotel before it opened; every one of them was most impressed. The Christofle silverware. The Baccarat glassware. The luxurious guest rooms, all in pale blues, pinks, yellows, and grays. Everyone noticed the lack of wallpaper, the lack of elaborate bed curtains, the lack of velvets and brocades. The walls in the bedrooms and bathrooms were painted with flat white Dutch paint; the guest-room floors were entirely covered with fitted carpets in light colors. Just as Ritz had demanded, the hotel was resolutely modern, even as Mewès's design sophistication and historical references permeated the building.

"You have created a *chef-d'oeuvre*!" said Robert Crawshay — a masterpiece. Ludwig Neumann had no interest in design or décor, but declared the new hotel to be "the last word in comfort." And Henry Higgins was effusive: "Kings and princes will be jealous of you, Ritz. And they will copy you. You are going to teach the world how to live."

This would turn out to be a prophetic

337

statement, one that went right to the heart of the genius of Ritz's hotel. Out of his intimate knowledge of wealth, his close observation and long association with the aristocracy, his obsequious fascination with the lives of his most glamorous customers, his intuitive understanding of the fantasy and drama and grandeur of the good life — out of all of this, Ritz had distilled the essence of luxury. Only someone like him, an outsider, a man who was sure his peasant hands and feet were far too big and would reveal him to be unworthy, only he could have created the magic of the Hôtel Ritz, the perfect simulacrum of wealth and privilege. And as Higgins noticed, the imitation was in fact superior to the real thing: the aristocrats would soon be copying what they saw at the Ritz, emulating a new and modern version of luxury. Not only aristocrats — everyone. The opulence that the Ritz represented was by definition accessible to all. Americans and Jews, industrialists and the nouveau riche — Ritz would teach them all how to live.

Ritz watched the workers as they hung the metal letters over the archways facing the Place Vendôme. The arcade formed a peristyle, where carriages could enter a recessed covered entrance to the hotel. The words

338

were in all capital letters, formed in wrought iron over an intricate design, one in each of four arches:

RITZ HOTEL RESTAURANT RITZ

Ritz was filled with overwhelming pride and, at the same time, a creeping sense of inadequacy. It was indeed brazen to hang one's name on a building. He couldn't help but see the sign, momentarily, from the perspective of his social superiors. The Prince of Wales, the Duc d'Orléans, Lady de Grey — what would they think of him, of his audacity? Would they laugh at the sight of his name displayed so boldly on the side of a building on the Place Vendôme?

Look what had happened to Barney Barnato: The "little East End Jew," they called him, so rich he carried loose diamonds in his pocket, so rich he had built one of the largest mansions in London, on Park Row, but he was never really respected or accepted — and then it had all fallen apart. A shaky market in South African gold-mining shares was all it took to put him over the edge: while on a ship back from Cape Town in the summer of 1897, Barnato threw himself overboard. Ritz could remember seeing the newspaper item; just a few lines

339

was all the death had merited. He felt a chill as he read the paper that morning. He had considered Barnato a friend.

Barnato had never even moved into that enormous house; it was still under construction when he died.

How high he'd flown, how quickly he'd fallen. . . . And was it really so surprising, given his humble background? And would the same thing happen to Ritz?

Ritz was a snob, he realized. He had internalized all the assumptions and prejudices of the social elite. But this line of thinking was ridiculous. His investors were right: the hotel was stunning. Surely Ritz's name was by now worthy of respect.

Still, he worried. He and Escoffier had left London under a cloud. The lawsuit they'd filed against the Savoy dragged on. And the world was small; his reputation was in doubt.

"What do you think?" he asked his old friend Baron Hans Pfyffer von Altishofen, the younger son of his first employer, Colonel Pfyffer, who came to visit Ritz in Paris just before the grand opening. Hans Pfyffer now ran the Grand Hotel National in Lucerne, where Ritz had worked as a young man; Ritz had hired Hans's brother Alphonse to run the Rome Grand; they had all grown up together.

"Will they come? So much depends upon that! I have sent out invitations to the most select people in Paris society — and to my old London friends. Are they still my friends? Will they come?"

"Of course they'll come," Pfyffer replied. "They'll come if only out of curiosity, Ritz!"

On the morning of Wednesday, June 1, 1898, the day the Hôtel Ritz was set to open, the restaurant's tables finally arrived. This was the last of the furniture — the dining room chairs had come the previous week — and the staff immediately placed them around the room at the direction of Ritz and Mewès.

As this was happening, Ritz sat down at one of the tables and pulled his chair beneath him. He could immediately tell that something was wrong.

"These tables are too high," he said. "They are uncomfortable. They must go back; they must be cut down at once!"

Mewès now joined him at the table. Ritz was right, he said: the tables were a few centimeters too high. But what to do? There was nothing to be done, not now. The hotel's opening reception was that night, and if there were no tables . . .

But Ritz was already out the door, chasing down the workmen who'd delivered the tables in multiple carriages and demanding they take them back.

When he was in a mood like this, Ritz was ferocious, unstoppable. This was exactly the kind of detail at his hotel that *had* to be right.

"These tables must be cut down, finished off properly, and sent back within three hours," he demanded, and no one dared contradict him. Three hours later, the tables were back, and they were the correct height.

The night was rainy, and through the windows of the restaurant the garden and its fountains looked miserable.

Ritz was anxious, as anxious as he'd ever been, as he stood in the small lobby of the hotel wearing his formal black frock coat and white carnation, awaiting the arrival of all "the most select people" in Paris and London he had invited to the reception.

Would they come? The answer was yes, even in the rain. They all came. The Place Vendôme was soon crowded with carriages and footmen, as French society turned out to see the new hotel: Here were the Duc and Duchesse d'Uzès, the Duc and Duchesse de Morny, the Duc and Duchesse de

Rohan; here were nobleman and bon vivant Paul Ernest Boniface de Castellane (universally known as "Boni") and his wife, Anna Gould, daughter of the American railroad tycoon Jay Gould, whom Ritz had served as a waiter twenty-five years earlier; here were society ladies Madame de Breteuil (the young American wife of the French marquis), Madame Jules Porgès (wife of the famous diamond trader), and countless other French noblewomen: the Comtesse de Pourtalès, Princesse Lucien Murat, the Vicomtesse Léon de Janzé, the Comtesse de Salverte, the Marquise de Ganay, the Comtesse de Chevigné, the Marquis Antoine du Bourg de Bozas, and Madame de Lévis-Mirepoix and her daughter.

There was a contingent from London, led by Lady de Grey, including the Hon. Evelyn Fitzgerald (he was a bachelor, and related to the Duke of Leinster); there were journalists: Arthur Meyer, of *Le Gaulois,* James Gordon Bennett Jr., publisher of the *New York Herald,* and Henri Blowitz of the London *Times.* There were Americans (Anthony Drexel Jr., the banker; Mrs. William Corey, wife of the steel magnate), Germans (the Prince of Fürstenberg), wealthy South Americans (the Souza Dantases; Saturno di Unzué), sportsmen (Brazilian aviator Alberto Santos-Dumont), and diplomats (Pierre de Fouquières). And beautiful women, all fans of Escoffier: Katinka was there, and so was Liane de Pougy. And Rothschilds in droves. And the nouveau riche, of course, including all Ritz's investors: Leopold Hirsch, Calouste Gulbenkian, and Louis-Alexandre Marnier Lapostolle. There were writers (among them a young and nervous-looking Marcel Proust) and the art collector Jean Groult.

Many of the out-of-town guests were staying at the hotel, and all were invited to the party. Many were longtime clients of Ritz and Escoffier.

Yes, all of Paris was there — *le tout Paris* — and just as quickly as it opened, the hotel had changed the very definition of the term. A new and cosmopolitan elite, mixing aristocrats and artists; Americans, French, and English; grandes dames and Les Grandes Cocottes; the wealthy, the raffish, the artistic, the well-dressed, the well-traveled — all were welcome at the Ritz. Paris was a city of the salon, of private entertaining, but the opening of the Ritz introduced a seductive, semipublic arena, a stage upon which all might be seen and admired.

■ ■ ■ ■

The opening of the Hôtel Ritz was a triumph, a brilliant success. The only criticism came from a columnist at London's *Truth,* who complained that there were too many flowers — a silly complaint, which Ritz ignored of course — and from Blowitz of the *Times,* who told Ritz that the sides of the bathtub in his suite were much too high. This Ritz took seriously. Blowitz was a very small man, and a longtime friend. Ritz found a small stepladder for him so he could climb into the large bath with ease.

Still, Ritz remained on edge. It was just as Pfyffer had said: everyone would come to an opening party, if for no other reason than curiosity. But would they come back?

The hotel was booked, the restaurant was busy, but Ritz craved more than that. The Ritz must establish itself at the very center of the city's social world, the center of urban sophistication. Paris was much smaller than London, which made things either harder or easier, Ritz wasn't sure. Parisians were set in their ways. But if the tide were to turn, it would turn quickly. Just as at the Savoy in London, the keys to such changes were the habits of society women, the

345

women who entertained.

What could be done, Ritz asked his old friend and client Lady de Grey, to induce chic Parisian women to dine in public? She invited her friends to the restaurant. It made no difference. It continued to rain. Ritz continued to worry.

Two developments proved decisive: The first involved a few glamorous dinner parties at the hotel that month. The Egyptian pasha Izzet Bey hosted a small dinner to which the elite of Parisian society was invited: the Duc and Duchesse d'Uzès, the Duc and Duchesse de Morny, the Duc and Duchesse de Brissac, Vicomte and Vicomtesse de Janzé, Comte and Comtesse Costa de Beauregard . . . When Ritz saw the names on the guest list his mood brightened immediately. The success of the hotel, he knew, required the approval, the imprimatur, of the aristocracy.

Soon enough there was another dinner, and many of the same people were there. Everyone was laughing because the Duchesse d'Uzès had just been arrested for speeding in her motorcar, going twenty miles an hour! The traffic in Paris was terrible, everyone agreed; automobiles and horse-drawn carriages did not mix well.

It was at this dinner, hosted by French

aviator Jacques Balsan and the Marquis de Montesquiou, that Boni de Castellane said to Ritz as he was leaving, "I'm going to dismiss my chef. It's foolish to try to compete with you and Escoffier!" Castellane's approval was significant, for he was known for his taste and style; he was a dandy, a man-about-town.

Castellane did not fire his chef as it turned out, but the point was made. The Hôtel Ritz was chic. Castellane was soon a regular visitor.

The second development was the sudden popularity of "Le Five O'Clock," the hotel's late-afternoon tea service. In good weather, the gardens at the Ritz filled with fashionable women drinking tea and eating tea cakes.

"It breaks my heart," said Escoffier. "The bread, the butter, the jam, the cake and pastries — oh, how can one eat and enjoy dinner, the king of meals, an hour or so later? How can one appreciate the cooking, the food or the wines?"

But the British import of afternoon tea was only cementing the hotel's position in the social order — and bringing the society women who Ritz knew were linchpins of his hotel's success. Escoffier would just have to cook for guests who were full of tea and sweets if need be.

The hotel attracted travelers from England and America in great numbers. More so even than the approval of the French aristocracy, it was the patronage of these wealthy, cosmopolitan travelers flooding the Continent in ever-greater numbers that would ensure the hotel's preeminence. There was no competition in Paris for a hotel that offered truly modern luxuries and conveniences — private bathrooms in every room, for example. Ritz took out advertisements in British newspapers to make his case. In the London *Times,* running the length of an entire column:

HÔTEL RITZ, Place Vendôme, Paris.

UNDOUBTEDLY the most perfect Hotel in Europe.

RESTAURANT RITZ, Place Vendôme, Paris.

A LA CARTE — ALL PRICES MARKED. The Grill Room will be opened very shortly.

OPEN TO NON-RESIDENTS. The most stylish Rendezvous in Paris.

THE HÔTEL RITZ is not a colossal hotel in which the traveler is lost. It has only 100 bed rooms, but each one is accompanied by its private bath-dressing room (hot, cold, shower, needle, etc.) and separate w.c.

CHOICEST COLLECTION OF WINES. Most excellent cuisine. Under supervision of Maître Escoffier.

THE HÔTEL RITZ is situated in the most fashionable quarter of Paris, next to the Ministry of Justice, overlooking its own gardens and those of the ministry.

BOOK YOUR TABLE by telephone before leaving London, No. 243.99.

EACH ROOM is perfectly furnished with a large bed, innumerable cupboards surround the walls, and every appliance for comfort and luxury.

OPENS on the long terraces and gardens, near the fountains. Luncheons can be served in the open air.

EACH ROOM has telephonic communication with Service Rooms, and is lighted by electricity. Pneumatic clocks in every room.

Business was good, and Ritz seemed to relax, finally. One night during the summer of 1899 — the hotel had been open less than a year — he and Marie ate dinner together in the hotel garden, watching the night sky. It was a beautiful June evening, clear and cool. There was a lunar eclipse that night, and they watched along with all the other guests in the garden as the pale moon came into view from behind the black, curved shadow of the earth.

Ritz held Marie's hand during the dramatic moment.

"I too have felt under a dark shadow, Mimi," he said. "You will never know how much my nerves have been on edge. I thought for a while that Dr. Cole was right." Dr. Cole, Ritz's London physician, had long counseled more rest and quiet for the overworked Ritz. Marie also had been worried about her husband working too hard over the past year. The Ritz had consumed him.

"I thought I was in for a real breakdown," he continued. He smiled at Marie reassuringly. "But now everything is right again. Clear sailing ahead!"

Just how wrong he was about that he could not possibly have known.

■ ■ ■ ■

PART 6
RETURN TO
LONDON,
1899–1902

■ ■ ■ ■

16
REVENGE IS SWEET

It was pride that brought them back to London: the chance to return triumphantly to the city they had left in shame. Escoffier and Ritz were both looking for redemption. Or was it revenge?

In 1896, as he was setting up the Ritz Hotel Syndicate, Ritz heard about a new hotel under construction on the corner of Haymarket and Pall Mall, to be called the Carlton. The initial developer of the building had run into financial trouble, and a new group of investors planned to take over the site. Among them were a number of Ritz Hotel Syndicate shareholders, including Henry Higgins and Lord de Grey, and they urged Ritz to get involved. They wanted him to run the place, but at the time, that was impossible. Ritz was free to pursue his own affairs, but working for a competing hotel in London was out of the question, per his agreement with D'Oyly Carte.

Still, they talked.

The Carlton was a grand, ornate, seven-story building with a cupola and an attached playhouse, Her Majesty's Theatre, to be managed by the well-known actor Herbert Beerbohm Tree. The hotel would be state of the art: large and luxurious, with two hundred fifty bedrooms, all with private bathrooms. There was no garden, unfortunately, but there was instead a large, glass-enclosed Palm Court. The Carlton's location was ideal: close to Trafalgar Square, in the heart of London, a ten-minute walk from the Savoy.

Soon after their tumultuous departure from the Savoy, as they were preparing to open the Hôtel Ritz in Paris, Escoffier and Ritz had agreed to go into business with the Carlton once it opened the following year. Ritz would organize and staff the hotel; Escoffier would do the same for the restaurant. A new company was formed, the Carlton Hotel Ltd., with Ritz and Escoffier on the board. (There was significant overlap in the ownership of the Ritz Hotel Syndicate and the Carlton Hotel Ltd., but they were separate companies.)

In the fall of 1898, soon after the Paris hotel had opened, Ritz convinced Mewès to come on board as the interior architect of the Carlton, and they began traveling to London to oversee construction, continuing their collaboration.

The bedroom closets must be much bigger, Ritz declared. And the bathrooms, too. The bathroom was not merely a functional space — it was a locus of luxury. Mewès, meanwhile, came up with the design scheme for the hotel's furnishings — the influences were mostly eighteenth century, mostly English (Chippendale, Adam, and Tudor), with some French touches, too. As at the Paris hotel, Ritz was scrupulous about lighting. There would be no excessive drapery or any wallpaper, needless to say. The walls would be painted white; the doors mahogany.

The opening date was set for July 15, 1899. Ritz wanted to make sure to steal some of the Savoy company's thunder: the previous year, it had rebuilt and reopened Claridge's (a small Mayfair hotel that Ritz himself had helped develop for D'Oyly Carte) and had just bought the Berkeley hotel, also in Mayfair.

The Savoy had struggled at first after the departures of Ritz and Escoffier, but now it was moving at full speed to regain momentum, expanding to meet the seemingly bottomless demand for new luxury hotels in

London. Profits were scarce, but now was the moment to grow, D'Oyly Carte realized, and the acquisition of the Berkeley came with an added bonus: the hotel manager there was a man named George Reeves-Smith. He was thirty-six, had trained in France, and was quite knowledgeable about wine. He would soon take over the management of the Savoy. In the restaurant, meanwhile, there presided a new chef, Monsieur Thouraud, and a manager, known only as Joseph, both from Paris. Thouraud was no Escoffier, but he knew how to cook.

The fight between Ritz and the Savoy had devolved into endless claims and counter-claims: who was at fault, who was blameless, who should have known. Depositions were taken, court dates came and went; neither side gave an inch. The value of shares in the Savoy company had fallen precipitously after Ritz, Echenard, and Escoffier were fired, but had recovered. The fitful financial performance of the Savoy was some consolation for Ritz, but opening a better hotel would be true vindication.

And the Carlton *would* be better than the Savoy — more modern, more luxurious.

As Ritz prepared for the launch, he found that it had become easier. There was by now a formula. Everything he had learned at the

Savoy and then at the Rome Grand and the Hôtel Ritz would be brought to bear at the Carlton. There was truly no one in the world better equipped to open this sort of hotel and restaurant than César Ritz and Auguste Escoffier.

They had invented a new form: The state-of-the-art building. The very best restaurant. The cosmopolitan clientele. Most of all, the sense of drama that infused the enterprise. There was an explicitly theatrical quality to Ritz's hotels: to enter the lobby, to walk into the restaurant, was to step onto a stage of sorts. At the Carlton, Ritz found an opportunity to heighten this feeling: going over the plans for the hotel, he'd seen a way to put the restaurant a short flight of marble steps above the Palm Court, which was at street level.

"This is an expensive idea of yours, Ritz!" said Mr. Waring, of Messrs. Waring, one of the construction firms working on the building. "You take away the street steps and then put the steps at the other end, on the dining room side. It doesn't make sense. What's the idea?"

"So that ladies entering the dining room or leaving it may do so dramatically," said Ritz.

He was, as always, thinking like a director

(and also, as always, not concerning himself too much about costs). A woman in evening dress, sweeping down the stairs into the Palm Court, all eyes on her . . . Yes, as far as Ritz was concerned, the lobby and the restaurant constituted a stage set.

"Don't stop him," said Henry Higgins. "He knows what he's about. Go ahead, Ritz. Have your drama — and we'll pay for it."

The Carlton building was fully electric, of course, and also outfitted with an innovative ventilation system: fresh air in summer would be passed over blocks of ice and cooled and then pumped into guest rooms with enormous fans; in winter, the air could be heated if necessary. According to the designer of the system, a Mr. R. G. Lovell, the air could even be scented if the hotel manager so desired.

The windows of the building were double-paned for soundproofing and mounted on a new kind of pivoting hinge, which allowed the exterior to be cleaned from the inside. The walls of the hotel were coated with fireproof plaster. Every guest room contained a telephone connected to all of the hotel offices and to the central exchange.

The main restaurant at the Carlton was grander and airier than that at the Savoy; the color scheme was cream and rose.

Downstairs was the Grill Room, and here Ritz had placed electric lights between panes of frosted glass for warm, indirect lighting.

"The Carlton Hotel is, without question, the most modern and up-to-date in its arrangements, its equipment, and its decoration of any hotel in Europe," reported the *Western Mail* in the weeks before the hotel opened. "The directors have spared no expense."

César and Marie Ritz arrived together in London in early July 1899 to prepare for the opening. They'd come across the Channel to Southampton and, on the way over, had seen Sir Thomas Lipton's new yacht, the *Shamrock,* anchored in Hythe. It was a stunning boat, and would be competing in the America's Cup race later that year.

Lipton had long fascinated Ritz; he followed the businessman's career in the newspapers. (He had admired the flamboyant Barney Barnato in the same way, although in the case of Barnato, Ritz actually knew him personally.) Like Ritz, Lipton was a self-made man. He'd been born poor in Glasgow and had founded a chain of grocery and provision shops called Lipton's Markets, and then made a fortune importing and selling tea.

They were the same age, Ritz and Lipton — contemporaries, Ritz would often say. When Lipton was knighted by Queen Victoria the previous year, Ritz had said to Marie, "We're both on top now!"

He wasn't entirely serious, of course. Ritz was not a millionaire, and he had not been knighted, but he had achieved some success, some recognition, and he, too, had come from nothing. To think that his parents had lived and died in Niederwald, had never even left Switzerland, not once, and here he was, the proprietor of the Hôtel Ritz in Paris, the most famous hotelier in the world, and now he was opening a new property in London.

He could still vividly remember his first trip to London, ten years ago, to attend the grand opening of the Savoy. How amazed he'd been at the sheer scale of the city, the vastness of it, the unfathomable wealth. He was electrified. He had seen the future, *his* future.

He could also of course remember his departure from the city the previous year: the burning shame at being dismissed, the indignation, the ignominy.

Here he was again, and how much had changed.

It was the memory of that humiliation that had brought him back. He had succeeded in Paris, and he would retake London. He was working harder than ever.

The Paris hotel was booming: it was on track to make a significant profit in its first year, £10,555, which the Savoy certainly hadn't done. Indeed, the Hôtel Ritz would be paying a 7 percent dividend to ordinary shareholders. More important, all the Savoy's best clients came to the Hôtel Ritz when they were in Paris: Nellie Melba, the Rothschilds, the Goulds, the Vanderbilts. The Prince of Wales had come to the Ritz, breaking his long tradition of staying at the Bristol when in Paris, and numerous members of the Marlborough House set came too. Ritz had every reason to expect his clients would follow him to the Carlton when they were in London.

Yes, the Carlton was magnificent. Grander, taller, more elegant than the Savoy, it was a true palace hotel. The public support of the Prince of Wales was invaluable: the Carlton would soon be a royal destination. In fact, Ritz had designed a semiprivate balcony area just off the Palm Court with the prince himself in mind. "There will be a few palms there," Ritz had explained to Henry Higgins — for privacy.

"The Prince of Wales will appreciate having a corner of the Palm Room to himself, and a little removed, where he and his friends can have their coffee and listen to the orchestra undisturbed."

This was a daring assumption on Ritz's part, and it was based on his intuitive understanding of the Prince of Wales and of the shifting crosscurrents of fame and privacy. By tradition and protocol, royalty ate and entertained in private, but Ritz knew that the prince thrived in public, and would welcome the discreet yet still visible semi-seclusion of the balcony.

César moved into the hotel two weeks before the grand opening, which was set for July 15, 1899. Marie and her mother were in Golders Green with the two boys, Charles and René, opening up the house in the country. This was the same property they had rented when Ritz worked at the Savoy. He would visit on weekends. In the meantime, he took a suite on the fifth floor, which was also where Escoffier was staying, along with other members of the staff.

The opening of the Carlton seemed easier to Ritz than the opening of the Paris hotel had been. Partly this was because it was less personal. The Carlton wasn't named for him, after all. Also, they'd gotten better at it. The grand opening was by now a routine. Still, there were endless details, and Ritz was up late every night, walking the halls of the hotel, just as he'd done in Paris, making last-minute adjustments, training new members of his staff. Marie would worry about his health — he was working too hard — but Ritz was racing to the finish. He had the uncanny ability to look at a newly made bed, for example, and immediately tell if something wasn't quite right.

"Something wrong here," he would say.

Marie later described what would happen next: "Sure enough, when the maid pulled back the covers it would be found that the blankets had not been tucked in sufficiently, or the sheet not folded back properly, or the pillows not puffed up to the right degree."

The night before the Carlton was to open, the staff held an impromptu party in the hotel restaurant. They were a family of sorts; many of them had worked for Ritz and Escoffier for years. Echenard, Autour, Kramer, and Branchini — all had been at the Savoy or the Grand, and then at the Hôtel Ritz, and were now in London for the next chapter. There was an equally devoted and experienced staff in Paris, too — longtime hands Ellès and Agostini; joined by the new chef, Gimon, who had distinguished himself

365

as Escoffier's deputy and been given the top job; the maître d', Olivier Dabescat; and at the reception desk, Victor Rey — all at the beginning of what would be long careers at the Ritz.

Indeed, Ritz and Escoffier's men were devoted. They came from working-class families, just as their employers had, and their lives were transformed by the success of the hotels and restaurants for which they worked. Escoffier, for example, had long made a point of fighting for decent wages, decent living conditions, and the recognition of the restaurant staff as professionals. He paid them a fair wage, and he did his best to ensure their accommodations were adequate.

Most of the staff lived in nearby apartments provided by the hotel. Such staff quarters were traditionally small and dingy — department stores and other large retail establishments in London, for example, housed their staff in warrens of rooms, sometimes in the upper floors of the same building. This was not the case at the newly built luxury hotels with elevators, for which the upper floors were valuable real estate. Instead, the staff was housed in separate residence halls; in the case of the Carlton, these quarters were surprisingly appealing.

Escoffier made sure of that.

One new recruit from Paris had been shocked to be shown to a pleasant, comfortable bedroom when he arrived in London. There was even a bathroom!

The luxury of a simple bathroom could not be overstated. Escoffier beamed when he heard about the new cook's amazement, and told Ritz about it.

Escoffier's pride in his work was infectious; his calm, gentlemanly demeanor showed a new way to be a chef. Ritz, meanwhile, was voluble and intense, a difficult boss, but also as ferociously loyal to his staff as they were to him. He had led them all to unfathomably elegant and quite profitable careers, in which they had daily contact with the good life, however tangential, with all the glamour of modern London. They shared a kind of reverence for the luxury they had created, even as it remained untouchable in some way, unreachable.

But the world of the kitchen, and of the waitstaff, was insular in its own way, too, as distinct and impenetrable as that of the restaurant's aristocratic clientele. They were a brotherhood, a tribe. They spoke their own language.

Now, as the staff gathered in the glittering

new restaurant, they drank champagne and celebrated a new beginning. Some of the waiters, after a few drinks, wrapped themselves in white bath towel togas and raised their arms in mock Roman salutes.

"Hail, César! Hail, César!" they cheered. "Hail, César!"

Ritz and Escoffier laughed, all the wound-up anticipatory tension of the previous weeks dissolving in the moment. Ritz gave a silly speech, in the style of a grand oration. Friends, Romans, countrymen! Everyone laughed some more. The Carlton will conquer London!

"Hail, César!"

Escoffier loved being back in London. He'd come in March 1899, after training Gimon to take over the kitchen at the Hôtel Ritz, and spent a few months preparing the Carlton kitchen and hiring staff. Just like Ritz in setting up new hotels, Escoffier was by now exceedingly proficient when it came to the necessary arrangements for a new hotel restaurant kitchen. He brought in key staff members from the Hôtel Ritz in Paris and poached numerous cooks he'd trained in the Savoy and Rome Grand kitchens.

He had missed London, of all places. Who would have thought? He'd always claimed to hate the place, but the truth was that in Paris, Escoffier was a great chef at a great restaurant, while in London he was *the* French chef. He was famous. And in his own modest way, he quite liked being famous.

As he had at the Savoy, Escoffier was offering prix fixe menus, customizing them according to guests' preferences. The restaurant at the Carlton almost immediately catapulted to the top ranks of restaurants in London. "Do you want to give your friend, your brother, or your cousin who is returning from the front with the C.I.V. one of the best meals procurable in London?" asked the *Daily Mail,* referring to City of London Imperial Volunteers fighting the Boer War in South Africa, which had begun soon after the hotel opened. Indeed, it was a common sight at the Carlton at the time: soldiers in full regalia, just back from the war, and others getting ready to ship out, celebrating a last great dinner in London.

The recipe book was on the back burner, temporarily. Escoffier was too busy at the Carlton. Also, he had found a new distraction: a woman named Rosa Lewis.

Like him, Lewis was a cook — a great cook. She was younger than Escoffier, in her early thirties, and she had found success as a private caterer in London in the 1890s. She'd come up as a servant, working for the Orléans family, among others, learning French cooking techniques. Later, she was hired to cook and serve dinners for various prominent hosts and hostesses in London: the Duc d'Orléans, Lady Randolph Churchill. The Prince of Wales had taken note of her cooking, and of her beauty, and her success had thus been assured. (He famously greeted her with a kiss at a Chieveley Park shooting party where she was cooking, not realizing that she was hired help. What happened to the lady in white? he asked the hostess. Told that she was the cook, he said, "But, I kissed her." The hostess replied, "Then we shall certainly have a very excellent dinner!")

Escoffier and Lewis had numerous clients in common; it was only a matter of time before their paths crossed. She was brash, outspoken, and strikingly beautiful. He was London's dean of French cooking. They talked about recipes, his work on his book, her desire to open a small hotel of her own. Their bond was food, but they talked about everything. They were soon close friends.

After the Carlton opened, Escoffier's daily routine was consistent: he was up at 6:30 a.m., leaving his fifth-floor apartment for his first-floor office, greeting Frank the night porter in the elevator. At around 7:00, he would walk down one of two staircases to the kitchen, to check on the breakfast service. The cooks were kept on edge, for they never knew which set of stairs Escoffier would use, or on which side of the kitchen he would appear. He would confer with the *chef de nuit,* just going off duty, and check on the day's deliveries: certain vegetables and fruits, cheeses, butter, foie gras, lamb, and fowl all came from France by train in baskets from Les Halles food market, marked "Reserved for the Carlton Hotel, London." Most fish (sole, trout, salmon, turbot) came from local suppliers.

Needless to say, Escoffier was scrupulous about the deliveries and payments; there would be no questions about commissions or bribes or anything of the sort. He had learned his lesson.

He took his breakfast and a French newspaper to his office, and checked in with Ritz and Echenard. Who was coming to lunch and dinner that day? Later in the morning, Escoffier would sit at his desk and draw up menus for all the prix fixe reservations. Then it was back to the kitchen for lunch. In the afternoon, he was free for three hours, and he would go for a walk in St.

James Park, not far from the hotel. Or he would play billiards, or read. Sometimes he would visit Rosa Lewis.

As with Sarah Bernhardt, there was an innocent romance and flirtation about Escoffier's friendship with Lewis. He loved women — cooking for them, seducing them with his talent, naming recipes for them — but he was a proper gentleman, courtly and correct. People may have talked about him and Bernhardt (he'd brought food to her room at the Savoy!) and they talked about him and Lewis, too. Escoffier didn't care.

For dinner, he was back in the kitchen, overseeing the *chefs de partie,* calling out the orders, examining each plate before it went out to the dining room. He himself would visit the dining room to greet certain guests, and to take the temperature of the room, smiling and nodding as he passed the crowded tables.

It was a long day, ending around midnight. He would make himself a nightcap: an egg yolk whisked with sugar, a bit of champagne, and a cup of hot milk. It was his own recipe — the secret to his good health, he was sure. His mind would turn to his cookbook as he drifted off to sleep. As soon as he had a bit more free time, he would finish what he'd started.

17

HE TOAST OF THE TOWN

1ary 3, 1900, about six months after
lton had opened, Ritz, Escoffier, and
rd finally ended their legal battle
Savoy. It was hopeless; they had no
of winning in court. Indeed, just the
e — if they went to court, they
be humiliated.

Savoy's countersuit had turned up all
of evidence against the three of them.
board of directors' Committee of
stigation, which had gathered the evi-
ce used to fire them, had continued its
rk after Ritz and the other two filed their
wsuit claiming wrongful termination. The
umerous interviews with the Savoy's food
suppliers, for example, were damning. All
the underweight deliveries, all the kickbacks.
Many of the suppliers had also been sued
by the Savoy, and agreed to repay the hotel
for the overcharges. The Hudson Brothers
grocers, for example, paid £3,179; Bel-

lamy's and the other vendors paid a t*al of*
£4,908.

Ritz had no interest in going to cour
losing. He'd been embarrassed en*d*
already. Fortunately for him, D'Oyly C
and the other board members at the S
had no interest in going to court either,
if they were assured of winning. They,
had had enough of the whole affair. A
the evidence did not exactly show them
the best light: The kickbacks had been g
ing on for years. Why had it taken them
long to notice? Wasn't it their duty as boar
members to guard the interests of th
shareholders, and hadn't they failed in this
Furthermore, the Savoy was doing reason-
ably well under the leadership of Reeves-
Smith, and D'Oyly Carte did not want to
distract his staff.

Ritz, Escoffier, and Echenard agreed to
sign confessions, and to repay the hotel
what they owed. The Savoy agreed to keep
the confessions a secret.

Escoffier's confession was the shortest but
also the most serious, admitting to actual
crimes. He confessed to being "on commission" and to having accepted bribes from
his suppliers. The Savoy's losses, according
to the auditors, totaled more than £16,000;
Hudson Brothers, Bellamy's, and the others

had agreed to pay £8,087; Escoffier was to pay the rest, a total of £8,000.

He did not have the money. He would sign the confession, he said, but he simply did not have the money. The Savoy agreed to accept a fraction of the amount in repayment: £500, which was all that Escoffier could come up with.

Ritz and Echenard, meanwhile, signed a confession listing numerous sins: failing to provide oversight of their staff, including Escoffier; giving away wine and food to customers for free; extending credit to their friends; pursuing outside business interests in violation of Ritz's contract; entertaining investors in the Savoy's private dining rooms; overpurchasing wine, cigars, and other goods from suppliers in which they had an interest. In their confession, Ritz and Echenard strenuously denied "that they have ever been guilty of appropriating or applying to their own use the monies of the Savoy Hotel Company, or taking monies by way of presents or commissions from the tradesmen of the Hotel."

Nevertheless, they agreed to repay a total of £4,173.

Ritz also agreed to buy an enormous quantity of wine from the Savoy cellars, much of it supplied by two friends of Ritz's, the wine dealers Mr. Strauss and Mr. Lesta-pis. The wine did not sell, and yet he had continued to buy it. Ritz would buy the remaining stock of these and many other wines, for a total of £6,377. (This money would come not from him personally but from the Carlton, which would take the wine.)

All told, the Savoy would recoup a total of £19,137 — a significant amount. By way of comparison, the hotel's total profits in 1898, the year Ritz, Escoffier, and Echenard were fired, had been £20,276.

Ritz was glad to put the past behind him. He had the future to contend with. Yes, it was a disappointment to lose, to sign a confession, to admit to wrongdoing. But he did not feel guilty, no matter what he'd signed. He was innocent — he had made the Savoy what it was. Besides, so much had changed since he'd filed his legal claim against the Savoy the week he was fired by the hotel. He had launched the Hôtel Ritz, the best hotel in Paris, and then the Carl-ton, the best hotel in London.

The Prince of Wales had already eaten at the Carlton more than once. As Ritz had predicted, the balcony of the Palm Court had become one of the prince's favorite spots for entertaining. And the prince had also eaten in public, right there in the restaurant, rather than in a private room. This had never happened before — and it set a new precedent. True to his word, the Price of Wales had followed Ritz.

Richard D'Oyly Carte had written a letter to the prince in February 1899, explaining his side of the story because of "the importance we all attach to the good opinion of your Royal Highness." He outlined the case against Ritz — the "gross negligence and breaches of duty and mismanagement" that had been found by none other than the Hon. Charles Russell, who'd been in charge of the investigation. The Prince of Wales never replied.

The Carlton became the center of social, glamorous London at the turn of the new century. Ritz and Escoffier were arranging elaborate dinners for aristocrats, Americans, and the nouveau riche; Indian maharajas were reserving entire floors of the hotel at once. As he'd done at the Savoy, Ritz instituted an "evening dress essential" rule for the dining rooms at the Carlton, guaranteeing a glittering, formal atmosphere. There was a certain amount of grumbling about this from some quarters — indignant letters to the editors of local papers, written by elderly upper-class gentlemen who'd been turned away from the Carlton for wearing tweeds. The hotel was catering to new money, they complained bitterly. Only uncouth Americans and the nouveau riche would want to dress up to enter a public restaurant.

The complainers may have been right, but Ritz didn't care. The restaurant was full.

And it wasn't only the Carlton that was doing well — so was the Savoy, and so were the other new hotels that had opened in recent years: the Cecil, an enormous hotel on the Strand; the Coburg (later renamed the Connaught), just off Grosvenor Square. London was booming.

In early June 1899, Sarah Bernhardt checked in to the Carlton for a six-week stay. She arrived in dramatic fashion as usual, sweeping into the lobby at 8:30 p.m. wearing a long, white traveling cloak, a white veil, and a sable muff, and carrying a large bouquet of flowers. Her ferry across the Channel had been delayed because of rough water — she was coming from Paris — and she'd been greeted at Charing Cross Station by a cheering throng of admirers, and numerous French and English newspaper reporters all hoping for a word from the actress. She smiled and said nothing, climbing into a waiting carriage that took her to the hotel.

Bernhardt would be performing in two plays, *Cyrano de Bergerac* and *L'Aiglon,* both by Edmond Rostand, at Her Majesty's Theatre, adjacent to the Carlton. She'd been followed to the hotel by the eager press, but went straight to her room with her entourage. Escoffier himself went to her room to welcome her.

It was a sign of the Carlton's status as the best hotel in London that Bernhardt would choose to stay there. And it was also a reflection of her long-standing friendship with Escoffier. He would soon have a chance to cook a dinner in her honor, hosted later that month by Benoît-Constant Coquelin, the French actor. It had been Coquelin, years earlier at the Savoy, who had congratulated Ritz and Escoffier for making England "fit to live in" by serving the sort of excellent food that a Frenchman needed in London.

Escoffier made what he called *Filets de sole Coquelin* for the amusing host — sole gently cooked in fish stock and served with a sauce made of the poaching liquid enriched with cream and egg yolks. Around the dish were small boiled potatoes. And for dessert, Escoffier created *Pêches Aiglon,* named for the play Bernhardt was then starring in. The peaches were poached in vanilla syrup, served over vanilla ice cream, and sprinkled with crystallized violets. The dish was presented in a carved ice sculpture in the shape of an eaglet — the "Aiglon" of the title.

Bernhardt's role had her playing scenes from the life of Napoléon II — "L'Aiglon" was his sobriquet — all drama, melancholy, anger, and despair. She had played male characters before (Hamlet, for example); still, it was this fact that had caught everyone's attention. How would the fifty-five-year-old woman play the man who had died at age twenty-one in 1832? Would it work? There had been much speculation.

Yes, it had worked, and triumphantly so, everyone at the Carlton dinner agreed, raising their glasses and cheering as Escoffier brought his dessert to Bernhardt. There were mostly theater people in attendance, including actors Sir Henry Irving and George Alexander, and the manager of Her Majesty's Theatre, Herbert Beerbohm Tree.

They discussed the stellar notices the play had received, and Bernhardt's daring, emotional performance. And they talked about travel and technology and how fast the world was transforming at the dawn of the new century.

Life seemed to move faster than it had even in the early 1890s, if that was possible. Automobiles and aviation, dirigibles and bicycles, telephones and X-rays and animated photographs — all inventions and advances that seemed to debut at world's fairs and then rather quickly become ubiquitous. Amateur photography was suddenly a popular hobby. Music halls had begun showing moving pictures projected on screens.

Women's rights was another perennial topic of conversation — the growing movement for women's suffrage, for example — as was dress reform. Gowns, meanwhile, had gotten tighter and more revealing; the Neena brand "bust improver" was "modeled on that of the famous Venus de Milo," its manufacturers claimed. The voluptuous "Gibson Girl" look had been imported from America. Dresses fit tightly across the hips, a shocking novelty.

It was all there to be seen and discussed in the dining room at the Carlton, the very center of sophisticated London.

Lt. Col. Nathaniel Newnham-Davis wrote up the Carlton restaurant for his syndicated column, "La Vie de Luxe." He loved it, describing the palm court with its "enticing wicker chairs, its deep, broad green sofas, its spread of palm leaves, its glistening floor spread with crimson rugs, its columns of creamy marble." He admired the lighting, so flattering, he said, to the ladies and their dresses. As usual, he took note of duchesses wearing diamond tiaras and American women and their pearls. "There are always interesting people to be seen dining in this great banqueting room," he reported, "and the world of society, the world of art, and the world of money meet here on equal terms."

Most of all, Newnham-Davis showered praise on Escoffier, on the lightness and delicacy of the cooking — "it is a work of art, and gives anticipatory pleasure and leaves all the pleasures of memory behind it." He ordered the borscht (his favorite), the *filet de poulet* in paprika, the lamb, the *mousse de jambon* ("Escoffier's mousse is always a dream of a delight"), and quails, ortolans, and asparagus. Dessert was the *Pêches Aiglon,* of course, added to the menu after debuting at Coquelin's dinner for Bernhardt. In this case, the presentation was even more dramatic: the eaglet ice sculpture upon which the peaches were served had glowing eyes, lit from within by a concealed lamp.

The review also mentioned Ritz: "He finds the management of this great hotel, of the Ritz in Paris, and half a dozen other caravansaries scattered about Europe, sits very lightly on his shoulders."

It was a gross exaggeration to say that Ritz was managing a half dozen hotels in Europe. Yes, it was true that he maintained informal contact with many hotels, places where he had worked or consulted in the past, and to which he would frequently refer guests. He would make sure his clients received excellent treatment at the Frankfurter Hof in Frankfurt — he owned shares in the hotel, which he'd helped open in the 1890s — the National in Lucerne, the Grand in Monte Carlo, the Grand Hôtel des Iles Britanniques in Menton, all places where he was known and respected.

Ritz was busy enough managing the two best hotels in Europe, the Carlton and the Ritz, and he and his backers had recently bought the Grand Hôtel des Thermes, a health spa in the tiny Italian village of Salsomaggiore in the Apennines, northeast of Genoa.

Salsomaggiore was nothing more than a spot on the map before Ritz bought and renovated the small hotel and, almost immediately, made it a fashionable destination. The village had long been a place where invalids came to recuperate in the hot springs. Now, suddenly, there was what was called the "English season," in the spring, and again in early fall. Clients of the Ritz Paris and Carlton soon heard that Ritz had opened a luxurious health retreat, and made their reservations. Train service from Bologna was extended to reach the town; new shops and hotels began to open on the tiny main street.

Ritz had again brought in Mewès to design the interiors: The hotel was to be ultra-hygienic, and painted all white. The windows were shaded with slatted screens rather than curtains; everything was designed to be easily cleaned. Each of the five floors had its own thermal bath, so guests need not wander about the hotel in their robes and blankets or be carried in bath chairs, a common sight at other resorts.

The Duke and Duchess of Devonshire were among the first visitors, and they were followed by the rest of English and Italian society, and by opera stars including Adelina Patti, Enrico Caruso, and Edouard and Jean de Reszke. The vapor baths were good for the throat, the singers said — and soon they were calling it the "Salso cure," to be taken before the dramatic or musical season.

Salsomaggiore was a place people came for their health, but equally a place for fun. Ritz arranged dinners and parties for his guests, just as he did in London and Paris. A dinner for the Duc d'Orléans, for example, featured a small evergreen tree as the table centerpiece, and perched on one of its branches was a goldfinch. The women at the dinner fed the bird crumbs — it was attached to the tree with a thread around its foot. Eventually, after dinner, the bird was freed by Princess Isabelle, but instead of flying away, it flew back and landed in her golden hair, causing everyone to laugh hysterically.

Ritz was traveling constantly among his hotels — April in Salsomaggiore, back to London for the start of the season, then to Paris for the "Grande Semaine" in June, then back to London, and back to Italy, and back to Paris again, with stops in Frankfurt and Switzerland along the way. It was a never-ending rush of trains.

Wherever he was, he stayed in touch with his staff at all the hotels, checking in on reservations, who was arriving and departing. He used the telephone and telegraph and kept up a large business correspondence, devoted mostly to the preferences and proclivities of his guests. (Mail was quite efficient, and still generally the way guests would make their reservations, although use of the telephone was more and more common.) Marie described her husband's letters:

Madame So-and-so abominated butter and ate dry toast for breakfast; Mr. So-and-so was inordinately fond of cherry jam for tea; Sir A. drank a certain mineral water and liked to have a bottle of it on his night table; Lord B. drank one brand of whisky and no other; the Duchess of Such-and-such slept but with one pillow; the Marquis de Tel et Tel could not tolerate music with his meals; Prince So-and-so liked his beefsteak almost raw; Baron von This or That was very tall and would require an eight-foot bed; Lady This or That wanted to be awakened every morning at half-past seven sharp. And so on and so on. Again and again gratified clients would arrive for the first time in some hotel recommended by Ritz, and again and again upon their return to us they would express with almost tearful emotion their delight at the way they had been received and treated, the magical way in which their least wishes had been anticipated.

Ritz had never been happier — despite working as relentlessly as ever. His influence spanned the Continent; his energy, perfectionism, and savoir faire had found their ultimate expression in his role as the mastermind of modern luxury. Ritz had long been admired, but now he was building an empire, one that embodied a new standard of service and comfort. His guests were heard to say, "I don't need a valet when I stop at a Ritz hotel." This was new, and a powerful sign of the changes the 1890s had wrought. The era of traveling with a coterie of servants was coming to an end. The world was faster, smaller, more cosmopolitan, more open to women, and ever more in need of practical, accessible comfort. The rise of the automobile had made shorter trips possible (from one's country estate to London and back again, for example) and increased the demand for hotels. Society was entertaining in restaurants as well as at home. Escoffier and Ritz were famous because they, along with those who followed them, were indispensable to this new way of life. Indeed, they had helped invent it.

The need for new hotels, meanwhile, was undiminished, as Henry Higgins and other of Ritz's backers continued to point out.

They had their eye on Piccadilly: the old Walsingham Hotel was for sale. The perfect site for a new Ritz.

18

A New King and a Nervous Breakdown

On January 22, 1901, Queen Victoria died. She was eighty-one.

It was the end of an era, and the beginning of a new one. The Prince of Wales would ascend to the throne. The playboy prince, the hedonistic gourmet, was now king.

The first thing that crossed Ritz's mind when he heard the news: he would be losing his best customer. No longer would the prince be eating dinner at the Carlton, his favorite restaurant, or listening to the orchestra beneath the palm trees, sitting semi-secluded with his friends and many beautiful women on the balcony. The free-wheeling days of the Marlborough House set would come to an end.

Or perhaps not; yes, of course, now that the Prince of Wales was King Edward V II he would be more restrained by protocol and tradition. But there was every reason to hope that high society more generally would flourish. For one thing, there would be no end of celebratory dinners and gala events toasting the new king. And the coronation itself would be the most lavish celebration London had ever seen. Ritz would make sure the Carlton was at the center of it.

The beginning of the twentieth century also saw the deaths of Arthur Sullivan and Richard D'Oyly Carte. Sullivan died in November 1900, of a heart attack; he was fifty-eight. He and Gilbert had been at odds again, ever since their final opera, *The Grand Duke,* flopped badly in 1896. They had recently attempted a reconciliation: Helen had proposed that Gilbert, Sullivan, and her husband, all of them ill, take the stage together at the Savoy Theatre during a revival of *Patience*. It was the first play ever performed at the Savoy, back in 1881 — their satire of the aesthetic movement. In a comic turn, Gilbert, Sullivan, and D'Oyly Carte were to be wheeled out in invalid chairs at the end of the performance — the crowd would go wild! Unfortunately, Sullivan was too ill. "Please tell Gilbert how very much I feel the disappointment," he wrote to D'Oyly Carte. "Good luck to you all. Three invalid chairs would have looked *very well* from the front."

Gilbert and D'Oyly Carte went ahead without Sullivan, hobbling onstage with walking sticks — they dropped the invalid chair idea — old men taking a valedictory bow.

Sullivan died a few weeks later. D'Oyly Carte died in April 1901, at home. He was fifty-six and had suffered through years of illness, cared for by Helen. She was devastated.

"You ask me not to write but I must just thank you for your kind, loving words," she wrote in response to a letter of condolence from Haidee Crofton, who had toured with the D'Oyly Carte company back in the 1880s:

I don't know how to write or speak of myself — I am practically dead. I don't ask anything now but to be let go quickly to join him. When I see how his dear old friends — like you — regret his going — I feel they will know a little of what it has meant to me. We had got so close through these years of suffering and weakness that of late he was more to me my dearly loved child — my one thing to protect and care for. It is all over now — and I suppose the less I say the better.

Helen moved into the Beaufort Buildings, part of the newly expanded Savoy Hotel. With the help of her stepson, Rupert D'Oyly Carte, she would continue to look after the hotel and theater, as she had for years. George Reeves-Smith, the new hotel manager, was promoted to managing director of the company.

The coronation of King Edward was announced during what would have been the height of the summer season in 1901. London society was still in mourning for the queen, putting a damper on entertaining in general, and certainly on the sort of grand dinners and galas routinely held at the Carlton. News of the coronation, therefore, was most welcome, and especially to Ritz. It would take place the following summer, on June 26, 1902.

The entire city, the entire empire, even, would celebrate as never before. Royalty and political leaders from around the world would be in attendance; there would be military processions (soldiers from every part of the empire), and there would be fireworks. The planning stretched out over months. The London *Times* reported:

The Central Coronation Bonfires Committee have issued a circular in which they suggest that the bonfires should all be lighted simultaneously at 10 o'clock, Greenwich time, on June 26. The committee recommend that for England, Ireland, and Wales, a detonating rocket should be sent from any principal height at 9:55 p.m. to call attention; that at 10 o'clock a magnesium star rocket should be fired, to be followed by other rockets, the bonfires be lighted, and the National Anthem sung. Where possible, the hills should be specially illuminated at the same time with red, white, and blue colored fires.

There followed an extremely long and detailed set of instructions about how to safely construct a bonfire and light fireworks, including information about the official "Royal pyrotechnicists to the King, Messrs. James Pain & Son," who would provide the rockets at a 25 percent discount to bona fide members of the National Bonfire Union.

Banks and law courts would all be closed on Thursday the twenty-sixth, and the following day as well. Carriage traffic in central London was to be shut down along the coronation procession route, from Buckingham Palace to Westminster Abbey and back again; enormous crowds were expected. The newspapers ran articles with headlines such as "How to See the Coronation," with advice about traffic, where along the route was the best place to catch a glimpse of the procession, and, for the six thousand people with invitations to the coronation itself, how and by which door to enter the abbey.

As it turned out, there was no better place to see the procession than from the Carlton Hotel, on Pall Mall: the king and queen would pass by on their way back to Buckingham Palace. Every room at the hotel was booked, as was every table at the restaurant. In honor of the king, there would be a gala dinner for five hundred people on the evening of the twenty-sixth, including numerous high-profile guests attending the coronation. Many of them would be wearing formal court dress; it was sure to be a glittering affair. There would be a large contingent of Americans present, including New York senator Chauncey Depew and his wife; members of the prominent Widener and Elkins families; the banker Samuel Reading Bertron and his wife; and San Francisco newspaper publisher M. H. de Young and his wife. Americans, anti-monarchic by nature, had not come to

London in great numbers to celebrate the coronation, but the Carlton still seemed to be full of them.

For Ritz, the gala dinner was a bittersweet occasion because the king himself would not be there. Indeed, the gala would be unlike any Ritz had ever organized: there was no client footing the bill and sending invitations. The Carlton hotel was the host — in the form of Ritz himself, and Escoffier, too, honoring their longtime client and most favored guest.

The weeks before the coronation were an unending rush of logistics and preparations. The flowers, the décor, the orchestra; the menu, the wines, the placement of tables — all the usual juggling, planning, and improvising.

And then there was the problem of the views.

Not every room at the Carlton had windows facing Pall Mall from which to see the royal procession. Bad luck for those facing the courtyard! But Ritz was determined that all of his guests should be able to see the historic event, and one by one, he prevailed upon those with Pall Mall–facing rooms to allow others to join them. These gatherings were being called "window parties." Inviting fellow hotel guests to your window was in the spirit of the occasion, Ritz said — the coronation was a once-in-a-lifetime event. It took all his persuasive tact, but Ritz succeeded. Every room in the hotel overlooking the street below would be filled. The hotel had also constructed an outdoor viewing stand on Pall Mall. One way or another, every guest would be able to witness the royal procession.

Ritz was always high strung, and even more so as the great event approached. He would return home to Golders Green in an exhausted state, completely drained. "Don't worry, Mimi," he would say. "I'm not ill, only tired. When this is all over I'll take a long rest, I promise you."

Ritz's physician and friend Dr. Cole had been admonishing him about his health for years. Ritz needed to relax more, to take walks in the country. That was indeed one of the reasons he and Marie had taken the house in Golders Green. Now, Marie feared, he was pushing himself too hard: the constant travel, the multiple hotels to oversee, the plans to open more, and, most of all, the coming celebrations at the Carlton to organize.

Ritz would sit in the garden with his eyes closed. And then he would say, as he often did, *"Eh bien!* We might as well face it. I'm an old man now!" (He was fifty-two.) Marie laughed, but found it harder than ever to rouse her husband from his periodic dark moods.

Escoffier had designed the ultimate menu for the royal banquet, a series of dishes that were elegant, classically French with international touches (the Chinese bird's nest soup), and, in some cases, named for Queen Victoria, Queen Alexandra, and the new king:

CAVIAR FRAIS
Fresh caviar

MELON CANTALOUP
Cantaloupe

❀

CONSOMMÉ AUX NIDS D'HIRONDELLES
Bird's nest soup

❀

VELOUTÉ ROYAL AUX CHAMPIGNONS BLANCS
Cream of mushroom soup

PAILLETTES AU PARMESAN
Puff pastry with Parmesan

MOUSSELINE DE SOLE VICTORIA
Sole mousse with lobster and truffle sauce

❀

POULARDE EDOUARD VII
Poached chicken with curry sauce

CONCOMBRES AU CURRY
Curried cucumbers

❀

NOISETTES D'AGNEAU DE GALLES SOUVERAINE
Medallions of Welsh lamb served on croutons

PETITS POIS À L'ANGLAISE
Green peas with butter

❀

SUPRÊMES DE CANETON DE ROUEN EN GELÉE
Roasted Rouen duckling breast in jelly, served cold

NEIGE AU CLICQUOT
Sorbet of Clicquot champagne

❀

ORTOLANS AU SUC D'ANANAS
Ortolans with pineapple juice

BLANC DE ROMAINE AUX OEUFS
Hearts of romaine salad with poached egg

COEURS D'ARTICHAUTS FAVOURITE
Gratinéed artichoke hearts with diced truffles

❀

PÊCHES ALEXANDRA
Poached peaches with vanilla ice cream
and strawberry puree

BISCUIT MON DÉSIR
Assorted ice creams

MIGNARDISES
Petits fours

❀

CAFÉ MODE ORIENTALE
Oriental coffee

❀

LES VINS ET LIQUEURS AU CHOIX DES DÎNEURS
Selection of wines and liqueurs

The *Poularde Edouard VII* was a version of a dish Escoffier had made for the new king many times, going all the way back to the Grand Hotel in Monte Carlo in the 1880s. He'd called it *Poularde Derby,* and the then Prince of Wales had declared it to be a "truly royal dish." It consisted of a young chicken stuffed with rice, poached, and served with foie gras and whole truffles cooked in champagne.

For the coronation dinner, Escoffier created a *poularde* dish that celebrated the British Empire in India, and the many maharajas in attendance. The chicken was stuffed with rice, chopped truffles, and foie gras and served with a curry sauce made with diced red peppers. Creamed cucumbers would be served alongside, also with curry.

In the days before the coronation, Escoffier and his staff were busy preparing what they could in advance — the cold duck-breast dish, for example, for which quantities of duck and chicken livers needed to be sautéed and pushed through a sieve to make a mousse, upon which slices of cold duck would be served under a coating of Frontignan aspic. Each piece of duck breast was garnished with a cooked cherry.

The kitchen was calm and intense, with the *commis* busy peeling artichokes, preparing consommé, mixing sorbet, and molding ice cream from egg yolks, sugar, and cream in brick shapes, which were then frozen and sliced before serving. Escoffier kept track of all the orders and deliveries: the sole, the ortolans, the lamb.

He was quite proud of his new dessert, the *Pêches Alexandra,* named for Alix, the new queen, a variation on *Pêches Melba.* It consisted of perfectly ripe peaches (the skin removed) doused with kirsch and maraschino liqueurs and then poached in a hot vanilla-flavored syrup. The peaches, cooled, would be served on a layer of vanilla ice cream covered with strawberry puree. The presentation was dramatic: he would sprinkle red and white rose petals over the dish and cover the peaches with a veil of spun sugar.

Escoffier planned to include the recipe for *Pêches Alexandra,* along with all the others from the banquet, in his cookbook, which he was now working on again quite seriously. He had hired an assistant, named Emile Fétu, a friend of Philéas Gilbert, to help compile and test the recipes. The book was growing: there would be more than five thousand recipes in all. Escoffier had decided to call it *Le Guide Culinaire,* and it would be definitive. It would be his magnum opus.

On Tuesday, June 24, two days before the coronation, London was already on holiday, the city electric with anticipation, the mood giddy. Crowds thronged the streets, many of the building façades decorated with flags and streamers. Street salesmen sold toy horns and peacock feathers (a symbol of royalty). Groups of soldiers milled about their encampments, and thousands of Christian Boys' Brigades had arrived in the city. Huge viewing stands had been erected on both sides of the Thames. The seats were being sold for anywhere from three to twenty guineas, which everyone complained was far too expensive.

In Victoria Park, in East London, a local politician had organized a day of music and entertainment for the poorer children in the neighborhood. Numerous actors and musicians had volunteered to take part, including Dan Leno, the famous music-hall comedian, who had assembled a slapstick cricket team for the occasion. Thousands of children aged nine to fourteen had been invited, "irrespective of creed," reported the London *Times.*

At Victoria Station, special trains carrying royal visitors from all over the world arrived every hour, it seemed, and were met by equally distinguished royal emissaries, who showed them to the royal waiting room, elaborately decorated with flags, flowers, and a red carpet, and then to their waiting carriages. Members of the public, meanwhile, lined up behind barricades to cheer the arrivals. Here were the Crown Prince of Denmark and the Grand Duke of Hesse,

Germany, being met by George, the Prince of Wales, and Prince Charles of Denmark. (George was the new king's second son, and heir to the throne; his older brother, Albert Victor, had died of the flu.) Here were Prince Henry of Prussia and the Crown Prince of Portugal, also being met by the Prince of Wales, who made multiple trips to the station. Then came Archduke Franz Ferdinand of Austria; the Prince of Asturias, in Spain; the Crown Prince of Sweden and Norway; the Crown Prince of Siam; Monsignor Merry del Val, the Spanish cardinal; and Gen. Ras Makonnen, of Ethiopia — all on one train from Dover. The men accompanying Makonnen looked striking in their long black robes and large green hats. Fifteen minutes later, another train from Dover brought Duke Albert of Württemberg, Germany; Prince Albert of Belgium; Prince Leopold of Bavaria; Prince Neuyed Ab Dallah (representing the Shah of Persia); Prince Muhammad Ali of Egypt; Prince Philip of Coburg, Germany; and the Prince of Monaco. There were more — groups of Greek princes; groups of Turkish pashas; Tsai-Chen, the son of Prince Ching of China; the Maharaja of Idar; the Duke of Aosta, representing the King of Italy; King

Lewanika, the paramount chief of Barotse-
land.

The crowd cheered as the various entou-
rages made their way to their open carriages, waving as they drove off, some to
private ambassadors' residences, others to
various hotels.

In the dining room of the Carlton that
Tuesday, some of the very royalty who had
been hailed in the streets were now preparing to eat — Indian maharajas, Italian and
German nobles. There was no raucous applause, but in its own way the hotel was
buzzing with a sense of history and excitement. Lunch was being served.

And it was at this moment that the news
arrived.

Ritz was in the lobby when he was handed
the telegraph tape:

**THE CORONATION CEREMONY
IS POSTPONED.
THE KING IS UNDERGOING A
SURGICAL OPERATION.**

He studied the words as if they were written in a foreign language. The coronation
postponed? The king undergoing surgery?
What did that mean? He looked around the
hotel lobby at all the people walking to

lunch, laughing, talking, as if nothing were wrong, and felt the shock of the news that only he knew. Ritz walked, then ran, to the telegraph office. What had happened? How could this be? Was it true?

Yes, it was true.

King Edward was gravely ill, undergoing emergency surgery. His life was in danger. The coronation was off — indefinitely. No one knew what the surgery was, or when it would be completed, or what the king's chances of survival might be.

It fell to Ritz to announce the news. He walked to the middle of the dining room and asked for quiet. There was something about his sober, stricken demeanor that caused those seated nearby to fall silent. A guest in the restaurant described the scene in a letter to the London *Times:*

Our rooms had been engaged at the Carlton Hotel. We went down to the luncheon room, which was quite full. We took the places which had been reserved for us and were struck by the animation that pervaded the spacious room. There were eager conversations, carried on in nearly all languages, bursts of laughter, a constant coming and going.

All at once there was an instantaneous

and striking silence. We looked with surprise and as the silence continued we rose from our seats. Everyone was standing motionless and as if petrified. In the middle of the room M. Ritz, the managing director of the hotel, pale and dejected, was speaking in a voice muffled but clearly audible to the taciturn gathering. He said: "The Coronation will not take place. The King, after a consultation of the leading physicians, is now undergoing an operation, dangerous, perhaps mortal, which has been declared absolutely and immediately necessary. His Majesty, on being consulted, said to his physicians, 'Obey your consciences and do your duty if you cannot spare me the pain of inflicting this great disappointment on the civilized world, whose representatives have honored me with their presence in London.'"

Everyone was stupefied. Then, after a moment's silence, there was a rush to the galleries, the Palm Court, the ground-floor saloons, and the Exchange Company's office, where the tapes continued to unroll, and where further information was hoped for.

The news ricocheted across London. Reporters and onlookers gathered at the

Buckingham Palace gates, awaiting news. Rumors spread: the king was dying; it was cancer. In fact, he was suffering from an inflamed appendix. He had resisted treatment for as long as he could. ("The Coronation *cannot* be postponed. I won't hear of it," he told his doctor. "I will go to the Abbey on Thursday if I die there." His doctor told him that if His Majesty were to go to the abbey on Thursday, he really *would* die there.) The operation took place early Tuesday morning.

At the Carlton, the cancellations poured in — by messenger, post, telephone, and telegraph. Every room, table, and window in the entire hotel had been booked, and now needed to be unbooked. Ritz and Echenard handled the onslaught. Ritz told Escoffier to stop all preparations in the kitchen, and to cancel any orders for provisions that he could. Of course, most everything for the gala dinner had already been delivered. Ritz also canceled the orchestra booked for the week. No one would be in the mood for waltzes.

Ritz remained serenely calm as he unwound the elaborate event. He was in shock. At about three o'clock that afternoon, in the middle of a conversation with his staff,

407

he collapsed, unconscious, falling to the floor.

When he woke up, he was delirious — incoherent. Echenard immediately sent him home to Golders Green in a carriage, and the coachman helped him into the house.

Marie was scared. She'd never seen her husband like this. He seemed not even to recognize her, and he lay in bed moaning. When Dr. Cole came, he gave Ritz a sedative. Sometime later, Ritz fell asleep.

The doctor called it a "complete nervous breakdown." It was what he had always feared, he said. Ritz had pushed himself too hard. And the shock of the sudden cancellation had been too much.

"How long will it be until . . . ?" Marie asked.

"Maybe a few months," the doctor replied. "Maybe a year. Maybe longer."

Ritz never recovered, not really. At least, he was never the same.

Six weeks later, on August 9, 1902, King Edward was crowned, and the royal banquet at the Carlton was finally served. The hotel was full, London a pageant of royal celebration. Ritz was not there. His doctors had prescribed rest, and a change of scenery. Marie had settled his affairs and taken him and their children to Lucerne, to stay with their old friends the Pfyffers, at the Grand Hotel National.

Echenard took over the management of the Carlton in Ritz's absence. It was only temporary, until Ritz recuperated.

He never did.

There were periods when Ritz seemed better, ready to get back to running his hotels. He would obsess about the press coverage of the Ritz, the Carlton, and the Grand Hôtel des Thermes. He would dash off notes to his staff: "You will be kind enough to charge Lieutenant Colonel Newnham-Davis prices as moderate as possible," he wrote to Henry Ellès, the manager of the Ritz Paris. "It's very important, as he will write articles for us." Newnham-Davis, the restaurant critic, had expanded beyond London and was now writing about his meals on the Continent. Ritz responded to job seekers and to potential customers, sending them brochures and giving out room prices. He took notes in a red leather notebook, outlining his plans for the future. On the first page, in bold calligraphy, he'd written:

MES PLANS — MES IDÉES.

He divided the notebook into sections, and wrote headings: "The Cairo Hotel," "Marseille," "Table Decorations," "Invitations for Cairo," "Ritz Development," "Construction of Hotels," "Provisional Receipts of Hotels," "Palais des Fêtes" (the Festival Palace).

At other times, though, Ritz was listless, apathetic. When Mewès came to visit, full of plans and questions and design ideas about the new Piccadilly hotel, Ritz looked off into the middle distance. "Do what you like," he said. "You know by now what my ideas are. Incorporate them. I know what your taste and ability are. Go ahead. Do what you like."

This was the London Ritz they were talking about, a hotel with his name on it. Ritz was the most fanatical and detail-oriented client Mewès had ever known. And now he was saying, "Do what you like"?

Escoffier, meanwhile, finished *Le Guide Culinaire* in November 1902 and published it in France in 1903. Translations soon followed: German, Italian, Swedish, Danish. The English edition was pared down to about three thousand recipes from the original five thousand, and published in England and America as *A Guide to Modern*

Cookery.

The success of the book was everything he'd hoped for, cementing his reputation as the foremost chef of his time. If Carême was the Old Testament, then Escoffier was the New Testament — that's what everyone said. He had written the first, definitive, modern cookbook of the new century. He had defined the art of French cooking.

And so just as the Edwardian era began, with Edward VII's emergency surgery and convalescence and triumphant coronation, the era of Ritz and Escoffier as a team came to an end. The partnership that changed the very nature of luxury, of hotels and restaurants, that had reshuffled and redefined the terms of taste, class, and prestige, was over. It was a partnership that spanned almost twenty years, from Monte Carlo and Lucerne to London, Paris, and London again, and had married the sophisticated pleasures of the aristocracy to the urgent desires of a new generation of travelers to create something entirely new. The dining rooms in their hotels possessed a magical quality (the lighting, the music, the flowers) and attracted everyone from the grande dames of high society to opera stars, artists, and actors to suddenly wealthy industrialists to politicians, Americans, financiers, princes, and nobility of all kinds.

Ritz, in particular, had intuited that the romance of the aristocracy could be translated for a broader audience, that wealthy Americans and the nouveau riche would desire, and pay for, the very best service and the validating stamp of "good taste" that his hotels provided. Escoffier's cooking was the key to the equation: the visceral, sensual pleasure of the food; the bottles of champagne that went with it; and the theatrical drama of the dining room, a place to see and be seen.

Ritz receded into a twilight of melancholy, brought low, at age fifty-three, by mental illness and exhaustion. Escoffier, meanwhile, continued to run the kitchens at the Carlton, and did so for years. They both looked back with amazement at what they had achieved together in the 1890s, how different the world was then, how they themselves had changed it.

It was Ritz who had brought them to London, who cajoled and convinced Escoffier to take a risk, to gamble on the unknown. And it was Escoffier who had ensured their success with his elegant, superior cooking. Together, just as Ritz had promised, they had conquered London and the world, alchemizing food and luxury into a new kind of glamour, a cosmopolitanism for the twentieth century and beyond.

AFTERWORD:
PARIS, 1925

Marie lived in the hotel, alone, in an apartment on the top floor. Every morning, she would look out her window at the Place Vendôme, a view unchanged in the many years she'd lived there. She was in her mid-fifties, about the same age her husband had been when he collapsed at the Carlton.

It was May 20, 1925. Victor Rey was now the general manager of the Hôtel Ritz. Henry Ellès had died earlier that spring, and Rey had taken over. Both men had worked at the hotel from the beginning: Ellès as general manager since 1899, when Ritz had left to open the Carlton in London; Rey as head of reception and later assistant manager, since 1900. Like Ritz, Rey was Swiss, and from the same region, the Valais. He was a connoisseur of good food and wine, and as suavely quick on his feet as his onetime boss.

Rey was preparing the hotel for an event

that evening: a grand reception to celebrate the debut of the American-Italian-French Grand Opera Company, which was performing Italo Montemezzi's *L'Amore Dei Tre Re* (*The Love of Three Kings*). The party would be hosted by an American, Mrs. Florence Millhiser, and would draw an international crowd, including Mary Garden, the star of the opera. The performance would be the Scottish soprano's first in Paris since the end of the war.

Marie was on the board of directors of the Paris Ritz, a forceful presence in running the company. She had always been smart; now she was also tough. She had lost a child — René, her younger son — and her husband both in the same awful year, 1918. René had died of spinal meningitis. Ritz had died in a private hospital in Switzerland after a long period of unconsciousness. Their elder son, Charles, meanwhile, had moved to the United States.

The war had been hard, in every way. Large portions of the hotel had been given over to the French Army for use as a hospital. Rey scoured Paris for coal to keep the building heated. There was no money; there were only insistent creditors. The Ritz shut down entirely for several months in 1914. Marie remembered that period quite vividly:

she had left Paris for Lausanne, to visit César in the hospital there. He was weak. And while she was in Switzerland, who should come to visit but one of Ritz's most devoted employees, the cashier Agostini.

Agostini had always idolized Ritz — he had done his best to dress like Ritz, behave like Ritz, trim his sideburns like Ritz. That day, he came to the hospital impeccably dressed, and sat with his well-brushed hat on his knees next to Ritz's bed and drank the tea Marie served him. They talked politely for an hour. He never mentioned money. As Marie would find out later, Agostini had no savings, and the temporary closure of the Ritz and the loss of his salary had put him in a bad spot. He had managed the hotel's books but not his own. He was desperate. If Marie had only known, she would have loaned him whatever he needed. But Agostini said nothing, nothing at all. He sat stiffly, overly formal, talking about the old days, the 1890s, and then returned to his boardinghouse in Vevey, not far away, where he killed himself with a gun. Another casualty of the war, Marie thought. There had been many.

Ritz had made periodic attempts to return to work, but it was impossible.

"I am worse than a dead man," he said to Marie a few years after he first fell ill, "for my working life is ended." His "Plans and Ideas" notebook remained mostly blank. He took a few pages of disjointed notes for a memoir, writing in a nearly indecipherable scrawl:

Joie de vivre — Belle-mère Alsacienne. Hongroise voluptueuse. Américains plus intelligents. Anglaises distinguées. Asquith. Duc Connaught. Mes plans — Paris — Bois Avenue — Palais — Opera — English, French, German, Russian. Marie délicieuse giftée. Melba — gourmet.

All notes to himself, memories to be expanded upon: his Alsatian mother-in-law; the voluptuous Hungarian; very intelligent Americans; distinguished Englishmen; his plans for Paris, and so on.

But his memory had begun to fail him. "Whole periods of his life seemed to go blank," Marie later wrote. "For fear of these lapses he dared not any longer mingle with people. He began to avoid all social contacts. For hours, he would remain shut up in his room, brooding. Nothing I could say would cheer him up or distract him." Ritz would sometimes shout at shadows only he could see, throwing things across the room in fits of delusion.

For a few years, he and Marie stayed in a small apartment on the Place des États-Unis in Paris, and Ritz took lessons in European history and sculpture, and avoided all talk about his hotels. His health worsened. By 1910, when King Edward died of a heart attack at age sixty-eight, Ritz had detached himself from reality almost entirely. He had become a kind of ghost. Not long after, he was moved to a private hospital in Lausanne, and later to another outside Lucerne.

It was Marie who oversaw the proliferation of the Ritz hotels in the early years of the century — in London, Budapest, Madrid. In 1906, the Hamburg–America Line, a German shipping company, approached the board of directors of the Carlton about licensing the company's name for a restaurant on board a new ship, the *Amerika*. They would call it the "Ritz-Carlton Restaurant." Escoffier, a member of the board, supported the idea; he would be hired by Hamburg–America as a consultant to the restaurant. Marie Ritz also agreed, allowing the use of the Ritz name, and thus was born a new luxury brand, one that was soon also licensed to a British-American hotel company, which opened the first Ritz-Carlton hotel in New York City in 1910. The building, on Madison Avenue and Forty-Sixth Street, was designed by Whitney Warren and Charles Wetmore, the architects who would design Grand Central Terminal a few years later.

Escoffier was also hired to consult on the new American hotel. He traveled to America for the first time in 1908, and again in 1910 for the opening, organizing the kitchen and the staff. He was celebrated as a "wizard of the kitchen" and the "Prince of Chefs" in profiles published in the *New York Times.*

Coincidentally, Sarah Bernhardt was in New York that same winter of 1910, on a grand valedictory tour in which she reprised many of her famous roles: Marguerite Gautier, Joan of Arc, Napoléon II. She was sixty-seven, an international celebrity, as was Escoffier, in his own way, at age sixty-four. He visited her in her room at the Hôtel Marie Antoinette, bringing a lunch of pâté de foie gras imported from Strasbourg. They talked about how long they'd known each other, and he noted how remarkably young she still seemed. What was her secret? he asked. "My dear Escoffier," she replied. "You are very nosy. There are secrets that a woman is born with, and that die with her." But she did tell him in the end: the secret to youth, she explained, was a half bottle of Moët et Chandon champagne with every meal. They laughed.

The war had changed everything, especially the hotel business. The revolution in Russia, the formation of the Weimar Republic in Germany, the dissolution of the Austro-Hungarian Empire — all the turmoil had curtailed leisure travel and, more fundamentally, upended the old European order. Aristocratic wealth and privilege could not be taken for granted; longtime clients of the Ritz Paris had seen their fortunes disappear.

But Paris came back to life, slowly at first, and then faster than ever. If old fortunes had disappeared during the war, now new fortunes were being made. The music halls, cabarets, and cafés were overflowing. The city was full of expats, artists, and jazz. Fashionable women wore knee-length dresses and silk stockings, and cut their hair in bobs. The mood was giddy, sometimes decadent. Americans were everywhere, it seemed.

At the height of the social season in June 1923, the *New York Times* reported:

GRANDE SEMAINE
AN AMERICAN WEEK
*
VISITORS CREATE A SEASON
OF THEIR OWN,
WITH LAVISH ENTERTAINING
*
GRAND PRIX IS RUN TODAY
*
FRENCH WRITER LAMENTS
FOREIGN INVASION,
BUT MERCHANTS PROFIT

Without the Americans and their money, the article explained, the "Grande Semaine" would have been a financial and social failure. That was certainly the case at the Ritz, which depended on wealthy foreign guests — serving cocktails to Americans who, back home, were suffering though Prohibition. "How far we have fallen from the days when Versailles gave the tone to the world," said the unnamed French writer quoted in the *Times* article. Now it was Cole Porter, playing piano at the Ritz, who was setting the tone. And F. Scott Fitzgerald, and Ernest Hemingway, and Gertrude Stein. The so-called Lost Generation, gathered in Paris, making art, talking about art, young expats from all over the world.

Ritz would have loved it, Marie was sure — the energy, the glamour, the daring sense of progress. Paris felt like the center of the world, and Ritz's hotel on the Place Vendôme felt like the center of grown-up Paris. The Ritz was not a café on the bohemian Left Bank, obviously, but the hotel welcomed artists and writers just as it did the wealthy and the aristocratic. The bar at the Ritz, opened in 1921, was called the Café Parisien, and the strict, authoritative bartender there poured drinks for everyone from the King of Spain to Hollywood star Douglas Fairbanks Sr. to Hemingway and Fitzgerald. The bartender's name was Frank Meier; he wore a pince-nez, kept his hair parted exactly in the middle, and treated everyone with the same solemn hauteur. Cocktails were in vogue, and Meier was good at inventing new ones, giving them names like the Royal, the Blue Bird, and the Green Hot.

Yes, Ritz would have reveled in Paris after the war, in the democratic glamour his hotel stood for — the aspiration his very name now represented, all over the world. Certainly, Escoffier enjoyed his fame: he had retired from the Carlton in 1920 and moved to his villa in Monte Carlo, surrounded by family. But he was restless, and traveled often (to Paris, New York, Zurich, London), visiting culinary exhibitions and receiving honors. He had published a revised edition of *Le Guide Culinaire* in 1921, and he towered over the food world, training a legion of protégés. When Escoffier visited Marie at the Ritz, they would laugh at the recognition he and César had achieved. "A Diamond as Big as the Ritz," for example — Ritz would have been amused and astounded to hear the title of the Fitzgerald story published in 1922. The story referred to the Ritz-Carlton Hotel in New York.

"César was always a little wistful in the presence of books," Marie noted — rueful at his lack of formal education. He would have been proud. And even more so at the word *ritzy,* a synonym for style and glamour, being bandied about in conversation. Could there be any greater compliment? Ritz had entered the lexicon.

Now Marie walked down the grand staircase into the lobby of the Ritz, a piano playing somewhere, as guests arrived for the American-Italian-French Grand Opera Company gala, the staff rushing purposefully about. Here were Giuseppe De Luca, a leading baritone at the Metropolitan Opera in New York; Alla Nazimova, the film and Broadway star; and Mr. and Mrs.

Evander Berry Wall, American millionaires, he a notorious, fantastic dandy and a regular at the hotel bar; Frank Meier had named a drink for him, a gin cocktail called the Berry Wall.

Life at the Ritz went on, just as it always had, a life of pleasure, a theater of luxury. Marie missed her husband, but now she joined the crowd, greeting old friends and new guests, welcoming them to the evening's festivities and to the Hôtel Ritz.

ACKNOWLEDGMENTS

I am deeply grateful for the help I received researching this book from staff members and archivists at the Savoy Hotel in London and at the Ritz Paris. My thanks to Emma Allam, Charlotte Faith, Susan Scott, and Kiaran MacDonald at the Savoy; at the Ritz, thank you to Anne Benichou, Matthieu Goffard, Anita Cotter, Wanda Tymowska, and Frank Klein. For their historical knowledge and guidance, I thank Michel Escoffier and the Escoffier Museum of Culinary Art in Villeneuve-Loubet, Paul Levy, Michel Rey, David Bowie, Andreas Augustin, and Derek Taylor. Melanie Locay and the staff at the New York Public Library provided important research support, as did the staff at the Victoria and Albert Museum Archives in London. To my brilliant editors, Doris Cooper and Rica Allannic, and to the entire team at Clarkson Potter, including Carly Gorga, Erica Gelbard, and Aaron Wehner:

thank you. My agent and friend David Kuhn made this book — and so much else — possible; thank you also to Dana Spector at Paradigm. Clea Bierman helped me with excellent research. For their generosity, support, and wisdom, I thank my friends Adam Lehner, Suzanna Petren-Moritz, Ocean MacAdams, Nancy Novogrod, Albert Wenger, Mark Leyner, Benoît Peverelli, Adrian Erni, Luke Dawson, Sean Gullette, Stephan Klasen, and Bruno Maddox. Finally, I could not have written this book without the love and support of my family — my late mother, Catrine, and my father, John Barr; my wife, Yumi Moriwaki; and my daughters, Sachi and Emi.

NOTES AND SOURCES

All of my sources for quotations are listed on the following pages. I am indebted to previous accounts of the era, and in particular to the memoirs of Marie Louise Ritz and Auguste Escoffier for all their intimate detail. In the case of unpublished material, the archive or library is listed: the Savoy archives and the Victoria and Albert Museum archives, both in London, and the Ritz hotel archives in Paris.

Part 1: The Grand Opening, 1889

1. The Hotelier and the Impresario

"This is the sort of thing": Marie Louise Ritz, *César Ritz: Host to the World,* p. 135.

"There is not a hotel": Ibid., p. 110.

"You'd make money": Ibid.

"£350": Andreas Augustin, Andrew Williamson, and Rupert Tenison, *The Savoy London,* p. 50.

"He wants the clientele": Ritz, *César Ritz*, p. 135.

"He wants to make his hotel": Ibid., p. 136.

"private viewing": *Morning Advertiser,* August 1, 1889, Savoy archives.

raised £200,000: Savoy Hotel Prospectus, 1889, Savoy archives.

"ascending rooms": Ibid.

"in the most perfect manner": Ibid.

"The theatre is protected": Savoy playbill, D'Oyly Carte Archive, Victoria and Albert Museum, London.

"You see there is no deception": *Electrical Times,* quoted in Brian Jones, *Helen D'Oyly Carte: Gilbert and Sullivan's 4th Partner,* p. 94.

"No charge for Baths": Advertisement, 1890, Savoy archives.

"Let us first take": Albert Smith, *The English Hotel Nuisance,* p. 18.

"The restaurant is intended": Savoy Prospectus, 1889, Savoy archives.

"A marked importance": Ibid.

2. A London Debut

R. D'OYLY CARTE, MUSICAL AND THEATRICAL AGENT, read the sign on the door: This title also appears on D'Oyly Carte's stationery, D'Oyly Carte Archive, Victoria and Albert Museum, London.

"Oh no": Jones, *Helen D'Oyly Carte,* p. 2.

"Worth now eschews": *Rational Dress Society Gazette,* quoted in Alison Gernsheim, *Victorian and Edwardian Fashion: A Photographic Survey,* p. 77.

"Now, women dress for dinner": *The Woman's World* quoted in Gernsheim, *Victorian and Edwardian Fashion,* p. 78.

Croustades de crevettes Dieppois: The menu is described in *World,* July 31, 1889, Savoy archives.

"I do not know that there is any view": *Stock Exchange,* September 28, 1889, Savoy archives.

"Clara Jecks": *Oracle,* August 2, 1889, Savoy archives.

"M. Ritz, proprietor": *Era,* August 3, 1889, Savoy archives.

"It will not succeed": Ritz, *César Ritz,* p. 142.

3. An Offer Too Good to Refuse

"It's a mathematical certainty": Ritz, *César Ritz,* p. 44.

"You'll never make anything": Ibid., p. 20.

"Oh, but I'm tired!": Ibid., p. 136.

"fever of excitement": Ibid., p. 141.

"So mannish!": Ibid., p. 138.

£1,200 per year: *Lighthouse,* October 4,

1890, Savoy archives.

"little army of hotel men": Ritz, *César Ritz*, p. 143.

"I am counting on your support": *L'Art Culinaire à Londres, Le Jubilé Escoffier*, November 1, 1909, quoted in Kenneth James, *Escoffier: The King of Chefs*, p. 128.

Part 2: Boomtown, 1890

4. Taking Charge

"The rush hour in the kitchen": Eugène Herbodeau and Paul Thalamas, *Georges Auguste Escoffier*, p. 77.

"they would find no flaws": Ritz, *César Ritz*, p. 145.

"Never bother a guest": Ibid., p. 75.

"The customer is always right": Ibid., p. 287.

"César le Rapide": Claude Roulet, *Ritz: A Story That Outshines the Legend*, p. 27.

"the Beau Brummel": Ibid., p. 112.

"the hotel de luxe": Savoy advertisement, Savoy archives.

Deux oeufs sur le plat Meyerbeer: This example is described in Herbodeau and Thalamas, *Georges Auguste Escoffier*, p. 79.

Surtout, faites simple: James, *Escoffier*, p. 109.

breakfast for two shillings: Restaurant prices quoted here are from an 1890 Savoy advertisement, Savoy archives.

a single room at the Savoy cost seven shillings: Room rates cited in Stanley Jackson, *The Savoy: The Romance of a Great Hotel,* p. 21.

5. A Celebrity Guest and an Infamous Dinner

"Unfortunately": Auguste Escoffier, *Memories of My Life,* p. 3.

"I was informed": Ibid., p. 7.

"Although we have all heard": *Licensed Vic Mirror,* June 10, 1890, Savoy archives.

"the man in the street": London *Times,* June 26, 1890, Savoy archives.

"the instrument of the future": *Whitehall Review,* June 14, 1890, Savoy archives.

"Good morning, mama": *Home News,* August 1, 1890, Savoy archives.

"Conversation during the repast": *Illustrated Sporting and Dramatic News,* November 1, 1890, Savoy archives.

"It must be superb": Ritz, *César Ritz,* p. 148.

gold and diamond millionaires: Ibid., p. 142.

"Dark Continent": Ibid., p. 170.

"Why it's enough": T. Martin Wood, *George*

du Maurier: The Satirist of the Victorians,
p. 138.

"Trust them to find": Ritz, *César Ritz,*
p. 142.

£100,000 in 1889: Jane Ridley, *The Heir Apparent: A Life of Edward VII, the Playboy Prince,* p. 328.

"We resented the introduction": Ibid.,
p. 330.

"Narrow Escape of Madame Bernhardt":
Liverpool Daily Post, June 25, 1890, Savoy
archives.

"Madame Bernhardt in Danger": *Dundee Courier,* June 25, 1890, Savoy archives.

"I have not been very well": *New York Herald,* June 26, 1890, Savoy archives.

"A Sensational Story Contradicted": *Leicester Post,* June 26, 1890, Savoy archives.

Hors d'oeuvres à la Russe: The menu was
published in *City Press,* July 5, 1890,
Savoy archives.

"For indeed": Auguste Escoffier, *A Guide to Modern Cookery,* p. 437.

"Magog, 1815": Wines listed in *City Press,*
July 5, 1890, Savoy archives.

"the cause of garlic": Escoffier, *Memories of My Life,* p. 15.

"A Dinner at £15 per Head": *Pall Mall Gazette,* July 8, 1890, Savoy archives.

"Even in these days": *The Figaro,* July 12, 1890, Savoy archives.

"a very large specimen": *Society,* September 27, 1890, Savoy archives.

"In times like these": *Pelican,* July 10, 1890, Savoy archives.

"It seemed to me a wonder city": Ritz, *César Ritz,* p. 165.

"They say Mrs. R—": Ibid.

"No whisper in a ballroom": Ibid., p. 119.

"What very odd music": Ibid., p. 166.

Part 3: Decadence and Suspicion, 1890–1893

6. The Shareholder Meeting

"It is hardly necessary": All quotes in this section from "Savoy Hotel, Limited," *Financial News,* September 27, 1890, Savoy archives.

"Mr. D'Oyly Carte's First Failure": *Lighthouse,* October 4, 1890, Savoy archives.

£4,500: Alan James, *Gilbert & Sullivan,* p. 133.

7. Flying High

"Paris! Switzerland!": Ritz, *César Ritz,* p. 163.

"Leave Paris at 3:45 p.m.": Ibid., p. 160.

"For the most part": Max Beerbohm, *Yet*

Again, p. 125.

"Many of them signified beautiful or famous places": Ibid., p. 137.

"Who wants an immovable": Ritz, *César Ritz,* p. 161.

"I maintain that for service": *San Francisco Chronicle,* August 30, 1891, quoted in ibid., p. 163.

"doubtful reputation": Ritz, *César Ritz,* p. 153.

"You can lay down the law": Ibid.

"You pass through wide, airy corridors": *Harper's New Monthly Magazine,* January, 1891, quoted in Antony Clayton, *Decadent London: Fin de Siècle City,* p. 125.

"Those burning nights": *The Memoirs of Arthur Symons,* quoted in Clayton, *Decadent London,* p. 124.

"accosted young gentlemen": *Daily Telegraph,* quoted in Clayton, *Decadent London,* p. 126.

"purity and clearness": London *Times,* December 9, 1891.

"England will soon be fit": Ritz, *César Ritz,* p. 150.

"We might": Ibid., p. 151.

"Why not bring him here?": Ibid., p. 152.

"Nymphs at Dawn!": Ibid., p. 150.

"This was not a novel dish": Escoffier, *Mem-*

ories of My Life, p. 103.

"Messieurs les Anglais": Ibid., p. 102.

"I started looking for words": Ibid., p. 9.

"I frequently had the occasion": Ibid., p. 78.

"But I know that he loves that fine amphibian": Ibid., p. 81.

"paradoxical": Ibid., p. 105.

"I may place some French characters": "M. Zola on London," Manchester Guardian, October 3, 1893.

8. Expansion Plans and New Pressures

"We need a new Savoy": Ritz, César Ritz, p. 174.

£2,000: Figure cited in Andreas Augustin, The St. Regis Rome.

"All this beauty": Ritz, César Ritz, p. 181.

"What a magnificent": Ibid., p. 183.

"Why are you not?": Ibid., p. 182.

"as a vain woman": Ibid., p. 122.

"He was a very short man": "Two Tricky Americans," New York Herald, October 3, 1889, Savoy archives.

"Two Tricky Americans": Ibid.

"Do palms grow in your hotels": Ritz, César Ritz, p. 131.

"Your taste is good": Ibid., p. 176.

"having lost control of myself": Derek Taylor, "Cesar Ritz and Auguste Escoffier vs the Savoy Hotel Company," International

Journal of Hospitality Management 15, no. 1 (March 1996).

"These foreigners": Ritz, *César Ritz,* p. 180.

"It means giving up my liberty": Ibid., p. 176.

"Thank God": Ibid., p. 122.

Part 4: Scandal, 1894–1898

9. The Prince of Wales vs. The Duc d'Orléans

"To the Rome of the antiquarian": Ibid., p. 184.

"the new César": Ibid., p. 183.

"Two such perfect princes:" Ibid., p. 146.

"Too bad": Ibid., p. 147.

"Not to be thought of!": Ibid.

"Go ahead": Ibid.

sliding scale commission: Taylor, "Cesar Ritz and Auguste Escoffier vs the Savoy Hotel Company."

"Advisory Expert to the Board": Augustin, *The Savoy London,* p. 68.

"César was excessively busy": Ritz, *César Ritz,* p. 192.

"received the emoluments": Augustin, *The Savoy London,* p. 66.

Cornish Club dinner: The menu is cited in Escoffier, *Memories of My Life,* p. 94.

Aosta-Orléans royal wedding dinner: Menu

cited in ibid., p. 92.

Amontillado, a dry sherry: Wines listed in ibid., p. 94.

"ponce and a sodomite": Neil McKenna, *The Secret Life of Oscar Wilde*, p. 342.

"What is the 'Love that dare not speak its name'?": Ibid., p. 391.

"Here was this man": Ibid., p. 392.

"Hello! Here's my Herbert": Ibid., p. 221.

"The hotelier who cannot learn": Ritz, *César Ritz*, p. 114.

"disgusting conduct": McKenna, *The Secret Life of Oscar Wilde*, p. 224.

10. Ritz Makes a Move

"He had a large place near London": Mrs. George Cornwallis-West, *The Reminiscences of Lady Randolph Churchill*, p. 283.

"Let us meet and shake hands": James, *Gilbert & Sullivan*, p. 135.

One Who Knows: Taylor, "Cesar Ritz and Auguste Escoffier vs the Savoy Hotel Company."

"Ritz, Echenard and Escoffier": Ibid.

"There is no doubt": Ibid.

"allow 5% off": Ibid.

11. A Secret Investigation

"It was a famous victory": *World*, September 22, 1895, quoted in Amanda Mackenzie

Stuart, *Consuelo and Alva Vanderbilt: The Story of a Mother and a Daughter in the Gilded Age,* p. 134.

"Age: Eighteen years": *World,* September 29, 1895, quoted in Stuart, *Consuelo and Alva Vanderbilt,* p. 1.

"Why Do Women Crave Titles?": *World,* October 13, 1895, quoted in Stuart, *Consuelo and Alva Vanderbilt,* p. 132.

"our vulgar moneyed aristocrats": Stuart, *Consuelo and Alva Vanderbilt,* p. 136.

"the rage of the season": Ibid., p. 208.

"but this did not last long": Frederick Townsend Martin, *Things I Remember,* p. 211.

"so full that they lack": *The Queen,* quoted in Gernsheim, *Victorian and Edwardian Fashion,* p. 80.

ten pounds per person: *Daily Mail,* Savoy archives.

"I remember what happened": Martin, *Things I Remember,* p. 160.

"a grand name": Roulet, *Ritz,* p. 44.

starting capital of £120,500: Ibid., p. 45.

profits had dropped to 24.5 percent: Taylor, "Cesar Ritz and Auguste Escoffier vs the Savoy Hotel Company."

"I am not allowed to walk": Ibid.

12. Calamity

"During that period": Quoted in James, *Escoffier,* p. 116.

"*L'École des Menus*": Ibid., p. 145.

"The 5 percent paid to Mr. Escoffier": Taylor, "Cesar Ritz and Auguste Escoffier vs the Savoy Hotel Company."

"When we got to the Savoy" and subsequent quotes: Paul Levy, *Out to Lunch,* p. 229.

"the stuffiest kind of English taste": Ritz, *César Ritz,* p. 190.

"No. 35,466, if you please": Lt. Col. (Nathaniel) Newnham-Davis, *Dinners and Diners: Where and How to Dine in London,* p. 26.

"The writing of ceremonious notes": Cornwallis-West, *The Reminiscences of Lady Randolph Churchill,* p. 55.

"The fancy dress ball at Devonshire House": Consuelo Vanderbilt Balsan, *The Glitter and the Gold: The American Duchess — In Her Own Words,* p. 102.

£37,549 worth of wine: Figures cited in Taylor, "Cesar Ritz and Auguste Escoffier vs the Savoy Hotel Company."

profits had fallen by £11,000: Ibid.

"forgot they were servants": Levy, *Out to Lunch,* p. 228.

"you have latterly been simply using the

441

Savoy": Taylor, "Cesar Ritz and Auguste Escoffier vs the Savoy Hotel Company."

"The Savoy, with its luxurious suites": Levy, *Out to Lunch*, p. 228.

"conducted practically day by day": "Under New Management; Startling Changes at the Savoy Hotel," *Daily Mail*, March 10, 1898.

"the astounding disappearance": Levy, *Out to Lunch*, p. 226.

"It is the imperative duty": Taylor, "Cesar Ritz and Auguste Escoffier vs the Savoy Hotel Company."

"By a resolution passed this morning": Augustin, *The Savoy London*, p. 69.

Part 5: Paris, 1898–1899

13. A New Beginning

"forgot they were servants": Levy, *Out to Lunch*, p. 228.

"During the last 24-hours": *The Star*, March 8, 1898, quoted in Augustin, *The Savoy London*, p. 70.

"Under New Management": "Under New Management; Startling Changes at the Savoy Hotel," *Daily Mail*, March 10, 1898.

"The Savoy Expulsions": *Daily Mail*, March 12, 1898.

"Where Ritz goes, I go": Ritz, *César Ritz*, p. 207.

"In times such as these": Ibid., p. 206.

"She was in a great hurry": Ibid.

"My hotel must be": Ibid., p. 208.

"I know nothing": Ibid.

Hotel Bristol: This hotel closed permanently during World War I, and is unrelated to Hôtel Le Bristol on Rue du Faubourg Saint-Honoré, which opened in 1925.

bath-at-home service: Ritz, *César Ritz*, p. 65.

"the atmosphere of a gentleman's town house": Ibid., p. 210.

"We cannot hope": Ibid.

"almost exalted voice": Ibid., p. 209.

"I have always had a passion": Ibid., p. 211.

"My wife knows all about linen!": Ibid., p. 121.

"The best is not too good": Ibid., p. 211.

14. THE COOKBOOK

"a luxurious work of art": Escoffier, *Memories of My Life*, p. 119.

"1. the various pheasants": Escoffier, *A Guide to Modern Cookery*, p. 535.

"Bone 2 woodcocks": Ibid., p. 540.

"This entree should be raised high": Marie-Antoine Carême, *The Royal Parisian Pastry Cook and Confectioner from the Original of M. A. Carême*, p. 241.

"Formerly, chaud-froids": Escoffier, *A Guide to Modern Cookery,* p. 491.

"is that most of my dishes": Ritz, *César Ritz,* p. 102.

"The number of dishes": Escoffier, *A Guide to Modern Cookery,* p. xiv.

"1. Salmon": Ibid., p. 245.

"Ways of cooking fish": Ibid., 240.

"Pieces cooked separately": Ibid., p. 250.

"I am not partial": Ibid.

15. The Perfect Hotel

"The last word in artistic lighting": Ritz, *César Ritz,* p. 212.

"nothing helps them to look their best": Ibid.

"When I first saw": Ibid., p. 191.

"reduced the appearance": Derek Taylor and David Bush, *The Golden Age of British Hotels,* p. 136.

"all the false curls": Ritz, *César Ritz,* p. 213.

"Ritz was always pleased": Ibid., p. 216.

"Was there ever a house": Ibid., p. 217.

The ovens were hulking: Photographs, Ritz archives.

"for the Fire Eternal": Ritz, *César Ritz,* p. 218.

"If I ever open a restaurant": Escoffier, *Memories of My Life,* p. 10.

les plats Escoffier: Photographs, Ritz archives.

"About the *Bortsch*": Newnham-Davis, *Dinners and Diners,* p. 30.

"Novelty by hook": Escoffier, *A Guide to Modern Cookery,* p. xii.

"Stock is everything": Ibid., p. 3.

"In cooking": Ibid.

"Remarks Upon the Different Causes": Ibid., p. 5.

"You have created a *chef-d'oeuvre!*": Ritz, *César Ritz,* p. 220.

"RITZ HOTEL RESTAURANT RITZ": Period photograph, Ritz archives.

"What do you think?": Ritz, *César Ritz,* p. 227.

"These tables are too high": Ibid., p. 225.

"These tables must be cut down": Ibid., p. 226.

"I'm going to dismiss my chef": Ibid., p. 234.

"It breaks my heart": James, *Escoffier,* p. 165.

"HÔTEL RITZ, Place Vendôme": London *Times,* October 8, 1898.

"I too have felt under a dark shadow": Ritz, *César Ritz,* p. 235.

16. Revenge Is Sweet

"This is an expensive idea": Ibid., p. 263.

"The Carlton Hotel": *Western Mail,* June 29, 1899.

"We're both on top": Ritz, *César Ritz,* p. 259.

£10,555: Roulet, *Ritz,* p. 64.

"There will be a few palms": Ritz, *César Ritz,* p. 263.

"Something wrong here": Ibid., p. 217.

"Hail, César!": Ibid., p. 268.

"Do you want to give your friend": *Daily Mail,* October 23, 1900.

"But, I kissed her": Daphne Fielding, *The Duchess of Jermyn Street: The Life and Good Times of Rosa Lewis of the Cavendish Hotel,* quoted in James, *Escoffier,* p. 189.

17. The Toast of the Town

£3,179: Amounts listed in this section from Taylor, "Cesar Ritz and Auguste Escoffier vs the Savoy Hotel Company."

"that they have ever been guilty of appropriating": Paul Levy papers.

"the importance we all attach": Taylor, "Cesar Ritz and Auguste Escoffier vs the Savoy Hotel Company."

"bust improver": Gernsheim, *Victorian and Edwardian Fashion,* p. 83.

"enticing wicker chairs" and following quotes: *Daily Mail,* July 1, 1901.

"Madame So-and-so": Ritz, *César Ritz,* p. 283.

"I don't need a valet": Ibid., p. 278.

18. A New King and a Nervous Breakdown

"Please tell Gilbert": James, *Gilbert & Sullivan,* p., 149.

"You ask me not to write": Jones, *Helen D'Oyly Carte,* p. 120.

"The Central Coronation Bonfires Committee": London *Times,* April 12, 1902.

"How to See the Coronation": London *Times,* June 24, 1902.

"Don't worry, Mimi": Ritz, *César Ritz,* p. 291.

"Eh bien!": Ibid.

Caviar frais: Menu described in Escoffier, *Memories of My Life,* p. 130.

"truly royal dish": James, *Escoffier,* p. 181.

"irrespective of creed": London *Times,* May 16, 1902.

"Our rooms had been engaged": Ritz, *César Ritz,* p. 292.

"The Coronation *cannot* be postponed": Ridley, *The Heir Apparent,* p. 442.

"complete nervous breakdown": Ritz, *César Ritz*, p. 291.

He would dash off notes to his staff: Examples in Ritz archives.

"You will be kind enough": Roulet, *Ritz*, p. 67.

"Mes Plans — Mes Idées": Stephen Watts, *The Ritz*, p. 66.

"Do what you like": Ritz, *César Ritz*, p. 293.

Afterword: Paris, 1925

L'Amore Dei Tre Re: The program is described in the *New York Times*, May 21, 1925.

"I am worse than a dead man": Ritz, *César Ritz*, p. 298.

"Joie de vivre": Watts, *The Ritz*, p. 67.

"Whole periods of his life": Ritz, *César Ritz*, p. 298.

"wizard of the kitchen": *New York Times*, December 27, 1910.

"Prince of Chefs": *New York Times*, April 24, 1908.

"My dear Escoffier": Escoffier, *Memories of My Life*, p, 152.

"Grande Semaine: An American Week": *New York Times*, June 24, 1923.

"César was always a little wistful": Ritz, *César Ritz*, p. 24.

BIBLIOGRAPHY

Asya, Ferdâ, ed. *American Writers in Europe: 1850 to the Present.* New York: Palgrave Macmillan, 2013.

Augustin, Andreas. *The St. Regis Rome.* Vienna: The Most Famous Hotels in the World, 2008.

Augustin, Andreas, Andrew Williamson, and Rupert Tenison. *The Savoy London.* Vienna: The Most Famous Hotels in the World, 2002.

Balsan, Consuelo Vanderbilt. *The Glitter and the Gold: The American Duchess — In Her Own Words.* London: George Mann, 1953.

Barr, Ann, and Paul Levy. *The Official Foodie Handbook.* London: Ebury Press, 1984.

Beckson, Karl. *London in the 1890s: A Cultural History.* New York: W. W. Norton, 1992.

Beerbohm, Max. *Yet Again.* London: Chap-

man & Hall, 1909.

Behrman, S. N. *Portrait of Max: An Intimate Portrait of Sir Max Beerbohm.* New York: Random House, 1960.

Bennett, Arnold. *Imperial Palace.* Garden City, NY: Doubleday, Doran & Company, 1931.

Berger, Molly W. *Hotel Dreams: Luxury, Technology, and Urban Ambition in America, 1829–1929.* Baltimore, MD: Johns Hopkins University Press, 2011.

Berman, Marshall. *All That Is Solid Melts into Air: The Experience of Modernity.* New York: Simon & Schuster, 1982.

Bernhardt, Sarah. *My Double Life: The Memoirs of Sarah Bernhardt.* London: William Heinemann, 1907.

Berry, Christopher J. *The Idea of Luxury: A Conceptual and Historical Investigation.* Cambridge, UK: Cambridge University Press, 1994.

Blume, Mary. *A French Affair: The Paris Beat, 1965–1998.* New York: The Free Press, 1999.

Boxer, Mark, and Pierre Salinger. *The Paris Ritz.* New York: Thames and Hudson, 1991.

Brereton, Austin. *The Literary History of the Adelphi and Its Neighborhood.* New York:

Duffield & Company, 1909

Broomfield, Andrea. *Food and Cooking in Victorian England: A History*. Santa Barbara, CA: Praeger, 2007.

Carême, Marie-Antoine. *The Royal Parisian Pastry Cook and Confectioner from the Original of M. A. Carême*. London: F. J. Mason, 1834.

Chastonay, Adalbert. *César Ritz, Life and Work*. Visp, Switzerland: The César Ritz Foundation, 1997.

Clayton, Antony. *Decadent London: Fin de Siècle City*. London: Historical Publications, 2005.

Cornwallis-West, Mrs. George. *The Reminiscences of Lady Randolph Churchill*. New York: The Century Co., 1908.

Davenport-Hines, R. P. T. *Proust at the Majestic: The Last Days of the Author Whose Book Changed Paris*. London: Bloomsbury, 2006.

David, Elizabeth. *An Omelette and a Glass of Wine*. New York: Viking, 1985.

Davidson, Alan. *The Oxford Companion to Food*. Oxford: Oxford University Press, 2014.

Denby, Elaine. *Grand Hotels: Reality and Illusion; An Architectural and Social History*. London: Reaktion Books, 1998.

451

Desmond, Shaw. *London Nights in the Gay Nineties.* New York: Robert M. McBride & Co., 1928.

Eden, David. *Gilbert and Sullivan: The Creative Conflict.* London: Associated University Presses, 1986.

Escoffier, Auguste. *A Guide to Modern Cookery.* London: Heinemann Cookery Book Club, 1966.

———. *Memories of My Life.* New York: Van Nostrand Reinhold, 1997.

Fielding, Daphne. *The Duchess of Jermyn Street: The Life and Good Times of Rosa Lewis of the Cavendish Hotel.* New York: Little Brown, 1964.

Friedman, David. *Wilde in America: Oscar Wilde and the Invention of Modern Celebrity.* New York: W. W. Norton, 2014.

Gernsheim, Alison. *Victorian and Edwardian Fashion: A Photographic Survey.* New York: Dover, 1963.

Hayman, Ronald. *Proust: A Biography.* New York: HarperCollins, 1990.

Herbodeau, Eugène, and Paul Thalamas. *Georges Auguste Escoffier.* London: Practical Press Ltd., 1955.

Hope, Annette. *Londoners' Larder: English Cuisine from Chaucer to the Present.* Edinburgh: Mainstream Publishing, 1990.

Jackson, Stanley. *The Sassoons.* New York: E. P. Dutton, 1968.

―――. *The Savoy: The Romance of a Great Hotel.* New York: E. P. Dutton, 1964.

James, Alan. *Gilbert & Sullivan.* London: Omnibus Press, 1989.

James, Kenneth. *Escoffier: The King of Chefs.* London: Hambledon and London, 2002.

Jones, Brian. *Helen D'Oyly Carte: Gilbert and Sullivan's 4th Partner.* London: Basingstoke Books Ltd., 2011.

Kaempfen, Werner. *Cäsar Ritz: Ein Leben fur den Gast.* Brig, Switzerland: Rotten Verlag, 1991.

Kelly, Ian. *Cooking for Kings: The Life of Antonin Carême, the First Celebrity Chef.* New York: Walker & Company, 2004.

Kingston, Beatty, Robert Hichens, Elizabeth Robins Pennell, et al. *Homes of the Passing Show.* London: Savoy Press, 1900.

Laburte, Pauline-Gaia. *Ritzy.* Paris: Éditions Albin Michel, 2016.

Levy, Paul. *Out to Lunch.* New York: HarperCollins, 1987.

Mackenzie, Compton. *The Savoy of London.* London: George G. Harrap & Co., 1953.

Martin, Frederick Townsend. *Things I Remember.* New York: John Lane Company, 1913.

Mazzeo, Tilar J. *The Hotel on Place Vendôme: Life, Death, and Betrayal at the Hôtel Ritz in Paris.* New York: Harper-Collins, 2014.

McAuliffe, Mary Sperling. *When Paris Sizzled: The 1920s Paris of Hemingway, Chanel, Cocteau, Cole Porter, Josephine Baker, and Their Friends.* New York: Rowman & Littlefield, 2016.

McKenna, Neil. *The Secret Life of Oscar Wilde.* New York: Basic Books, 2005.

Mennel, Stephen. *All Manners of Food: Eating and Taste in England and France from the Middle Ages to the Present.* Urbana and Chicago: University of Illinois Press, 1985.

Montgomery, Maureen E. *Displaying Women: Spectacles of Leisure in Edith Wharton's New York.* New York: Routledge, 1998.

Montgomery-Massingberd, Hugh, David Watkin, and Keith Collie (photos). *The London Ritz: A Social and Architectural History.* London: Aurum Press, 1989.

Nadelhoffer, Hans. *Cartier.* San Francisco: Chronicle, 2007.

Newnham-Davis, Lt. Col. (Nathaniel). *Dinners and Diners: Where and How to Dine in London.* London: Grant Richards, 1899.

————. *The Gourmet's Guide to Europe.* New York: Brentano's, 1911.

————. *The Gourmet's Guide to London.* New York: Brentano's, 1914.

Nowell-Smith, Simon. *Edwardian England: 1901–1914.* London: Oxford University Press, 1964.

Page, Edward, and P. W. Kingsford. *The Master Chefs: A History of Haute Cuisine.* New York: St. Martin's Press, 1971.

Read, Donald. *The Age of Urban Democracy: England 1868–1914.* London: Routledge, 1994.

Ridley, Jane. *The Heir Apparent: A Life of Edward VII, the Playboy Prince.* New York: Random House, 2013.

Ritz, Marie Louise. *César Ritz: Host to the World.* London: George G. Harrap & Co., 1938.

Roulet, Claude. *Ritz: A Story That Outshines the Legend.* Paris: Quai Voltaire/La Table Ronde, 1998.

Sassoon, Siegfried. *Letters to Max Beerbohm.* London: Faber & Faber, 1986.

Shaw, Timothy. *The World of Escoffier.* New York: Vendome Press, 1995.

Smith, Albert. *The English Hotel Nuisance.* London: Bradbury & Evans, 1858

Stuart, Amanda Mackenzie. *Consuelo and*

Alva Vanderbilt: The Story of a Mother and a Daughter in the Gilded Age. New York: HarperCollins, 2006.

Taylor, Derek. *Ritzy: British Hotels, 1837–1987.* London: The Milman Press, 2003.

Taylor, Derek, and David Bush. *The Golden Age of British Hotels.* London: Northwood Publications, 1974.

Watts, Stephen. *The Ritz.* London: The Bodley Head, 1963.

Wilde, Oscar. *Essays by Oscar Wilde.* London: Methuen & Co., 1950.

————. *A Life in Letters.* New York: Carroll & Graf, 2006.

Willan, Anne, and Michael Boys (photos). *Great Cooks and Their Recipes: From Taillevent to Escoffier.* New York: Bulfinch Press/Little, Brown, 1992.

Williams, Mrs. Hwfa. *It Was Such Fun.* London: Hutchison & Co., 1935.

Williamson, Jefferson. *The American Hotel: An Anecdotal History.* New York: Alfred A. Knopf, 1930.

Wood, T. Martin. *George du Maurier: The Satirist of the Victorians.* London: Chatto & Windus, 1913.

ABOUT THE AUTHOR

Luke Barr is the author of the *New York Times* bestselling *Provence, 1970*. Raised in the San Francisco Bay Area and Switzerland, Barr attended Harvard College and was formerly the features editor at *Travel + Leisure* magazine. He lives in Brooklyn with his wife and their two daughters.